Theory of Social Process:
An Economic Analysis

Theory of Social Process:
An Economic Analysis

BLAINE ROBERTS

BOB R. HOLDREN

The Iowa State University Press, Ames, Iowa

THIS BOOK is dedicated to those who challenge dogma and stimulate the rupturing of the frontier of knowledge for a better life for all mankind.

BLAINE ROBERTS is assistant professor of economics at the University of Florida, on leave (1972–73) as Deputy Director of Price Analysis, U.S. Price Commission.

BOB R. HOLDREN is professor of economics at Iowa State University.

Library of Congress Cataloging in Publication Data

Roberts, Blaine, 1944–
    Theory of social process.

    Based on Roberts' thesis, Iowa State University, 1970.
    Bibliography: p.
    1. Utility theory. 2. Economics—Mathematical models. I. Holdren, Bob R., joint author. II. Title.
HB201.R58   330.1   71–171169
ISBN 0–8138–1355–7

Contents

Preface

ALL PREFERENCES are learned. All preference changes are the result of learning, but not all learning results in preference changes. The operation of an economic system is a potent source of learning experiences. The occurrence of learning signifies that knowledge was not perfect; that either the total of human knowledge or the knowledge available to a decision unit has changed or expanded.

Heretofore all of economic theory has, either implicitly or explicitly, had as a foundation a theory of utility based on perfect knowledge and given preferences. We regard risk and uncertainty as perfectly informed situations since learning is not admissible. Our world is a world of imperfect information first and only secondarily, if at all, stochastic.

We are not suggesting that no one has heretofore considered or written about imperfect knowledge and its consequences. Rather, we are saying that formal economic theory as now constituted cannot encompass the implications of imperfect information.

We have constructed a mechanism which makes the received utility theory a special case. If we think of the utility function as a parameter of the system, we have changed the parameter into a variable and created a new set of parameters one step removed. This system does permit learning and connects the consequences of learning to economic theory. Its implications for all of economic theory are profound.

We have used the language and artifacts of stimulus-response learning theory because they seemed most apposite to us. Nothing in the model is dependent on the particular type of learning theory utilized. Some readers may not like our use of the concept of "drives" rather than "motivation." The reasons for this choice should be obvious from the context.

Blaine Roberts developed the mathematical models and did virtually all the writing; this book grew out of his doctoral dissertation. The theory grew out of an idea Holdren had been developing for several years. It, however, existed as only a flow chart and a collection of random notes when Roberts began working on it. Our interaction was long and arduous. We both contributed many additions to the basic idea, and by now it is difficult to say who contributed which ideas. In any case, this work bears the indelible stamp of both of us as well as each of us.

We are offering a new foundation for economic theory. Whether we have made a viable offer only time and our colleagues will tell.

Both authors owe thanks to the General Electric Foundation, which supported some of the work on this book. Bob R. Holdren owes thanks to the National Science Foundation for a grant and to the Ford Foundation for a Ford Foundation Faculty Fellowship, both of which afforded him support to work on some of the ideas which are incorporated in this book.

The production of a book depends upon the efforts of many people, from those who commented on rough drafts to the final proofreaders. The contributions of all are gratefully acknowledged. Nancy Bohlen, as editor, warrants a special note of appreciation for her concern and understanding.

BLAINE ROBERTS
BOB R. HOLDREN

Theory of Social Process:
An Economic Analysis

chapter 1

Science, Theory, and Analysis: A Preliminary Discussion

ALL SCIENTIFIC ANALYSES are based upon normative criteria to some degree. The results are dependent upon the opinions and subjectivity of both those who do the research and those who accept it as valid. Often these value judgments are implicit and cryptic but nevertheless are necessarily extant as a basis for any analysis. In spite of disclaimers of ever including personal ethics and opinions in research, the contrary is inevitable. It is in fact impossible even to describe something without recourse to certain subjective value judgments.

THE NATURE OF THEORY

Science is a body of knowledge accumulated in a systemized and classificatory manner. A student of science faces an extremely complex and abstruse environment, one in which literally billions of agents and factors are continually interacting. The simplest phenomena are products of many atoms, molecules, particles, organisms, and bodies. But man has a tremendous capacity to simplify and organize. In order to "know" or to understand this environment, the scientist separates the relevant from the irrelevant. Precisely what is and what is not relevant or important to comprehend, explain, predict, and control this environment depends upon man's sensations and his reactions to them. In other words, what is or is not relevant depends upon what gives satisfaction (broadly defined) to an individual. Even the initial act of deciding to explore an aspect of man's environment implies that it is worthwhile to do so, that such activity is fruitful and valuable to the individual. The next decision of what to study or describe, and in what way or in how much detail, again requires the use of personal value judgments. For an individual to comprehend such a complex environment, it is necessary to "select" the aspects which are the most important, to study the underlying trend which determines, or at least relates to, the process under investigation. This process of scientific simplification continues in such a way that often in the most recent stage of a scientific development the value judgments and opinions generated along the way are perhaps as ineluctable and esoteric as the phenomena being studied.

Since all analyses contain opinions and value judgments, the question becomes one of specification and degree; that is, what are these judgments and to what extent do others find them agreeable. The generality of a scientific discovery depends upon the agreeableness of its assumptions. One theoretical model produces results which are different from another, as the basic criteria vary between models. A particular problem is that these bases often are not made explicit. As a consequence, two models could differ by only a very obscure value judgment used as a building block and could produce conflicting conclusions. All this may appear very paradoxical and frustrating; and even if it is possible to reconcile the two, a great deal of time and effort may be required. A similar problem arises when a model is extended or expanded to additional problems. Unless the assumptions and postulates of the model are clear, it is quite easy to violate an implicit assumption in "expanding" the model. This gives further impetus to clearly and accurately stating the theoretical basis of a model.

As long as an individual is aware of the assumptions, value judgments, and subjective evaluations of different models, the one considered best depends upon the individual and his preference. Consequently, theory is at best nothing more than a precise and rigorous form of communication. And further, the more precise this communication is, the better, other things being equal. In its ultimate form theory reduces itself to a tautology which relates one concept to another. The value of establishing such tautological relationships depends in part upon their obviousness, a priori. Clearly and precisely relating intricate concepts of apparent diversity can greatly improve man's knowledge of his environment. To show the minimal assumptions, axioms, and postulates which imply a result and to show that a result is equivalent to making particular value judgments should be ultimate goals of theory if communication is to be in its most precise form.[1]

1. Some sources on this question of methodology are Friedman (1953); Koopmans (1957), second essay; Houthakker (1961); and Melitz (1965). Koopmans and Houthakker basically take this same position except that they make

DEPENDENCE OF THEORY ON THE STATE OF THE SOCIAL SYSTEM

When an economist builds a model by selecting the relevant aspects from millions of phenomena, he and those who agree with his analysis are making a decision as to what is important and are accepting criteria for personal and social welfare. When it is decided what problems should be analyzed and time and effort (hence resources) are allocated to any particular facet of social interaction, an implicit price or opportunity cost exists. Whether overt or not, the scientific analyses undertaken at any point in time become a measure of priorities, a weighting of what is relevant, and thus a manifestation of criteria for social welfare. To deny that problems selected are a product of a constrained maximization technique and hence that they represent an accurate measure of the discipline's social welfare criteria not only violates basic axioms of human behavior accepted since Adam Smith but is a violation of a tautological description of that behavior.

Thus the rational bases for social scientific studies considered acceptable at any point in time depend upon the stage of development not only of the academic profession of the social sciences but of the social system as well. A relevant model in a society which is starving, or nearly so, is not a relevant approach in a more affluent social system. In a poor society whether one considers the existence of single individuals is not important; in fact, the effort necessary for such detail is a waste of time and other resources. It is sufficient to consider the welfare of the state and to develop more rational ways for the state to survive. Thereby, individuals will survive as well.

Empirically, as a society becomes richer, it behooves those in effective decision-making positions to take into account the preferences of others. The greater the degree of wealth, the more worthwhile it is to protect that wealth. Once a social system attains a particular level of riches, the solution for even greater levels requires that models explicitly consider singular individuals as relevant detail, and thus the implicit social welfare criteria of theoretical analyses must become more magnanimous. Just as the rich have padlocks and the poor do not lock their doors, the actions of individuals in a technologically advanced and wealthy society become increasingly effective toward preservation and further augmentation of that

---

no allowance for the gestation period of theory to be refined and sharpened to its ultimate form. Friedman argues, on the contrary, that the assumptions are irrelevant; only the conclusions are of significance. However, theory is a method of communication and no criterion exists as to which concept is the assumption and which is the conclusion. Consequently, each are of equal relevance.

wealth. A rich society is forced to adopt a more and more egalitarian approach to theoretical rationale. A rich society's "best" solution for viability and continued progress is one which is cognizant of all decision-making units.

HISTORICAL DEVELOPMENT OF ECONOMIC THOUGHT

This general course of social welfare criteria can both explain the evolution and revolution of paradigms in economic analysis of the past and predict the general nature of future developments.[2]

Historically, the general path of the relevant social welfare criteria utilized in the mainstream of economic analysis has changed from a structure which analyzed the state as an entity, often personified in the form of a sovereign, to one where individual preferences influence the scope and method of economic analysis. Then this path has evolved to the present state where these preferences should have some general weighting associated with them.

What is termed the "marginal revolution" in economics, occurring in the latter years of the nineteenth century, is the manifestation of a change from accepting the state as the rationale for analysis to one where individuals take its place. For example, relative prices become much more crucial if the implicit welfare criteria are based upon individuals rather than the state. The concern with the state is whether resources are being utilized to maximize its wealth. In this context the value (market price) of commodities which are not being continually reproduced is irrelevant and can be ignored. The definition or assumption of what is a commodity is limited to those goods which are being continually reproduced by the physical and human resources of the state. Under these restrictive assumptions of limited commodities, the general equilibrium solution is consistent with a labor theory of value. And in this system, where only the welfare of the nation-state is important, this is the most useful way to describe, analyze, and control relevant variables which affect the power and position of the state. To say that the labor theory of value cannot explain the price of a painting by da Vinci is totally uninteresting to the strength of the state. In fact, including a painting in the definition of what is valuable would obscure recognition of the industrial-mercantile wealth of a nation.

As wealth accumulates and technology expands in a society, individuals must also attain greater levels of skill and knowledge.

2. See Kuhn (1962) and Coats (1969) for a discussion of the changes in scientific paradigms over time.

Their knowledge sets expand and often become specialized. Consequently, not only must the decision-making process become more democratic, it is more efficient to make it so. Wealth can be further enhanced only with specialization and the development of expertise among the individuals providing the human resources for production. Thus the emphasis begins to change from the power of the state as an entity to the power of individuals. Concomitantly, the relevant social welfare criteria or value judgments for economic analysis must change in the same direction. Individuals become increasingly crucial to meaningful analysis and so do the prices of nonreproducible as well as reproducible items.

This evolution in the relevant basis for analysis coupled with various other minor influences, such as individual genius and developments in mathematics, culminated in a marginal revolution. It is quite clear that such analyses were possible before the metamorphosis of the economic paradigm. Various individuals had used the concept of utility and marginal analysis for over a century before the marginal revolution came about.[3] But it was not until individual preferences became important (became part of the relevant social welfare criteria) that marginalism and supply and demand analysis replaced the labor theory of value.

As marginal analysis was extended, production and the tendencies of the market became an integral sector of the economic paradigm. Still the emphasis of the consequences of these market tendencies remained directed toward the implications of the well-being of individuals in the long run. Individual preferences were important but only to the extent of general long-run tendencies.

Shortly after the turn of the century, the additional accumulation of wealth and the increasing rate of technological expansion forced the relevant social welfare base to shift to more short-run problems. Market imperfections began to receive more and more attention in the structure of economic models. The idea of control of the capitalistic marketing process and collective intervention became feasible and was debated at length. This shift to short-run problems and concern with collective goods implies that the assumptions of the basic economic models were implicitly giving more weight to the mass of consumers than to the monopolist or the monopolistic competitor to be regulated. Individual consumer groups had attained a sufficient amount of time and leisure so that their

---

3. Especially noteworthy is the work by Daniel Bernoulli and Gabriel Cramér, 1731, and Cournot, circa 1738. See Fellner (1965) and Blaug (1969) for further details. Also Baumol and Goldfeld (1968) provide a clear picture of the lead of expertise over acceptability.

potential collective activity had become a relevant force in the social system and accordingly had to be considered in the models of scientific analysis.

Although the Keynesian revolution and consequent change in the paradigm of economic analysis was an apparent radical shift in policy recommendation, especially from an analytical point of view, the evolution of social welfare criteria was not quite so marked. From the concept of government control of monopoly for the benefit of consumers it is but a short, logical step to altering these criteria to include an individual's level of income or to develop governmental policy against unemployment. And as in the case of marginal revolution these "Keynesian" ideas, which received much social currency in the 1930s and after, were essentially nothing more in spirit than the theories of Malthus and other underconsumptionists. These Keynesian precursors were almost entirely ignored until the conditions were sufficient to allow the social welfare criteria to move toward a more equal weighting of the wellbeing of individuals. For example, defining full employment as 4% of the labor force being unemployed and concomitantly structuring governmental policy toward this goal implies sanctifying a particular institutional arrangement; it is also a change of the implicit criteria for social welfare present in the marginal paradigm.

To illustrate this change, suppose that a falling-off of autonomous investment occurs (a large investment project is completed). This requires an institutional adjustment to transfer those engaged in the investment industry (construction workers and carpenters) to move into other industries (to become lawyers or artists). However, these individuals do not possess the requisite skills to move immediately into these other areas. Since they are out of work, they do not have any income and the demand for artists and lawyers does not increase as it would if these individuals (laborers) were a homogeneous commodity in all areas of production. Yet this situation is still quite consistent with the marginal paradigm. Supply and demand are in equilibrium. Workers are looking for jobs but do not possess marketable skills and hence do not have a supply of labor to offer.

The Keynesian solution is to give these unemployed persons more weight in the social welfare criteria and conclude that these individuals should have an income. The result is government spending which makes use of these skills, for example, government works programs such as the CCC or WPA. The arbitrary definition of full employment must be relative to some presumed conditions, namely, skills, knowledge, and particular institutional arrangements; the use of government spending to meet this definition carries a particular implicit weighting of individuals in the definition of social welfare.

An alternative solution to the above problem of technological unemployment is to question the institutional system which created such conditions. One could question the origin of skills and the knowledge of individuals relative to the institutional mechanism which generates these skills. By recognizing that labor is not homogeneous but that individual skills depend upon the knowledge set of the individual laborer, it is possible to ask whether this educational institution should be altered. For example, an alternative proposal to the Keynesian spending and interest rate manipulation policy would be to establish training centers and to encourage individuals to participate by providing an adequate income subsidy while retraining takes place.

Economic models do not generate such an explicit solution because the implicit basis of social welfare has not evolved to the stage of considering the origin and creation of preferences and motivations. The level of wealth and associated technology has not been sufficient in the past to make considerations of the origin of knowledge relevant to economic analysis. There have been sufficient problems with analysis and prediction assuming given preferences. This has led many economists to argue that preference formation is not in the domain of economic analysis but belongs to psychology or sociology. It is not that preference formation is unimportant, but, it has been argued, it is irrelevant to economic analysis. However, this is completely analogous to the argument that individual preferences are irrelevant to the welfare of the state, which was typical before the marginal revolution.

Social welfare criteria will continue to evolve, and economic inquiry can begin to question the generation of knowledge in a meaningful way. Individual wealth and the general state of knowledge has reached such a level that for society to further advance at its most rapid rate, knowledge and information must be transmitted more rapidly and efficiently, and explicit comparisons must be made between improving the abilities and circumstances of institutional rejects and not doing so.

This implies that the paradigm of economic analysis must depart from its current position to one where preference formation is integral to the process. The models of analysis must necessarily specify the value judgment base in greater detail as the models begin to range over various institutions rather than merely within institutions. Vastly different types of data will be needed for such analyses, just as for Keynesian analysis and national income data.

The role of theory and methodology is that it be relevant, and explicitly so, to the levels of affluence and knowledge of the social system within which it is operating. The implications are that theory, when applied to analysis within a social structure, should also be acutely attuned to the changes in this structure and the mechanisms which produce them.

THREE BASIC ASSUMPTIONS

Three implicit assumptions are used in this book. They are not new, unique, or exhaustive but the reader should be aware of the extenuating aspects which may not always be explicitly discussed.

The first aspect basic to the study is that of individualism, or the fact that individuals are assumed to play a crucial role in any economic analysis. This has not always been the case in economic theory. Analyses based upon the "state" or the "church" have been frequent in man's history. These studies have not mentioned that individuals exist or comprise the state or the church or whatever. Thus the emphasis in this book on individual actions and reactions is a value judgment considered crucial for a relevant understanding of the forces which determine a large portion of the environment.

The primary level of aggregation is taken to be that of the individual. Many other levels are possible, both higher and lower. One could begin with protons, neutrons, and electrons as the most relevant level of analysis. A bit higher level of aggregation would be the role level of individuals—analyzing various roles independently of one another. Higher still, would be a group of individuals with its own personality, motives, and so forth.

The analysis of society to be developed in the following chapters views the most useful method of understanding various aspects of the environment as one which begins with a single integrated individual as an independent decision maker. Although his freedom of choice is constrained in many ways, he has sufficient ability and control over variables that the best way to explain, predict, and control social phenomena is to concentrate on the individual. The individual will be viewed as having conscious control over activities in which he participates. While these may be subject to various constraints and may evoke responses from others in the social system, the individual is free to rationally regulate his activities.

The second assumption which requires subjective interpretation of the history of man is that economic aspects are sufficiently crucial to the determination of any social system to warrant their being isolated and given particular analysis. One can understand a significant portion of social evolution by isolating the economic factors at work.

The third basic belief implicit to this theoretical analysis is that knowledge is fruitful toward attaining the goals of every individual. That is, by simplifying, conceptualizing, and organizing the real-world phenomena, man is able to explain, predict, and consequently control his environment. The end result is an achievement of desired states by mankind. This constitutes a subjective evaluation that scientific research and the consequent effects upon the state of the individual have been beneficial and will continue to be so.

Often statements similar to the foregoing are taken for granted as being obvious and undebatable. Indeed, there is not room in time or space to develop a complete and exhaustive discussion of such under-pinnings to the theory presented here. However, the reader should be conscious of the very large and complicated base which is assumed as given for this theoretical departure.

SCOPE OF THE STUDY

The inclusion of personal preferences in economic theory dates back implicitly at least to Adam Smith's *Wealth of Nations* and ex-plicitly to the work of Menger, Jevons, and Walras in the midnine-teenth century. Since the turn of this century utility theory, the hypothetical construct of personal preferences, has come to be in-corporated in virtually every facet of the discipline. It provides a theoretical basis from which operational hypotheses are derived and a myriad of models are constructed. However, its application is presently restricted to an assumed static knowledge set. In order to develop a theory of social interaction and social process, one must be cognizant of knowledge change. Indeed, this is the very essence of the dynamic evolution and revolution of social structures. There-fore, in what follows, utility theory is extended to fit in the broader matrix of a theory of individual behavior which will be applicable to the problems associated with changing preferences.

The received theory of consumer behavior assumes that prefer-ences are given. For such traditional uses as explaining consumer be-havior in a market system this present theory is quite sufficient, and questions as to preference formation are simply not relevant. Throughout history the majority of mankind has struggled merely to maintain bodily functions. There can be very little questioning of the direction of human endeavors when day-to-day existence is con-stantly in doubt. In a subsistence environment personal freedom and choice are severely restricted as compared to an environment which provides a cornucopia above and beyond the basic necessities to sus-tain life. Physiological needs such as water, food, clothing, and shel-ter are relatively stable and subject to much less variation from learn-ing experiences vis-á-vis the psychological exigencies which are generated once the former are fulfilled. In an affluent society when physical requirements become almost guaranteed for everyone and constitute a comparatively small portion of total produce, the much more subjective, psychological aspects of individual behavior become the prime determinants of social activity.

As the range of economic activity expands and as society changes from an essentially static environment (as far as individual preferences are concerned) to a dynamic confluence of increased complexity and developing technologies, the efficacy of products is continually altered by changes in the product set and the multiplicity of learning activities which occur. The capabilities of current economic theory are simply inadequate to deal with many of the relevant questions which arise in this context.

For example, utility theory does not include decision variables which are specifically designed to alter one's information state. Decisions to gain additional information concerning the mix of products available, the prices of products, or their quality are not included.

But learning, in and of itself, is an economic activity which utilizes a significant and ever-growing portion of society's resources. (Machlup (1962) estimated the expenditure for knowledge in the United States in 1958 to be approximately 30 percent of the gross national product.) In addition to the educational system (which is about 7 percent of the GNP) corporations, branches of government, and other organizations devote a substantial amount of their activity toward the quest of knowledge and learning, advertising to alter people's knowledge, research and development to generate increased technological skills, and activities to define and identify their current position and status relative to the markets in which they are operating.

Thus there is a clear necessity for extending utility theory so that it is relevant both to current social problems and to the understanding of the dynamics of social change. Preferences are formed, shaped, and altered not only by the amount of goods and services but also by their array, quality, and complexity, through the many facets which are conceptually effective on the decision processes of the individual. This effect on the satisfaction or "utility" of the human organism is paramount to the explanation of individual behavior. Therefore, the first step will be to extend the generality and applicability of utility theory as an explanation of individual actions. This generalization will be essentially twofold: (1) to analyze the conditions and results of viewing the individual as consciously choosing among numerous activities in which he can engage, subject to the various constraints and conditions which he feels are imposed on him by his environment and (2) to allow, within this theory of choice, for learning to occur and for the consequences of such learning and changed opinions to affect the activities which the individual pursues.

This amounts simply to an extension of utility theory to a more robust analysis, with the current concept of utility as a special case. Preferences imply a knowledge set, and the theoretical models to follow explicitly consider the formation of such knowledge and consequently permit analysis of preference change. The individual is viewed as possessing a set of drives which provides a hypothetical construct for the motivating force within him. These drives can be satisfied by various activities which the individual is free to select, subject to the constraints imposed by technology and society. Activities are partitioned into two categories: economic, those which require an exchange of goods and services, and noneconomic, those which do not. The essence of this approach can be seen more readily by the use of a schematic diagram (Fig. 1.1).

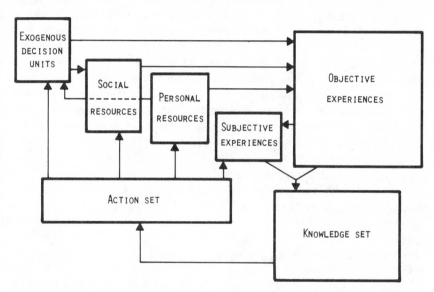

Fig. 1.1. Schematic formulation of individual actions, their effects, resulting experiences, and the individual's knowledge set.

Given a set of knowledge, the individual decides on a set of actions. These actions affect his subjective experiences, personal resources, social resources, and other exogenous decision units, both directly and indirectly through use of his personal resources. This environment provides the individual with a set of objective and subjective (or imagined) experiences. These experiences, then, alter the knowledge set. Current utility theory views the process of going from the knowledge set to the action set as utility maximization. The objective of the next three chapters is to generalize the process of going from the knowledge set to the action set and to specify the process of going from experiences to the knowledge set.

CRITERIA OF SOCIAL WELFARE

Throughout this book an attempt is made to limit the criteria of social welfare to the individual and improved rationality. That is, an individual is better off if he can more efficiently attain a given set of basic goals or level of satisfaction. Since different methods of goal or satisfaction achievement require different amounts of valuable and scarce resources, it is assumed that an individual, a group, and the whole of society would be better off to use the most economical one.

Improvements in individual welfare are based solely upon the internal maximizing criterion of the individual, namely, drive reduction. It is further postulated that actions such as altruism and magnanimity are a translation of an internal desire for personal welfare with an associated particular understanding of the interrelatedness of individuals. For a given individual in a given situation, the best way to achieve personal drive reduction may be through others. A multimillionaire may become philanthropic because the recognition and gratitude he hopes will be forthcoming from others can create greater satisfaction for him than other possible uses of his resources.

Criteria for judging aggregates of individuals are similarly based on rationality. A group action will be judged as inefficient if it does not result in the best method of achieving individual ends by group means. A market could result in the production and distribution of a product in an inefficient manner vis-á-vis a situation where those engaged in the market had more information. In general, an aggregate activity will be considered inefficient if it could be improved by more information, other things being equal.

For a person to find such criteria of welfare acceptable as value judgments (criteria which are void of ethics, morals, and so forth) he must believe that he will be better off if everyone acts rationally. He must feel that greater knowledge will bring greater rationality and hence greater ability to achieve basic goals rather than merely derived ones. In other words, a belief is necessary that the aggregate effects of knowledgeable individual choices are beneficial to that aggregate and in turn to the individual.

It should be clarified that the above criteria do not prohibit one group from destroying another, for example. Therefore, for those who abhor violence, these criteria require a belief that if all groups were knowledgeable of their drives and the methods of satisfying them, one group would not destroy another.

SUMMARY

The foregoing brief discussion of methodology demonstrates the general objectives of this book. The review of the existing structure of utility theory in the next chapter serves as a benchmark for the generalization of individual choice and knowledge change. Then with this base of individual behavior, social interaction and social process can be analyzed.

chapter 2

The Current State of Utility Theory

AN UNDERSTANDING of the applicability of utility theory in economic analysis and some of the criticisms of it serve as a springboard to conceptualizing and analyzing individual behavior in a manner which is relevant for the theory of dynamic social interaction and progress.

TRADITIONAL STATIC UTILITY MODEL

After 200 years of successive application of Occam's razor, which removed all the irrelevant postulates,[1] utility theory today stands as a prime example of how to extract the minimum results from the minimum of assumptions. The bibliography contains a listing of representative articles which is intended to cover all phases of utility theory but is not exhaustive.[2] The current state of utility theory can be summarized thus: If individuals have preferences over different commodity bundles, the sign of the substitution effect of a price change will be negative. Stated this way, the result seems almost trivial;[3] but nevertheless, the theoretical structure—the product of years of development and thought—provides economists with a sub-

1. For excellent surveys of the development of utility theory see Stigler (1950) and Blaug (1968), Ch. 8 and 9. Stigler's article is reprinted in Page (1968) along with several other articles from Bentham to Samuelson.
2. Good survey articles include Houthakker (1961), which reviews utility and demand theory from 1939 to 1961. For more rigorous mathematical treatment of current utility theory see Uzawa (1960) and Chipman (1960). Articles which deal with utility over several time periods and somewhat broaden its scope would include Koopmans (1960) and Koopmans, Diamond, and Williamson (1964). Also see Chipman et al. (1971).
3. See Johnson (1958).

stantial wealth of intuitive feel and insight and a knowledge of the actual capabilities of utility theory.

To provide an explanation of market demand, for example, it is only necessary to postulate the existence of a preference ordering by the individual over the commodities which are available. One needs no further psychological analysis of why this preference ordering exists or how it came about. Without access to information such as the intensity of individual likes and dislikes among commodity bundles, the economist can derive operational hypotheses which explain a certain range of empirical phenomena; he is also able to construct criteria which have limited application to questions of social welfare and efficiency by merely knowing the general nature of individual preferences.

Model 2.1 presents the traditional static model of utility maximization for a given income and given prices.

Model 2.1

Maximize

$$U = U(x_1, \ldots, x_n)$$

subject to

$$M = \sum_{i=1}^{n} P_i x_i$$

where M = money income and U is a utility indicator with the property that

$$U(x_1, \ldots, x_n) > U(x_1', \ldots, x_x')$$

if and only if the commodity bundle $(x_1, \ldots, x_n)$ is preferred to $(x_1', \ldots, x_n')$, and usually U is assumed to be continuous with defined first and second partial derivatives.[4]

The following conditions must hold for a regular constrained maximum to exist:

$$\frac{\partial U/\partial x_i}{\partial U/\partial x_j} = P_i/P_j, \text{ and } \sum_{i=1}^{n} P_i x_i = M$$

4. For conditions necessary for such a function to exist, see Debreu in Thrall, Coombs, and Davis (1954), Ch. 11.

If there is a small change in the price of commodity i, $dP_i > 0$, then the Slutsky equation follows.

$$\partial x_j / \partial P_i = (-1)^{i+j} \lambda (|U_{i,j}|/|U|) - x_i (\partial x_j / \partial M) \qquad (2.1)$$

where $|U_{i,j}|$ is the bordered Hessian determinant of the cofactor matrix of second-order partial derivatives.

If $i = j$, the first term of the Equation 2.1 can easily be shown to be negative, and this is the substitution effect of a price change. The second term, $x_i(\partial x_i / \partial M)$, is the income effect and in general can be either positive or negative. Thus the central tenet of utility theory is that the effect of an income-compensated price change will be negative (Equation 2.2), and consequently, an income-compensated demand curve will slope downward.

$$\partial x_i / \partial P_i + x_i(\partial x_i / \partial M) = \lambda (|U_{i,i}|/|U|) < 0 \qquad (2.2)$$

In spite of apparent meagerness, the effort which has gone into extracting it from the minimum of assumptions—and consequently placing utility theory in a proper perspective in economics—has been enormous, and justifiably so in view of the vast application of such theories of preference. Regardless of the amount of application of this very simple construction and the amount of literature associated with it, the usefulness is noticeably restricted. Suppose the set of available products expands such that a new product very similar to others previously available is introduced. What effect will this have on demand? The above analysis provides no answer. What is the relation between the complex of commodities available and the income of the individual? Again the theory is silent.

SOME TRADITIONAL CRITICISMS

The abstract theorists of economic thought have long been the object of criticism from "institutionalists" who feel that the abstract, simplified construction of utility theory omits much of what is relevant in the explanation of consumer behavior.[5] Although their approach is often eloquent and stimulating criticism, unfortunately they have offered no alternative analysis which rigorously upgrades the failings of current theory. If institutions play a significant and relevant role in determining the course of society and the nature of its economic system, these aspects should be included in the theoretical analysis in a specific and rigorous manner. Many have argued that often prices cannot be divorced from the nature of a good itself

5. For example see Commons (1934) or Ayres (1962) for the general flavor of institutional critics. Viner (1925) presents the traditionalists' point of view.

or that economic theory is oversimplified and man is something much more than the cold, calculating *homo oeconomicus* implied by economic theory.[6] If this is true, the relevant characteristics of the individual's environment which impose these constraints should be included and clearly analyzed. Economic theory, and more specifically utility theory, is a simplification of the forces operating in the economic system; currently, it is the best analysis available. Thus the institutionalists have often been excoriated for dealing in mysticism and failing to provide a better alternative. Nevertheless, they have provided some food for thought in that the questions they have raised point out weaknesses and incapabilities of current economic theory.

Economists who have been actively engaged in marketing analysis and research are quick to point to the failings of modern utility theory. Doyle (1968a) states, "The theory of consumer demand is seriously inadequate. The consumer is faced with conditions of supply which are dynamic; new products are appearing while old ones disappear or change. In this situation the assumptions that wants are static and uniformly perceived and that information requirements are simple, are clearly misleading." Further, he states, "The most valuable contribution of behavioral science [is that] learning is accepted as a central feature of buying behavior." In spite of this there have been few if any attempts to incorporate this learning process rigorously into the theory of consumer behavior; an immense amount of correlation and experimentation have been undertaken without such a theory to provide the structure necessary for meaningful analysis.

Since learning has been omitted from economic analysis, one might feel that psychologists would have a theory which would neatly fit into economic analysis. Unfortunately, this does not appear to be the case. The approach by mathematical psychologists such as Luce et al.[7] differs in principle from the theoretical analysis of this book, since the postulate of the mathematical psychologists is that utility or preference maximization gives rise to stochastic behavior. The deviation between the mathematical psychologists and the principles to be developed in later chapters derives from a difference in interest. Traditionally, psychologists have been interested in the individual aspects of learning and the formation of preferences, while economists have been concerned with aggregate effects of individual units. For reasons connected with measurement problems, a stochastic approach is necessary at the individual level. However, for

6. See Veblen's *Theory of the Leisure Class* (1899) or Scitovsky (1962).
7. See for example Luce (1959); Suppes (1961); and Luce, Bush, and Galanter (1965), vols. 1, 2, and 3.

theoretical clarity and since this random element is not a central force at work in aggregate relationships, a deterministic approach will be followed here.[8]

SOME RECENT DEVELOPMENTS

Only recently have significant developments occurred in economic theory which extend and generalize the traditional utility theory as stated in Model 2.1.

Kalman (1968) generalized utility analysis to include the situation where prices influence preferences. More specifically, the implications of the assumption that the higher the price the better the quality are analyzed in the comparative statics of consumer demand theory using the Slutsky format. In essence, Kalman argues that preferences shift in a specified manner with a change in price or that learning takes place so that the individual has an increase in knowledge with a change in prices in an unchanging way. While this is a step forward in generalizing utility theory, the implicit assumptions contained in the mathematical developments are quite restrictive and not likely to hold except in rare situations.

Specifically, Kalman's assumption is that for a preference indicator, $U = U(q_1, \ldots, q_n, p_1, \ldots, p_n)$, $\partial U/\partial q_i \geq 0$ for all i, and $\partial U/\partial p_i > 0$ for at least one i. If $\partial U/\partial p_i > 0$ for wheat, and the price of wheat rises, it is assumed to be more preferred than before. Intuitively, this formulation is intended to represent the consumer's cognition of a positive relation between price and quality. While this approximation to learning and changing preferences may hold in a particular situation, it is indeed a limited and restrictive assumption. Kalman's article is indicative of a failure to explicitly recognize that the specification of a preference ordering implies a certain state of knowledge, as does specification of the product set and all other parameters which are implicitly assumed in such a theoretical analysis. Any change in these parameters of the model represents new information and must be analyzed by the decision maker for its meaning and implications. Suppose an economy is perfectly competitive and prices in one industry rise relative to all other prices. While this increase could be the result of an increase in quality of the product, it could be due to many other factors as well, such as a change in the price of factors of production. If the price of the commodity should fall relative to other commodities so that it is at its former level, does utility fall? It would seem unlikely. Thus a change

8. The economic literature of utility theory under uncertainty beginning with von Neumann and Morgenstern (1947) is discussed in Appendix A.

in price may or may not represent a change in the quality of the product, and quality changes rather than price changes would be incorporated in a theory of consumer demand which allows for changing preferences.

Another significant step in furthering the breadth of utility analysis was achieved by Lancaster (1966) in two articles. Lancaster views products as having characteristics which satisfy the wants and needs of individuals. In this sense, products are inputs possessing characteristics which are desired by the individual. This analysis, among other things, significantly increases the ability of economic theory to distinguish among complements and substitutes and to a certain extent assesses the value of technological change to the consumer. The approach in this book, more generalized and encompassing than Lancaster's, derives somewhat similar conclusions, namely, that the characteristics of economic goods and services are important to the individual. Lancaster assumes that individuals have preferences over the characteristics of the various products, whereas in Chapter 3 of this book the individual is viewed as reducing drives by means of activities which require a certain bundle of commodities. Thus, although similar, the two approaches are subtly different. The preponderance of psychological evidence is in favor of the more Gestalt approach of viewing preferences as dependent upon the total activity rather than as isolated characteristics.[9] As an extreme but illustrative example, consider a concert. The Lancaster analysis would imply that the individual had preferences over the tone of the violins, the rhythm of the timpani, and so on, while the theoretical structure developed in Chapter 3 would view the individual as deriving satisfaction from the total activity, which would include the entire orchestra, the concert hall, the comfort of the seat, and so on.

Lancaster restricts his analysis to the assumption that the functional relation between products and characteristics is linear, while the analysis in this book is not so restricted. As with Lancaster, an evaluation of technological change is presented which includes a broader range than Lancaster's model is capable of handling. Also, the inclusion of an assumed constant knowledge set (albeit over characteristics rather than commodities) eliminates many relevant economic problems which can be discussed with the models developed here.

Anspach (1966) analyzes the disutility associated with the effort of obtaining additional information about the utility afforded by different goods. This approach was also applied by Baumol and Quandt

9. For example see Maslow and Mintz (1956), Dember (1961), Nelson (1964), or McKeachie and Doyle (1966).

(1964) to firms and their usage of "rules of thumb" because of the cost associated with gathering information. Anspach restricts the analysis by assuming that the individual obtains information about one product at a time. His extension of utility analysis to include effort remains in the utility format, and considerations of time constraints and learning over time are not considered. Anspach's article as well as Kalman's analysis are restrictively set in a situation which might hold as time passes, but they are not sufficiently rich to allow for a more complete felicific calculus by the individual.

Becker (1965) presents a theory of the allocation of time. He argues that commodities have two relevant characteristics, the intrinsic utility of the commodity and the time associated with its consumption. Although never specifically mentioned, the description of such a commodity more closely resembles the description of an activity as ordinarily conceived. Again the approach is to view individuals as having "production" functions, producing leisure and income for the individual, for which commodities are factors of production. When the individual is viewed as a maximizing producer with some freedom of choice, the accepted distinction between firms and households vanishes for the most part. (In Chapter 7, the relevant distinction between the individual and the firm is developed as a process of mutual benefit from group formation.) The advantages of including a time constraint in the analysis of individual behavior are many, as Becker explicitly points out.

Becker's analysis is an important and relevant development for the theory of economic behavior. However, the approach is restrictive in that only given preferences over commodities with an associated time dimension exist. The theoretical structure developed in this book includes Becker's analysis as a very special case in a much broader framework and proceeds to analyze the effects of learning experiences on the preferences of the decision-making unit.

SUMMARY

The theory developed in the following chapters includes all the aforementioned extensions of utility theory as well as the traditional theory of utility maximization of a given income as special cases. It is, then, an extension and generalization of individual behavior resulting in a model with a much greater power to explain, analyze, and predict behavior in situations which cannot be handled within the traditional framework.

Generalized Preference Model

THOMAS HUXLEY has said, "Science is, I believe, nothing but trained and organized common sense, differing from the latter only as a veteran may differ from a raw recruit: and its methods differ from those of common sense only so far as the guardsman's cut and thrust differ from the manner in which a savage wields his club."[1]

If Huxley is correct, this implies that common sense in turn is nothing but a rough form of scientific calculation. Common sense is an implicit decision by an individual of how he is affected by his environment and how he can best adapt to it to fulfill his needs as he sees them. Indeed, this is how rationality is defined—acting in a manner which will best achieve a myriad of goals.

This assumption of the rationality of man will be adopted here. (This should not be confused with the connotations of the often used "rational 'economic' man.") It will be assumed that the individual can consciously calculate and carry out plans formulated in light of his environment so that the result is an attainment of desirable goals subject to the constraints upon the individual. The person, typified by such a paradigmatic approach, is assumed to have some freedom of choice to select variables which will achieve some sort of constrained maximum. However, this technique of analysis is incidental to what is of genuine interest. The heart of the analysis is a specification and delineation of the quantity maximized, the range of the variables, the relevant constraints, and the consequent effect upon economic activity.

1. Thomas Huxley, *Weiner* (1953), p. 130, quoted in Ackoff (1962), p. 3.

The methodology will be one of developing a series of models, rigorously specified mathematically, with a discussion and an interpretation of the special conditions and implications associated with each model. As a necessary first step toward the development of a general analysis of changes in the knowledge set, the view that an individual has preferences over commodities will be expanded to one where preferences are embedded in a more general matrix of all possible activities and actions. Within the theoretical structure this will permit the individual to select activities which are designed to alter his preference ordering (that is, information-gathering activities); this will be developed in Chapter 4. However, the models of the individual calculus in this chapter will be limited to a comparative static framework in this expanded format for individual preferences.

CHOICE AS A GENERAL MATHEMATICAL PROGRAMMING PROBLEM

Model 3.1 is the full generalization of a nonlinear programming approach to the maximizing process in the static sense. $x_1, \ldots, x_n$ represent the variables under control of the maximizing unit, and equations $g_1(x_1, \ldots, x_n) \geqslant 0, \ldots, g_m(x_1, \ldots, x_n) \geqslant 0$ are the constraints the maximizing unit must obey. The data variables are parameters in the maximizing and constraint equations. It is assumed that S is quasi-concave[2] and the constraint set is convex.

MODEL 3.1

Maximize

$$S = S(x_1, \ldots, x_n) \tag{3.1}$$

subject to

$$g_1(x_1, \ldots, x_n) \geqslant 0$$

$$\vdots$$

$$g_m(x_1, \ldots, x_n) \geqslant 0$$
$$x_i \geqslant 0, i = 1, \ldots, n \tag{3.2}$$

The Lagrangian equation is

$$\lambda = S(x_1, \ldots, x_n) + \lambda_1 g_1(x_1, \ldots, x_n) + \ldots + \lambda_m g_m(x_1, \ldots, x_n)$$

2. $f(x)$ is quasi-concave if the set of all x such that $f(x) \geqslant c$, a constant, is a convex set.

The Kuhn-Tucker conditions[3] for a maximum are

$$\partial\lambda/\partial x_1 \leqslant 0, \text{ if } \partial\lambda/\partial x_1 < 0, \text{ then } x_1 = 0$$

$$\vdots \qquad\qquad\qquad\qquad\qquad \vdots$$

$$\partial\lambda/\partial x_n \leqslant 0, \text{ if } \partial\lambda/\partial x_n < 0, \text{ then } x_n = 0$$

$$\partial\lambda/\partial\lambda_1 \geqslant 0, \text{ if } \partial\lambda/\partial\lambda_1 > 0, \text{ then } \lambda_1 = 0$$

$$\vdots \qquad\qquad\qquad\qquad\qquad \vdots$$

$$\partial\lambda/\partial\lambda_m \geqslant 0, \text{ if } \partial\lambda/\partial\lambda_m > 0, \text{ then } \lambda_m = 0$$

or that $x_i(\partial\lambda/\partial x_i) = \lambda_j(\partial\lambda/\partial\lambda_j) = 0$, for all i and j

Interpreting Model 3.1 in terms of conventional utility analysis, Equation 3.1 would be the utility function or preference indicator and the only constraint (Equation 3.2) is that money income must be equal to the total value of goods and services purchased, that is,

$$\sum_{n=1}^{n} P_i x_i = M$$

With the above technique of analysis, all that remains for the development of any static theory of consumer behavior is to specify and interpret the completely general nature of Model 3.1. While there are many different possibilities, the methodological criteria will be to interpret Model 3.1 in a relevant manner which will lead to useful insights and operational hypotheses.

AN INTERPRETATION OF MODEL 3.1

The first step is a specification of the objective function. The basic tenet of this book is to view the consumer as possessing a set of psychological drives. And the sole motivating force within the individual is to reduce these drives. In other words, from Equation 3.1 of Model 3.1, S will be interpreted as the amount of drive reduction obtainable and $x_1, \ldots, x_n$ are the variables under the control of the individual.

The essence of this concept is that reasons exist behind preference formation. If more information were available as to these reasons (for example, greater detail of the chemical process of neu-

---

3. Under the assumptions, these conditions are both necessary and sufficient for a maximum. This is proved in Arrow and Enthoven (1961).

rology, the confluence of impulse generation from various stimuli and consequent cognition processes, and so on), economic theories based upon the individual would take on a great deal more predictive power and possess a greater operationally relevant nature. This, then, is somewhat of a philosophical distinction from the former role of utility theory, which was to completely ignore preference formation as if preferences were innate to the human organism or were conjured up by an intractable process—not only one incapable of explanation but one with theistic characteristics to be revered with awe, but not contemplated nor discussed for fear of some sort of eternal damnation. The consequence is not a mathematical alteration in a demand function nor an altered graphical analysis but an entirely different concept—one which can be tied closely to former methods of analysis yet offers an extensive expansion of the applicability of economic analysis to the problems of society.

The next question is, What exactly is a drive and how does it differ from the hypothetical construct of utility used by economists for over one hundred years? A drive is the resultant of any sufficiently strong stimulus. That is, any drive is a stimulus but not vice-versa, since some stimuli produce no drives. The level of the various stimuli necessary to produce a drive within the individual would vary in general among persons, depending upon their neurophysical-chemical makeup. Thus, the concept of drives is a hypothetical relation between stimuli and activities on the part of the organism. The use of drives is a general surrogate for an incompletely specified data-processing and decision-making process which is largely unknown at this time. If more detail were available as to how the individual perceives his environment, the precise chemical processes which constitute mental and physical activity, and on throughout the entire range of bodily processes, the concept of drives could be completely replaced by a system of functional relations between the environment and the consequent actions of the organism. Given a complete specification of the environment, the system of equations would specify the actions of the individual.

The essence of this statement is that "free will" as popularly used does not exist. The individual, given a particular body chemistry, is solely a product of his environment and his experiences. Given two people with like body chemistries who are subjected to identical experiences, the resulting individuals would be identical. But of course no two people have the same bodily makeup nor the same set of past experiences upon which to judge, and this variety of human experience results in unique individuals with apparent free will. The metaphysical abstractions of ordinary utility theory are thus replaced by a mechanistic and specific process. This process is then amenable to analysis of preference generation and preference change.

It is postulated that S, or drive reduction, is a cardinal quantity. That is, the individual can measure alternatives and compare the drive reduction attainable in a manner which is unique up to a linear transformation. Differences in levels of S are important but the origin and unit of measure of S is arbitrary. In the terminology of measure theory the individual's empirical relational system is such that the mapping from activities to the real line is a cardinal scale.[4]

The assumption of the cardinality of S, or drive reduction, is clear as to its origins. Since S is a simplification of stimuli processing, if the stimuli are perceived "quantitatively," the resulting drives would be quantitative and comparable. If the individual perceives stimuli in cardinal quantities, the processing of this data would give cardinal values to these stimuli; therefore, drive reduction would have similar cardinal properties.

This difference is quite significant, not so much as an extension of existing economic analysis, but as it makes economic analysis applicable to a host of social problems which were heretofore untouchable by economists. Specifically, it opens up the area of preference formation which is more or less sacred and untrodden by economists. In some sense this departure from traditional economic theory is analogous to the difference between the development of marginal utility analysis by Menger and Jevons. Jevons used the pleasure-pain calculus approach of Bentham and the utilitarians, while Menger insisted that economic analysis accept preferences as given and ordinal in character only. Without the availability of recent advances in medicine and psychology in understanding the chemistry of the human organism, Menger's approach was preferable to the political and philosophical overtones of the concept of pain-pleasure calculus espoused by the utilitarians of the 1800s as well as by Jevons, an enlightened utilitarian. However, since the early 1900s significant strides in scientific inquiries outside economics have been developed which can be incorporated into economic analysis, enriching its potential and areas of applicability.[5]

It should be noted that the models generated by the approach to preference formation presented here reduce the individual to an organistic mechanism of chemical and neurological processes, gathering

---

4. See Roberts and Schulze (1972) or Pfanzagl (1968).

5. See Jevons, "Brief account of a general mathematical theory of political economy," reprinted in Gherity (1965); "*Grundsatze der Volkwirthschafts-lehre,*" in Menger (1881); and Robbins, "The place of Jevons in the history of economic thought," also in Gherity (1965), pp. 328–45.

data (environmental stimuli), processing this data (drive creation), and acting upon this information (carrying out activities to reduce these drives).

The difference between minimizing drives and maximizing drive reduction is rather important. The logical conclusion of the former is simply to isolate the organism from stimuli for the desired goal. The second approach allows the organism to actively pursue stimuli solely for the purpose of reacting to them. In other words, the concept of maximizing drive reduction is consistent with any set of activities which appear to be drive enhancing in and of themselves. For example, the setting of personal criteria and specific goals produce stimuli effective upon the activity mix carried out by the individual. It enhances drives; and in turn the program of action undertaken by the individual is oriented toward these self-created drives. The result is self-satisfaction of personal goals and standards of excellence. This would be a system of action and reaction totally inconsistent with the proposition of minimizing drives, the solution of which would have been to avoid the entire situation in the first place by not creating drives.

Although this chapter utilizes the terminology of drive-reduction theories of motivation and learning as a basic hypothetical construct, the models developed here and the variable preference models in Chapter 4 are sufficiently general to be compatible with the specifics of either. The specific assumption of drive reduction is incorporated into the model because it adds significant scope and power which would otherwise not be possible. (This basic approach supported by a large number of psychologists is one of hedonism which suggests that animals behave and learn because of bodily needs.)[6]

Concomitantly, however, many of the results can be established with a more general formulation where the basic motivating-choice function is not presupposed to contain the specific welfare implications of drive reduction. Specifically, a necessary and sufficient assumption for the models developed in this chapter is that the individual possess a binary preference ordering over all choice variables, one which has the usual axiomatic properties of completeness, reflexiveness, and transitivity. This logically implies the existence of a function S such that $S(x) \geqslant S(x')$ if and only if x is preferred or indifferent to x' and furthermore S is unique up to any monotonic transformation; that is, one can abstract from the language of drives

6. In general the various theories of learning can be segregated into drive-reduction theory expounded by Hull (1943) and further developed by others, especially Dollard and Miller (1950), and a cognitive theory of learning, for example, Lewin (1942) and Tolman (1955).

and drive reduction and remain in the theoretical format. The welfare implications of a more unique function which has meaningful cardinal properties are, among others, (1) the cardinal number has a meaningful "intensity of feeling" interpretation and (2) this represents one possible cardinal criterion on which to base social policy.

The maximizing behavior on the part of the individual with a cardinal objective function assumes that he can measure the change in drive status in a quantitative sense and compare this with the change in another drive in like units; that is, $S = \phi(x_1, \ldots, x_n)$ where the x's are variables the individual can control. Thus let D be equal to a set of finite drives, and assume that some function σ maps the set of drives onto the real line and that ϕ^* maps the set of activities into the set of drives which changes the levels of the various drives. Since ϕ is a measure of drive reduction, ϕ is a composite function of ϕ^* and σ; that is, $\phi = \phi^* \cdot \sigma$. This implies that the maximization criterion S is independent of the origin, and a numerical measurement of drives is unique up to a positive linear transformation. Furthermore, it is assumed that the unit of measure can be meaningfully compared, but limited to a numéraire activity, among persons in terms of empirical observation. That is, it is meaningful to say that individual i relative to individual j is twice as motivated in terms of the value of S such that if i will spend one hour writing to his congressman, j will spend only half an hour.

Drive reduction is postulated as resulting directly from engaging in activities, the arguments of the objective function. Those variables which can be manipulated by the maximizing unit are a general concept meant to correspond theoretically to the range of individual actions. The activity set is partitioned into two subsets, economic and noneconomic activities. Economic activities are defined as those which entail the exchange of goods and/or services. This activity set is construed to be sufficiently classified to separately include any activity which has a differentiating characteristic from another activity. Each good or service would in general affect more than one activity, and in general each activity would be serviced by more than one good or service.

A few aspects of this approach should be noted immediately. First, given a classification of the various drives, each activity could be quantitatively evaluated as to its drive-reducing effects. In the final analysis the precise measurement of the drive-reduction value of any particular activity would be left to the subjective calculation of the individual. However, it would also seem that an approximation would be possible on objective criteria established by past experiences and psychological measurement. Thus, given past information of an individual or an aggregate of such individuals, an aggregative evaluation of the worth of new activities would be possible, providing that some interpersonal weighting scheme were constructed. Thus in some sense S would be analogous to a cardinal utility function. This is not to say that it would be a meaningful method of making interpersonal comparisons, but it would be a criterion. It is worthwhile to remember that the assumption of cardinality was dropped from economic theory, not so much because no one had any hope of ever quantitatively measuring utility, but because it was superfluous to the logical implications of demand theory. Its reincarnation here in a somewhat disguised form of drive reduction is necessary and useful in applications of learning theory as well as other relevant economic problems of present-day society.

Second, the class of activities, when defined in rather general terms, would tend to be much more stable than the complex of commodities which fulfills these activities. For example, activities such as eating and being entertained would tend to remain constant over the lifetime of the individual relative to the products which fulfill them. Also, the demand for an activity such as transportation would tend to be much more stable than the cars, trains, or airplanes which change over time to fulfill this particular desired activity.[7]

The models developed in this analysis are not intended to explain the individual's psychological state. Attention is devoted solely to the activities and commodities which are consciously considered by the individual. This is not to say that dreams, fantasies, delusions, various involuntary actions, and other forms of autistic behavior are ignored, but merely that the analysis does not attempt to explain such behavior. From an economic standpoint these aspects can be dismissed from several standpoints: (1) the effect of unconscious (or involuntary) behavior on economic activity is relatively unimportant vis-à-vis a rational felicific calculus; (2) these random effects will cancel out in an aggregate empirical application; or (3) idealistically, people will conform to the actions as predicted by the "rational" aspects of their psyche as they become more and more aware of their environment. Socially programmed behavior (such as rituals, ceremonies, pastimes, maneuvers, and games) is implicitly incorporated in the model as aspects of the individual's decision process, and the aggregate implications are considered in later chapters.

The individual is assumed to maximize his overall drive reduction as best he can at any point in time, that is, to maximize $\int_0^\infty S\, dt$, where the maximizing function used in the models is a translation of

7. Lancaster (1965, 1966) discusses this aspect by speaking of "characteristics" of economic goods and services.

this overall calculus to a more easily measurable or manageable equation, max $S = \phi(x_1, \ldots, x_n)$ at time t, which is the condition that must hold for all t in order that overall welfare is maximized.

$$S = \phi(x_1, \ldots, x_n)$$

is a necessary point on the path at time t in order to maximize $\int_0^\infty S\, dt$. In the calculus occurring at time t, all parameters and values in the maximizing function and the constraint functions are assumed to be converted to time t values and parameters.[8] The intuitive interpretation of this assumption is that the individual is capable of discounting and evaluating activities which last for a considerable period if they are known with sufficient certainty. For example, the purchase of an automobile or other durable good would be in consideration of the lifetime of transportation or other service the durable commodity would yield. On the other hand, an activity such as buying and eating lunch two weeks in the future would carry such a high discount as to give it a zero value in the objective function. In general, it is possible that several paths, each with different characteristics at time t, would result in the overall welfare maximization goal. In this case the individual would be indifferent among the various optimal solutions.

With the addition of specified learning activities introduced in Chapter 4, the individual is viewed as continually searching for the optimal path and recalculating its characteristics whenever sufficient information makes such a reevaluation necessary. In the constant preference models a person could calculate his entire lifetime of activities once and for all. In a comparative static sense he would recalculate only when an exogenous change in the data occurred. In the more general variable preference model, activities specifically designed to alter the data (for example, search activities), deliberate attempts to convince others of one's point of view, and so forth, are included.

Thus activities chosen at any point in time may be of various time duration. Some, such as purchasing an automobile, are made with concern for a longer period of time than are others, such as buying a hamburger. This difference in time duration is subsumed into the discounting process, that is, the converting of all values occurring at a time not equal to t into time t values. Thus everything, regardless of its time of occurrence or its duration, is converted to one point in time.

Similarly, at any point in time the consumer, upon selection of

8. See Pontryagin (1962).

an optimal activity mix, concomitantly selects an optimal commodity mix as well. The function which maps commodities onto activities is solely concerned with those which are necessarily involved in a transaction, the economic act of exchange. In other words, given no initial wealth, sleep might be an economic activity which would perhaps entail an exchange of labor for a bed. At a subsequent period of recalculation the same desired activity (sleep) would not require another bed to be purchased and thus no concomitant activity of exchange would be necessary in light of accumulated wealth (the bed).

In the overall calculus of welfare $\int_0^\infty S\, dt$, the activities chosen throughout this period w_{i,t_o,t_i} (where t_o is the time the activity commences and t_i is the time the activity is concluded) would depend upon both the trade undertaken during the period $t_o - t_i$ and the stock of commodities on hand throughout the period, that is,

$$w_{i,t_o t_i} = \gamma_{i,t_o t_i}(x_{1,t_o t_i}, \ldots, x_{k,t_o t_P}, X_{1,t_o t_i}, \ldots, X_{k,t_o t_i})$$

where x_{1,t_o,t_i} represents an amount of x_1 traded during $t_o - t_i$, and $X_{1,t_o t_i}$ represents the stock of the commodity on hand during $t_o - t_i$. The relation between these stocks and flows and the optimal stock accumulation from the point of view of the consumer are not relevant for the purposes of Model 3.2. In Model 3.2 the stocks $X_1, \ldots, X_k$ are absorbed as parameters in the equations, and the time subscripts are omitted for purposes of clarity.

For the individual the consumption of a free good would not be an economic activity. If the activity entailed use of a public good or one which was partially public and partially private, no particular problem is posed for the model. In each case the calculus would be in light of the information possessed by the individual and his expectations. Suppose that a particular good in question were a Samuelsonian pure public good where consumption could be restricted by ownership. In this case the cost to the individual might be P/n, where n is the number of people willing to combine to make the purchase. The calculus might dictate that it would be beneficial to the individual to proceed with the noneconomic activity of convincing others of the worth of the public good, and thus increase n and lower the price which he has to pay, P/n. The point here is that whether the good is purely private, purely public, or some combination, it poses no particular problem for the analysis; the acquisition of products in the models need not be physical in nature but more generally should be considered as the acquisition of the ownership or rights to the activity value of the good or service.

Model 3.2 represents a rigorous extension of utility theory and consumer behavior to include a simultaneous consideration of activities and the consequent product demand. It is a generalization of the conventional utility maximization approach to consumer behavior and market demand theory. It is not intended to replace utility theory in the areas where utility theory is quite adequate, namely, static market demand derivation under perfect information. Following the basic presentation of Model 3.2, conventional demand theory is worked out demonstrating that this approach in no way negates the utility approach but that indeed utility analysis is a special case. The primary intent of Model 3.2 is to develop an expanded theoretical structure, not to generate hypotheses and conclusions where the conventional analysis is a valid but special case. The scope and power of Model 3.2 will be beneficial in proceeding to greater problems of individual and group behavior.

MODEL 3.2

Maximize

$$S = \phi(w_1, \ldots, w_n, \omega_1, \ldots, \omega_m) \qquad (3.3)$$

where

$$w_i = w_i(x_1, \ldots, x_k); \qquad i = 1, \ldots, n \qquad (3.4)$$

and subject to

$$T = \psi(w_1, \ldots, w_n, \omega_1, \ldots, \omega_m) \leqslant T_o \qquad (3.5)$$

$$M = \sum_{i=1}^{k} P_i x_i \leqslant 0 \qquad (3.6)$$

Model 3.2 assumes that the individual can evaluate the effect of activities on a basic set of drives. This evaluation for a given level of activities is the real value of S. Drives may be reduced or enhanced by the various activities undertaken by the individual. Some activities may enhance drives while others reduce them. It will be assumed that the individual is continually trying to maximize drive reduction.

Whether these drives can actually be measured and compared is not in question here. The assumption is that the individual can compare the drive reduction from one activity with that from another and base his decision on those values. The actions of an individual can best be described as if he did a similar form of calculation, implicitly or explicitly. For further uses of this theory in empirical application, it is postulated that it is possible to construct a measure of drive reduction.[9] The debate as to whether this measurement of drive reduction would be equivalent to the welfare of the individual is indeed a moot one. Such a measurement would be expected to provide a cardinal measure of empirical observations of intensity of preference and motivation. Whether this is what is meant by welfare is an opinion and, in the final analysis, a value judgment to be made by the individual. However, there is a certain distinction between motivation as expressed by the value of S and what would in general correspond to welfare. For example, many needs or deprivational states never result in drive creation. There are no sense receptors sensitive to these deprivational states; thus there can be no arousal of the hypothalamic centers and no efferent impulses producing internal responses. Carbon monoxide produces no motivation for the individual to obtain purer air. In a state of ignorance the individual would place a low value on purer air, when in fact his very existence depends upon it. Is the individual the best judge of his own welfare?

Within the set of all possible activities, there is a set of known activities, $w_1, \ldots, w_n, \omega_1, \ldots, \omega_m$. The known set of possible activities is invariant under Model 3.2. Also contained in this knowledge set are the various functional relations in the model, which are also assumed constant.

Known activities are partitioned into subsets of economic activities $w_1, \ldots, w_n$, (those which necessitate the exchange of economic commodities) and noneconomic activities $\omega_1, \ldots, \omega_m$. The concept of an activity is an aggregate of actions on the part of the individual which he views singularly. Consider eating as an activity; there are various ways in which this could be fulfilled: by going out to a restaurant; going to a grocery store, purchasing the food, and cooking it at home; or dropping in on friends at mealtime. By classifying all these examples as servicing a single activity, it is implicitly assumed there are no quality differences among them. Similarly, each of these different methods of servicing the activity concomitantly implies a certain money expenditure and use of time. Alternatively for this example, each method of eating could have been classified as an activity if the individual believed there was a quality difference among them. In this case the commodities which would service the activity of eating out would be the various restaurants, each with a different service and a different required time usage.

Noneconomic activities are identical to economic activities in their intuitive interpretation except that they do not require the exchange of commodities. Noneconomic activities are an aggregate of

9. For the theoretical development of such measurement problems see Suppes and Zinnes in Luce, Bush, and Galanter (1963), vol. 1, Ch. 1, pp. 1-76.

personal actions which the individual perceives or thinks of as a single item. Consider the noneconomic activity of outdoor recreation; here the only cost to the individual is the opportunity cost of the time spent. Another example would be the decision to persuade a group of voters to vote in favor of a particular proposal. At any point in time the individual has an assumed relation between the time expended in argumentation and the consequent results. Again the cost involved is the drive enhancement (if arguing is not a preferred activity) plus the opportunity cost of the time used. If the activity of persuasion gives the individual drive reduction in and of itself, the cost would be the time used as valued by its shadow drive-reduction price minus the drive reduction from the act of debating.

Equations 3.3 through 3.6 represent the individual's set of beliefs or state of knowledge. Equation 3.4 is a function which maps commodities onto some subset of the activity space. This relation is basically one of technology and environment. In other words, Equation 3.4 represents the extent the individual believes that commodities will efficiently service the activities under consideration. Suppose that a desired activity was transportation. This activity could be serviced by various commodities available on the market, from shoe leather to jet aircraft. Equation 3.4 specifies the knowledge the individual has of these commodity-activity relations. Different individuals who have the same information sets could be expected to have similar opinions of product-activity relations. This is not to imply that in fact this relation is exogenous to the individual or that expectations do not play a large role in everyday activity. But this is more or less factual data and would include such things as the length of time required or necessarily associated with a particular product-activity combination.

Traditionally, the analysis of the consumer in demand theory has presumed that the individual has only one constraint, a budget constraint. The individual is free to select any combination of commodities he wants as long as the budget constraint is satisfied. However this is clearly not a valid assumption since, for example, the set of permissible products has been limited by society since earliest history. The importance of personal calculus and consequent commodity selection in determining the commodity mix which society produces, and thus, to some extent the course of social process, depends upon the number of constraints imposed upon the individuals and the extent of their knowledge sets. If the constraint set is relatively large as dictated by technology and social laws and mores both explicitly and implicitly stated, the effect of individual selection is insignificant upon the overall mix of commodities produced.

The general construction of Model 3.1 allows for explicit delineation of each constraint effective upon the individual. In Model 3.2 it is assumed that there are two relevant constraints which the individual must face, a time constraint, Equation 3.5, and an institutional budget constraint, Equation 3.6. Equation 3.6 assumes that the individual cannot buy more in value than he sells. In general, activities have more dimensions than simply a time dimension. That is, the quality or intensity as well as the duration of an activity could vary. Each activity is defined such that its dimensionality is time. Two similar activities differing in quality are defined as separate activities.

The Lagrangian for Model 3.2 is

$$\lambda = \phi(w_1, \ldots, w_n, \omega_1, \ldots, \omega_m)$$
$$+ \lambda_1 [T_0 - \psi(w_1, \ldots, w_n, \omega_1, \ldots, \omega_m)] \tag{3.7}$$

$$- \lambda_2 \left(\sum_{i=1}^{k} P_i x_i \right) \tag{3.8}$$

The Kuhn-Tucker conditions for Model 3.2 are

$$\frac{\partial \lambda}{\partial x_i} = \frac{\partial \phi}{\partial w_1} \frac{\partial w_1}{\partial x_i} + \ldots + \frac{\partial \phi}{\partial w_n} \frac{\partial w_n}{\partial x_i} - \lambda_1 \left(\frac{\partial \psi}{\partial w_1} \frac{\partial w_1}{\partial x_i} + \ldots + \frac{\partial \psi}{\partial w_n} \frac{\partial w_n}{\partial x_i} \right)$$

$$- \lambda_2 P_i \leqslant 0, \quad i = 1, \ldots, k$$

$$\text{if } \partial \lambda / \partial x_i < 0, \text{ then } x_i = 0$$

$$\partial \lambda / \partial \omega_j = \partial \phi / \partial \omega_j - \lambda \, \partial \psi / \partial \omega_j \leqslant 0, \quad j = 1, \ldots, m$$

$$\text{if } \partial \lambda / \partial \omega_j < 0, \text{ then } \omega_j = 0$$

$$\partial \lambda / \partial \lambda_1 = T_0 - \psi(w_1, \ldots, w_n, \omega_1, \ldots, \omega_n) \geqslant 0$$

$$\text{if } \partial \lambda / \partial \lambda_1 > 0, \text{ then } \lambda_1 = 0$$

$$\partial \lambda / \partial \lambda_2 = \Sigma P_i x_i \geqslant 0, \quad \Sigma P_i x_i \geqslant 0$$

$$\text{if } \partial \lambda / \partial \lambda_2 > 0, \text{ then } \lambda_2 = 0 \tag{3.9}$$

From Equation 3.9 if the equality holds,

$$\frac{\partial \phi}{\partial w_1} \frac{\partial w_1}{\partial x_i} + \ldots + \frac{\partial \phi}{\partial w_n} \frac{\partial w_n}{\partial x_i} - \frac{\partial \phi / \partial \omega}{\partial \psi / \partial \omega}$$

$$\left(\frac{\partial \psi}{\partial w_1} \frac{\partial w_1}{\partial x_i} + \ldots + \frac{\partial \psi}{\partial w_n} \frac{\partial w_n}{\partial x_i} \right) = \lambda_2 P_i \tag{3.10}$$

For all i where $\partial \lambda / \partial x_i = 0$,

$$
P_i / P_j = \frac{\displaystyle\sum_{k=1}^{n} \frac{\partial \phi}{\partial w_k} \frac{\partial w_k}{\partial x_i} - \frac{\partial \phi / \partial \omega}{\partial \psi / \partial \omega} \left(\sum_{k=1}^{n} \frac{\partial \psi}{\partial w_k} \frac{\partial w_k}{\partial x_i} \right)}{\displaystyle\sum_{k=1}^{n} \frac{\partial \phi}{\partial w_k} \frac{\partial w_k}{\partial x_j} - \frac{\partial \phi / \partial \omega}{\partial \psi / \partial \omega} \left(\sum_{k=1}^{n} \frac{\partial \psi}{\partial w_k} \frac{\partial w_k}{\partial x_j} \right)}
$$

Since

$$
\partial \phi / \partial x_i = \sum_{k=1}^{n} (\partial \phi / \partial w_k)(\partial w_k / \partial x_i)
$$

$$
\partial \psi / \partial x_i = \sum_{k=1}^{n} (\partial \psi / \partial w_k)(\partial w_k / \partial x_i)
$$

then

$$
P_i / P_j = \frac{\dfrac{\partial \phi}{\partial x_i} - \dfrac{\partial \phi / \partial \omega}{\partial \psi / \partial \omega} \cdot \dfrac{\partial \psi}{\partial x_i}}{\dfrac{\partial \phi}{\partial x_j} - \dfrac{\partial \phi / \partial \omega}{\partial \psi / \partial \omega} \cdot \dfrac{\partial \psi}{\partial x_j}} \tag{3.11}
$$

A basic conclusion of Model 3.2, from the first-order conditions for a maximum, is Equation 3.11. $\partial \phi / \partial x_i$ is the effect of a small increment in product x_i on drive reduction S. $\partial \psi / \partial x_i$ is the effect of a small increment of x_i on the time used. $\lambda_2 = (\partial \phi / \partial \omega)/(\partial \psi / \partial \omega)$, the marginal drive satisfaction from any noneconomic activity relative to its time cost, since $(\partial \phi / \partial \omega_i)/(\partial \psi / \partial \omega_i) = (\partial \phi / \partial \omega_j)/(\partial \psi / \partial \omega_j)$, at the optimal solution for all i and j.

From Equation 3.11 one can see that any set of commodities which maximizes a constrained utility function also maximizes the constrained ϕ function. In Equation 3.11 the traditional concept of marginal utility is broken down into the marginal drive reduction $\partial \phi / \partial x_i$ and the shadow price, expressed in drive reduction terms, of the marginal time use of the commodity. The traditional concept of preference as expressed by a utility indicator has been delineated in Model 3.2 into actual drive reduction minus the opportunity cost of marginal time use.

Under the assumptions of Model 3.2 let the maximum attainable S be

$$S* = \phi(w_1^*, \ldots, w_n^*, \omega_1^*, \ldots, \omega_m^*)$$

then $w_i^* = w_i(x_1^i, \ldots, x_k^i)$, where x_j^i is equal to the amount of commodity j necessary to fulfill activity w_i at a level w_i^*. If x_i^* is equal to the amount of commodity x_i exchanged in the time period under consideration, where $\Sigma_{i=1}^k P_i x_i^* \leqslant 0$, the conditions on x^* are the following:

$$x_j^* \geqslant \max_i x_j^i, \quad j = 1, \ldots, k$$

$$x_j^* \leqslant \sum_{i=1}^n x_j^i, \quad j = 1, \ldots, k$$

If $x_j^* = \max_i x_j^i$ for any combination of economic activities selected, then x_j can be defined as a *purely general good*. That is, an amount x_j will service several activities without additional units of x_j being necessary. If $x_j^* = \Sigma_{i=1}^n x_j^i$, then x_j can be defined as a *purely divisible good* in that if x_j is used for any one activity, it cannot simultaneously be used for another. In general, the nature of any commodity would fall between these two extremes.

To analyze the effect of a price change on the optimal commodity-activity mix, assume there is a small change in the price of commodity i, $dP_i > 0$, where all commodities are purely divisible. Rewriting Equation 3.10 as

$$(\partial\phi/\partial x_i) - \lambda_1 (\partial\psi/\partial x_i) - \lambda_2 P_i = 0; \text{ where } x_i \neq 0$$

where

$$\partial\phi/\partial x_i = \sum_{k=1}^n (\partial\phi/\partial w_k)(\partial w_k/\partial x_i)$$

$$\lambda_1 = (\partial\phi/\partial\omega_j)/(\partial\psi/\partial\omega_j)$$

$$\partial\psi/\partial x_i = \sum_{k=1}^n (\partial\psi/\partial w_k)(\partial w_k/\partial x_i)$$

then for simplicity, assuming $x_i \neq 0$ for $i = 1, \ldots, k$ and differentiating Equation 3.10 with respect to P_i, yields Equation 3.12 which is expressed in matrix notation:

$$[\phi] \ [\partial x/\partial P_i] = [\partial v/\partial P_i] \qquad (3.12)$$

$[\phi]$ is a $(k+m+2 \times k+m+2)$ matrix of second partial derivatives of ϕ, bordered by prices and the first derivative of the second constraint with respect to the decision variable. Typical terms in the Hessian matrix are

$$\phi_{i,j} = (\partial^2 \phi/\partial x_i \partial x_j) - \lambda_2 (\partial^2 \psi/\partial x_i \partial x_j), \qquad \text{if } i,j \leqslant k$$

$$\phi_{i,k+j} = (\partial^2 \phi/\partial x_i \partial \omega_j) - \lambda_2 (\partial^2 \psi/\partial x_i \partial \omega_j), \qquad \text{if } i \leqslant k; j \leqslant m$$

$$\phi_{k+i,k+j} = (\partial^2 \phi/\partial \omega_i \partial \omega_j) - \lambda_2 (\partial^2 \psi/\partial \omega_i \partial \omega_j), \qquad \text{if } i,j \leqslant m$$

$[\partial x/\partial P_i]$ is a $(k+m+2 \times 1)$ vector with typical terms.

$\partial x_j/\partial P_i$, in positions 1 through k

$\partial \omega_j/\partial P_i$, in positions $k+1$ through m

$\partial \lambda_j/\partial P_i$, in positions $k+m+1$ and $k+m+2$

$[\partial v/\partial P_i]$ is a $(k+m+2 \times 1)$ vector with all zeros save for the ith place and the $k+m+1$-th place, which are λ_2 and x_i respectively. (Greater mathematical detail is presented in Appendix B.)

$$\partial x_j/\partial P_i = (-1)^{i+j} \lambda_2 (|\phi_{i,j}|/|\phi|) + x_i(-1)^{j+k+m+1} (|\phi_{k+m+1,j}|/|\phi|)$$
(3.13)

Equation 3.13 is the familiar Slutsky equation with the income and wealth effects, where $|\phi_{i,j}|$ is a cofactor determinant and $|\phi|$ is the determinant of the full-bordered Hessian matrix.

The traditional results from utility theory as to the sign of $\partial x_i/\partial P_j$ follow without qualification. In terms of Model 3.2, $\partial^2 U/\partial x_i \partial x_j$ is $(\partial^2 \phi/\partial x_i \partial x_j) - \lambda_1 (\partial^2 \psi/\partial x_i \partial x_j)$ and the substitution effect of an own price change is negative.

An analogous effect to the income effect in the traditional Slutsky equation would arise if the individual were faced by a change in the budget restriction by replacing 0 in the budget restriction above by a more general M_o. This is interpreted as market credit conditions which could be greater than, equal to, or less than zero. If society required positive balances to be maintained, $M_o > 0$. If the social system allowed its members to go into debt, $M_o < 0$.

With an exogenous change in the initial budget constraint $dM_o > 0$, then $[\phi] [\partial x/\partial M_o] = [\partial v/\partial M_o]$, where $[\partial v/\partial M_o]$ is a vector with all zeros except in the last place which is -1. Thus

$$\partial x_i/\partial M_o = (-1)^{i+k+m+2} (|\phi_{k+m+1,i}|/|\phi|)$$
(3.14)

follows by Cramér's rule. The wealth effect in Equation 3.13 is identical to a change in the budget restriction's effect (Equation 3.14), on the optimum x_i chosen. For a consumer with initial wealth a change in the price level creates a wealth effect, and this is identical to a change in market credit conditions. Either case gives the individual more purchasing power.

From Equation 3.10 several interesting observations can be derived from assumptions about the terms therein. Five cases are examined below.

Case 1

Since

$$P_i/P_j = \frac{\dfrac{\partial \phi}{\partial x_i} - \dfrac{\partial \phi/\partial \omega}{\partial \psi/\partial \omega} \cdot \dfrac{\partial \psi}{\partial x_i}}{\dfrac{\partial \phi}{\partial x_j} - \dfrac{\partial \phi/\partial \omega}{\partial \psi/\partial \omega} \cdot \dfrac{\partial \psi}{\partial x_j}}$$

then if

$$(\partial \phi/\partial x_i)/(\partial \phi/\partial x_j) = (\partial \psi/\partial x_i)/(\partial \psi/\partial x_j)$$

then

$$P_i/P_j = (\partial \phi/\partial x_i)/(\partial \phi/\partial x_j) \qquad (3.15)$$

That is, let $p = (a - kb)/(c - kd)$, if $a/c = b/d$ then $ad = cb$. Then since $p(c - kd) = a - kb$ or $(p/a)(ac - kda) = a - kb$, and since $da = cb$, $(p/a)(ac - kcb) = a - kb$; then $(pc/a)(a - kb) = a - kb$. Thus $p = a/c$. In other words, if the marginal tradeoff between the satisfaction of two commodities is equal to the marginal tradeoff between the time usage, the price ratio of the commodities must be equal to the marginal rate of commodity substitution with respect to drive reduction alone.

Case 2

If

$$\partial \phi/\partial w_k = \partial \phi/\partial w_j, \text{for all } k, j$$

then

$$\partial \phi/\partial x_i = \sum_{k=1}^{n} (\partial \phi/\partial w_k)(\partial w_k/\partial x_i) = \partial \phi/\partial w \sum_{k=1}^{n} \partial w_k/\partial x_i$$

and if

$$\partial \psi/\partial w_k = \partial \psi/\partial w_j, \text{for all } k, j$$

then

$$\partial \psi/\partial x_i = \sum_{k=1}^{n} (\partial \psi/\partial w_k)(\partial w_k/\partial x_i) = \partial \psi/\partial w \sum_{k=1}^{n} \partial w_k/\partial x_i$$

Therefore,

$$P_i/P_j = \cfrac{\dfrac{\partial \phi}{\partial w} \sum\limits_{k=1}^{n} \dfrac{\partial w_k}{\partial x_i} - \dfrac{\partial \phi/\partial \omega}{\partial \psi/\partial \omega} \cdot \dfrac{\partial \psi}{\partial w} \sum\limits_{k=1}^{n} \dfrac{\partial w_k}{\partial x_i}}{\dfrac{\partial \phi}{\partial w} \sum\limits_{k=1}^{n} \dfrac{\partial w_k}{\partial x_j} - \dfrac{\partial \phi/\partial \omega}{\partial \psi/\partial \omega} \cdot \dfrac{\partial \psi}{\partial w} \sum\limits_{k=1}^{n} \dfrac{\partial w_k}{\partial x_j}}$$

or

$$P_i/P_j = \cfrac{\sum\limits_{k=1}^{n} \partial w_k/\partial x_i}{\sum\limits_{k=1}^{n} \partial w_k/\partial x_j} \tag{3.16}$$

That is, if the marginal satisfaction of all economic activities is equivalent and the time used by all economic activities is equivalent, the price ratio of two commodities i and j is equal to the ratios of the sum total effect of the commodity on activity levels.

Case 3

If $\partial w_k/\partial x_i = \partial w_j/\partial x_i$ for all k, i, and j,

$$P_i/P_j = \cfrac{\sum\limits_{k=1}^{n} \dfrac{\partial \phi}{\partial w_k} \dfrac{\partial w_k}{\partial x_i} - \dfrac{\partial \phi/\partial \omega}{\partial \psi/\partial \omega} \sum\limits_{k=1}^{n} \dfrac{\partial \psi}{\partial w_k} \dfrac{\partial w_k}{\partial x_i}}{\sum\limits_{k=1}^{n} \dfrac{\partial \phi}{\partial w_k} \dfrac{\partial w_k}{\partial x_j} - \dfrac{\partial \phi/\partial \omega}{\partial \psi/\partial \omega} \sum\limits_{k=1}^{n} \dfrac{\partial \psi}{\partial w_k} \dfrac{\partial w_k}{\partial x_j}}$$

$$P_i/P_j = \cfrac{\dfrac{\partial w_k}{\partial x_i} \sum\limits_{k=1}^{n} \dfrac{\partial \phi}{\partial w_k} - \dfrac{\partial \phi/\partial \omega}{\partial \psi/\partial \omega} \sum\limits_{k=1}^{n} \dfrac{\partial \psi}{\partial w_k}}{\dfrac{\partial w_k}{\partial x_j} \sum\limits_{k=1}^{n} \dfrac{\partial \phi}{\partial w_k} - \dfrac{\partial \phi/\partial \omega}{\partial \psi/\partial \omega} \sum\limits_{k=1}^{n} \dfrac{\partial \psi}{\partial w_k}}$$

or

$$P_i/P_j = (\partial w_k/\partial x_i)/(\partial w_k/\partial x_j), \qquad k = 1, \ldots, n \tag{3.17}$$

Equation 3.17 states that the price ratio of any two commodities must be equal to the ratio of the effects of the commodities on any one activity if each commodity affects all activities equally.

Case 4

If $\partial\phi/\partial\omega = 0$, then

$$P_i/P_j = (\partial\phi/\partial x_i)/(\partial\phi/\partial x_j) \qquad (3.18)$$

Equation 3.18 is the general intuitive interpretation of utility theory; that is, noneconomic activities have a zero effect on satisfaction at the margin. Although the marginal time use by noneconomic activities is not necessarily zero, this is negated since the marginal value of these activities is zero.

Case 5

Finally, if the time restriction is not relevant in that additional commodity purchasing requires no use of time; that is, if

$$\partial\psi/\partial x_i = \partial\psi/\partial x_j = 0$$

then again as in Equations 3.15 and 3.18:

$$P_i/P_j = (\partial\phi/\partial x_i)/(\partial\phi/\partial x_j) \qquad (3.19)$$

As society becomes more affluent, the assumptions of cases 4 and 5 become less realistic. Noneconomic activities begin to assume a positive marginal value evaluated at the optimal solution, while the time consumed in acquiring more commodities becomes more relevant.

GRAPHICAL INTERPRETATION OF MODEL 3.2

The above results will now be interpreted in a graphical manner in order to develop a fuller understanding of the scope of Model 3.2's expansion to demand theory. First, a slight digression to prove a simple theorem will aid the graphical presentation. The theorem is couched in terms of the traditional utility theory but is equally applicable to the concepts of Model 3.2 with a change in terminology.

Define an independent consumption process as one where for any bundle of goods $(x_1, \ldots, x_n)$ the individual has a choice of independently consuming any or all goods or consuming them in combinations. That is to say, for any subset $S \subset \{1, \ldots, n\}$ of commodity types, function $V_s(x_1, \ldots, x_n)$ exists such that

$$U(x_1, \ldots, x_n) = \max \sum_{\text{all } s} V_s(x_1, \ldots, x_n)$$

Theorem 3.1 If all consumption processes can be independent and each V_s is concave, then $U(x_1, \ldots, x_n)$ is concave.

Proof of Theorem 3.1 follows directly since the sum of concave functions is a concave function.

Theorem 3.2 If $U(x_1, \ldots, x_n)$ is a concave function, then an indifference curve, the locus of all points

$$\overline{x} = (\overline{x}_1, \ldots, \overline{x}_n), \overline{y} = (\overline{y}_1, \ldots, \overline{y}_n), \ldots$$

such that $U(\overline{x}) = U(\overline{y}) = \cdots = U$ is convex to the origin.

Proof

Let $x = (x_1^*, \ldots, x_n^*)$
$y = (x_1', \ldots, x_n')$
$x \neq y$, and
$U(x) = U(y)$

then by definition of a concave function,

$$U[\lambda x + (1 - \lambda)y] \geqslant U(x) \text{ for } 0 < \lambda < 1$$

This is shown graphically in Figure 3.1.

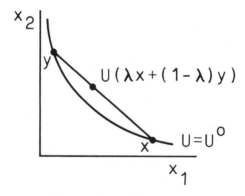

Fig. 3.1. A convex indifference curve.

Theorems 3.1 and 3.2 add a bit of intuitive appeal to the drawing of convex indifference curves. An interpretation would be that if each commodity taken singly has diminishing marginal utility and a commodity can be consumed individually or in a group with other commodities, the indifference curves must be convex to the origin. That is, two (or more) commodities would never be combined in a consumption process if consuming each separately would produce more satisfaction.

Assuming that independent consumption processes and independent activities exist and that there are only two activities and two goods, Model 3.2 can be reduced to a two-space analogy in graphical form. By these assumptions and Theorems 3.1 and 3.2, the locus of all points where any combination of activities w_1 and w_2 create equal amounts of drive reduction is mapped in Figure 3.2 and labeled S^o. $T_o' T_o$ is the time constraint. The linear nature of the time constraint in Figure 3.2 assumes that the activities do not interact. If both activities could be carried out simultaneously, $T_o' T_o$ would be a right angle. One would expect $T_o' T_o$ to be concave to the origin.

Also implicit in Figure 3.2 is a budget constraint which is omitted for purposes of clarity. The individual maximizes drive reduction by selecting w_1^* and w_2^*, both of which in turn imply that a particular commodity bundle will be purchased.

The commodity bundle purchased by w_1^* and w_2^* will be on the expansion or cost-minimizing path of activity w_1 in Figure 3.3 and

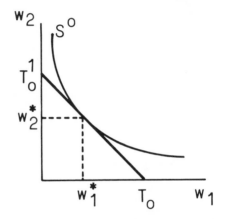

Fig. 3.2. Two activities and a time constraint.

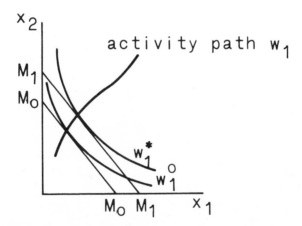

Fig. 3.3. Two commodities and an activity expansion path.

on the expansion path of activity w_2 in Figure 3.4. Again, Theorem 3.1 and the assumption of independence are implemented since the isoactivity curves are drawn convex to the origin. The relationship between economic activities would not necessarily be along the cost-minimizing path if the commodities were not purely divisible. Given some commodity which is concomitantly utilized in two activities, the total cost of the two activities would be minimized.

Figure 3.5 assumes that the expansion paths of activities w_1 and w_2 are linear with respect to products x_1 and x_2. At this point the analogy between this model and linear programming, if

$$w_i = \gamma_i (x_1, \ldots, x_k)$$

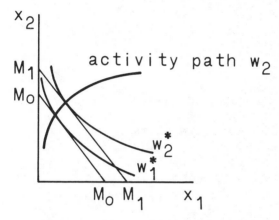

Fig. 3.4. Two commodities and an activity expansion path.

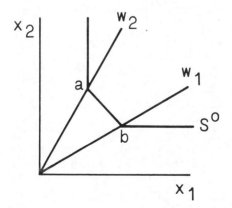

Fig. 3.5. Two commodities, two activity expansion paths, and an isodrive-reduction curve.

is linear and homogeneous, as applied to the firm or linear activity analysis is obvious.

Figure 3.5 makes a very special assumption that the marginal effect on drives of an additional unit of activity is constant. Graphically it assumes that the isodrive-reduction curve is a straight line as in Figure 3.6, that is, $(\partial\phi/\partial w_1)/(\partial\phi/\partial w_2) = $ constant.

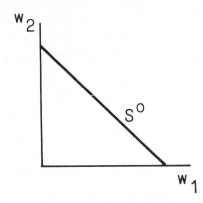

Fig. 3.6. Linear isodrive-reduction curve between two activities.

Thus combining Figures 3.2 and 3.5, an isodrive-reduction curve is traced out much the same as isoprofit curves are drawn for a firm which has a linear production technology and faces constant prices. If the time constraint were drawn in, the maximum would occur at point a, point b, or any point between and including a and b in Figure 3.5.

The geometrical analysis can be pursued further with a simple model of two activities and two products by assuming that each activity is solely a function of one product and this relation is linear.

Assume:

1. 2 activities: w_1 = consumption, w_2 = labor activity
2. 2 commodities: x_1 = food, x_2 = hours of labor
3. $w_1 = b_1 x_1,$ $w_2 = b_2 x_2$
4. $S = \phi(w_1, w_2)$
5. $T = t_1 w_1 + t_2 w_2$

In Figures 3.7–3.9, the graphical solution to the problem is presented. In Figure 3.7 the implicit assumption is that carrying out no activities is a feasible solution and that the S function is linear with respect to the tradeoff between w_2 (work) and w_1 (consumption). Figure 3.8 assumes that the marginal rate of substitution between w_2 and w_1 is constant. In Figure 3.9 the marginal rate of

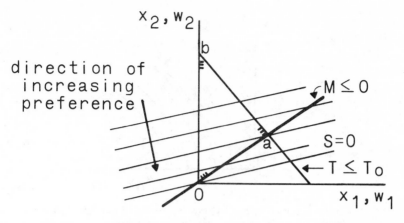

Fig. 3.7. Two commodities, two activities, and time and budget constraints with a linear drive-reduction map.

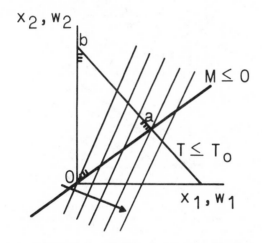

Fig. 3.8. Two commodities, two activities, and time and budget constraints with a linear drive-reduction map.

substitution between activities is decreasing as more and more w_1 is taken. In Figure 3.10 the situation again is presented where there is a diminishing marginal rate of activity substitution, but the solution is one where the time restriction is not relevant.

In all cases above

$$\partial\phi/\partial w_2 < 0, \qquad \partial\phi/\partial w_1 > 0,$$

$$(\partial/\partial w_2)[(\partial\phi/\partial w_1)/(\partial\phi\partial w_2)|S = \text{constant}] \leqslant 0$$

Under these conditions the solution must lie along $0a$, in Figure 3.10, including the end points.

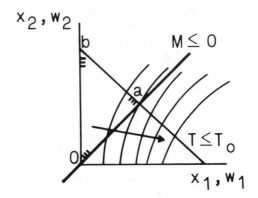

Fig. 3.9. Two commodities, two activities, and time and budget constraints with isodrive-reduction curves convex to the x_2, w_2 axis.

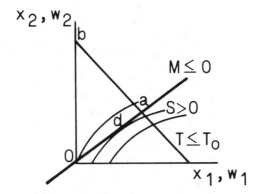

Fig. 3.10. Two commodities and two activities with a maximizing solution on the budget constraint, but less than the time constraint.

Expanding the analysis to three activities gives

$$w_1 = \gamma_1(x_1), \qquad w_2 = \gamma_2(x_2), \qquad w_3 = \gamma_3(x_3)$$

where $\partial \gamma_i / \partial x_i$ is constant. If $i = 1, 2, 3$, then the feasible set becomes $0abc$ in Figure 3.11, a tetrahedron with faces $0ab$ and $0cb$ at right angles to each other along the x_2 axis.

If both activities w_1 and w_3 are to be relevant, then the indifference curves between w_1 and w_3 will have to have the traditional convex form. If the tradeoff between work w_2 and either of the other activities is constant, the optimal solution will lie on ca or $c'a'$ projected down onto the $w_1 w_3$ plane.

$c'a'$ is an induced budget restriction in that it depends not only upon the prices of activities w_1 and w_3 but upon the wage rate, the

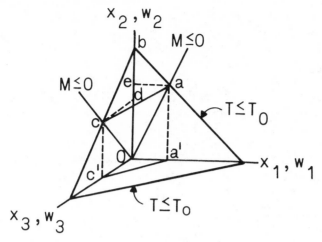

Fig. 3.11. Three commodities and three activities.

total time available, and the "willingness" to work. $c'a'$ is the budget constraint if and only if the optimal solution lies along ca and the individual will work between $0d$ and $0e$ units of time. This is the analogous solution to those of Figures 3.8 and 3.9. A solution of the Figure 3.10 type, a nontime-relevant solution, would place the solu-

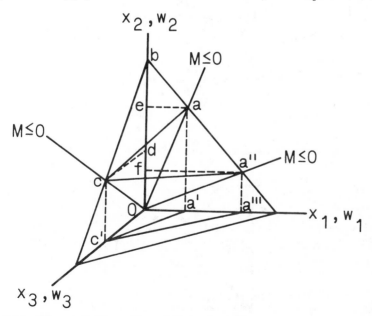

Fig. 3.12. Three activities with a shift in the budget constraint due to a price change.

tion closer to the origin than ca and correspondingly the time spent working would be less than $0c$.

Now suppose there is a change in the relative prices of x_1 and x_2 such that the amount of time spent working to attain a given level of activity w_1 is now less. This is pictured in Figure 3.12.

The budget restriction in the x_1x_2 plane shifts from $M \leqslant 0$ to $M' \leqslant 0$ which causes the induced budget restriction on the x_1x_3 plane to shift outward from $c'a'$ to $c'a'''$. Under the traditional assumption of the undesirability of working, activity w_2 (the maximum time the individual could spend working) would change from $0e$ to $0d$. Note that before the price change, labor output is maximized if the solution is at a, and after the price change the solution for maximum labor output would be at c.

In Figure 3.13 the induced budget restriction as projected onto the x_1x_3 plane is shown as the heavily shaded line. Nominal income is highest at a' and falls as you move along $c'a'$ from a' to c'. $c'a'$ represents an upper bound on the feasible limits of activities w_1 and w_3, using commodities x_1 and x_3.

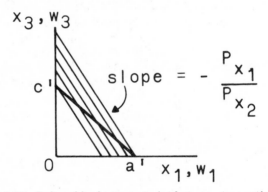

Fig. 3.13. Induced budget constraint between two activities.

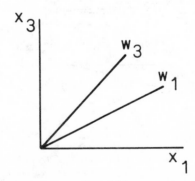

Fig. 3.14. Two linear activity paths which use some of two commodities.

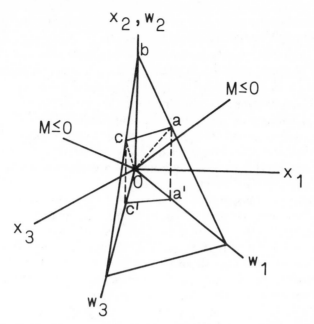

Fig. 3.15. Three activities, two of which use two commodities.

The instant that any of the above assumptions are relaxed, the graphical analysis quickly becomes quite cluttered. Suppose that activities w_1 and w_3 are a function of x_1 and x_3 but that the least-cost activity expansion paths remain linear as in Figure 3.14. Since these activity expansion paths are derived under a given set of prices, any change in relative prices of x_1 and x_3 will shift the activity paths as well. In Figure 3.15 the three-dimensional diagram showing the feasible set $0abc$ is presented.

With a rise in the price of x_3, there will be a shift in the optimal

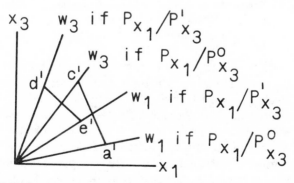

Fig. 3.16. Shift in the induced budget constraint between activities, using two commodities due to a commodity price change.

activity expansion paths. Such a shift is shown in Figure 3.16, along with the shift in the induced budget constraint from $c'a'$ to $d'e'$.

AN EVALUATION OF KNOWLEDGE CHANGE USING MODEL 3.2

From this cursory presentation the effects of a change in the knowledge set can be evaluated. Using Model 3.2, a comparative static analysis contrasting equilibrium states can be analyzed. A more rigorous model of learning will be presented in Chapter 4. At this point a certain evaluation is possible without further information as to how change in the knowledge set occurs.

A change in knowledge could result from a myriad of circumstances. It could represent a gain of information to the individual, which was available previously but simply unlearned. On the other hand, it could result directly from a technological change in the state of the arts. Each of these situations represents a change in the knowledge set for the individual. Some aspect of the calculus process must give way to a new aspect. Thus what follows is sufficiently general to include the evaluation of technical change as a special case of a more general change in the knowledge set.

Technological change in its most general sense is simply a change in knowledge. This change can be embedded either in a particular product or a certain manufacturing process, or it can be change in the uses of existing products, services, and resources. The first type is usually termed embodied technological change, while the second is termed disembodied. The distinction between technical change and any general change in knowledge is essentially twofold. First, technological change is limited to those changes in the knowledge set associated with commodities, either directly as improved products or product use or indirectly as a change in the methods of manufacture or commodity creation so that the commodity can be more cheaply produced. Second, technological change is generally limited to those knowledge changes which occur at the boundary or frontier of knowledge.

In the following analysis the more robust consideration of any change in the knowledge set will be pursued with illustrative examples of the evaluation of technological change as special cases. It will also be assumed that all changes in knowledge are beneficial. That is, new knowledge leads one to a higher level of drive reduction. This does not dismiss the possibility of changes in knowledge which result in a deterioration of satisfaction, but the analytical argument would be symmetrical. Further, increased drive-reduction feasibility is the more important case. As a motivating force for rational individuals, the tendency would be in the direction of increasing potential satisfaction rather than the masochistic pursuits implied by the latter.

In terms of Model 3.2 a change in the knowledge set can be classified into five different types. The basic equations of the model are

$$S = \theta\,(w_1, \ldots, w_n, \omega_1, \ldots, \omega_m)$$

$$w_i = \gamma_i(x_1, \ldots, x_k) \qquad i = 1, \ldots, n$$

$$\sum_{i=1}^{k} P_i x_i \leqslant 0$$

$$(w_1, \ldots, w_n, \omega_1, \ldots, \omega_m) \leqslant T_o$$

Knowledge change can occur by five types of action: (1) the product set $(x_1, \ldots, x_k)$ expands or changes so that for some activity w_i there is now a new optimal activity expansion path;[10] (2) there is a change in the functional relation between the product set $(x_1, \ldots, x_k)$ and the activity level w_i; (3) there is a change in the functional relation between activities and time used, so that activities can be carried out more intensively; (4) the knowledge set of known activities expands or changes such that there is a shift in the optimal drive-reduction path; or (5) there is a change in the perceived functional relationship between activities and drives. In addition to these pure cases, types 1-5, it is possible that any specific change will occur simultaneously in combination with other types.

Types 1-5 represent a change in knowledge which is independent of others' knowledge sets. However, in the situation where the individual's action depends upon the knowledge sets of others (for example, in a game strategy context) the types of change would have to be considerably enlarged. The decision by individual i to purchase commodity j which was to be used in status attainment would depend upon others' knowledge about the commodities available. A commodity acquired for purposes of status, by the very nature of status, requires knowledge on the part of those to be impressed. The following analysis will be restricted to changes in the knowledge set which have no dependence upon the knowledge sets of others.

Type 1. For a type 1 change in the knowledge set to have a relevant effect upon the constrained maximum position of the individual, the optimal activity expansion path must shift in the direction of a cheaper good.

The simplest case is illustrated in Figure 3.17. A new product x_3,

---

10. This is the sole kind of technical change analyzed by Lancaster (1966).

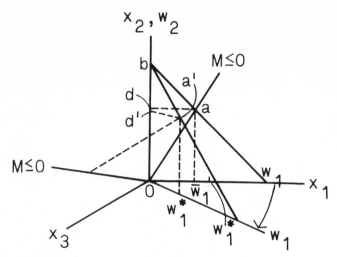

Fig. 3.17. Shift in activity expansion path due to a change in the known commodity set.

becomes known; in combination with x_1 this will fulfill the requirements for activity w_1, whereas before only x_1 would fulfill w_1. Since the price of x_3 is less than the price of x_1, the new feasible maximum activity level of w_1, w_1^*, is greater than $\overline{w}_1$.

The maximum time worked under an irksomeness of labor as-

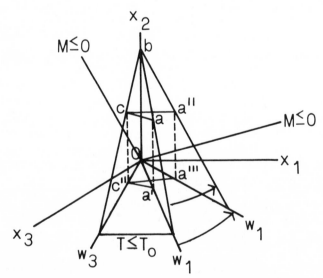

Fig. 3.18. Shift in the activity path due to a change in the knowledge of the efficacy of commodities, shown in three dimensions.

sumption drops from $0d$ to $0d'$ as the feasible set shifts from $0ab$ to $0a'b$ in Figure 3.17. Obviously the old $\overline{w}_1$ level can now be attained with labor less than $0d'$ which is less than $0d$.

Figure 3.18 shows a type 1 change where the products x_1 and x_3 were known before the knowledge change, but a shift occurs in the cost minimizing expansion path of w_1 toward the axis of the cheaper good x_1. Figure 3.19 shows the $x_1 x_3$ plane along with induced budget shifting from $c'a'$ to $c'a'''$.

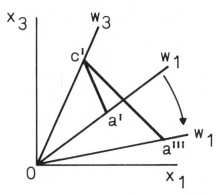

Fig. 3.19. Shift in the activity path shown in two dimensions.

Figure 3.20 shows the same knowledge change as Figures 3.18 and 3.19, as well as showing the shift of the budget line from $c'a'$ to $c'a'''$, but in terms of the $w_1 w_3$ plane. S^o and S^1 are arbitrary iso-drive-reduction curves.

The more general mathematical equivalent of the graphical pre-

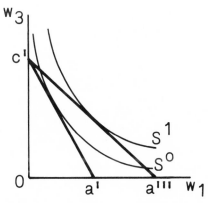

Fig. 3.20. Shift in the induced budget constraint between activities due to a change in the knowledge set.

sentation of type 1 technical change (Figs. 3.17–3.20) follows. Let

$(x_1, \ldots, x_k)$ = known commodities before knowledge change
$(x_1, \ldots, x_k, x_{k+1})$ = expanded known commodity set
S^* = max S with $(x_1, \ldots, x_k)$ known
S^{**} = max S with $(x_1, \ldots, x_k, x_{k+1})$ known

Without loss in generality assume $S^{**} > S^*$. In all cases of type 1, where the increase in knowledge has a relevant effect upon max S, the analytical equivalent is a reduction in the price of activities affected by the newly discovered commodities. The effect can be analyzed in the Slutsky equation format. Define the price of activity w_i as Pw_i. Then a change in the knowledge set is mathematically equivalent to dPw_i. Thus a change in the knowledge set is mathematically equivalent to $dPw_i < 0$ for the affected activity if $\partial\phi/\partial w_i > 0$. Therefore in this case from the Slutsky equation one can solve for dw_i/dPw_i as

$$dw_i/dPw_i = \lambda(|\phi_{i,i}|/|\phi|) - w_i(dw_i/dM_o) \qquad (3.20)$$

where $|\phi|$ is a bordered Hessian determinant. (For greater detail see Appendix B.) The first term in Equation 3.20 is the substitution effect and the second term is the income effect on activity selection. The concept Pw_i is composed of both the actual money expenditures on commodities to service activity w_i and the value of time measured by its shadow price. In this expanded format the analytical results are analogous to the traditional Slutsky analysis.

Analogously, normal and inferior activities can be defined, depending upon the sign of the income effect. If the activity is an inferior one and, further, if the income effect more than offsets the substitution effect, the activity is a Giffen activity. However, the general case would be $dw_i/dPw_i < 0$.

To analyze the effect upon commodity demand, assume that w_i is the only activity affected by the change in the knowledge set and, further, that w_i is a function of two goods x_k and x_{k+1} which are purely divisible, that is, $w_i = \gamma_i(x_k, x_{k+1})$.

Since $dw_i > 0$, then

$$dw_i = (\partial\gamma_i/\partial x_k)\, dx_k + (\partial\gamma_i/\partial x_{k+1})\, dx_{k+1} > 0$$

Since the newly discovered commodity x_{k+1} has a relevant effect $dx_{k+1} > 0$ and assuming that both $\partial\gamma_i/\partial x_k$ and $\partial\gamma_i/\partial x_{k+1} > 0$, then $dx_k \geqslant 0$. If the demand for x_k is adversely affected by the knowledge change, that is, if $dx_k < 0$, then

$$(\partial\gamma_i/\partial x_k)\, |dx_k| < (\partial\gamma_i/\partial x_{k+1})\, |dx_{k+1}|$$

Thus the fall in quantity demanded of x_k will be directly proportional to the increase in demand for x_{k+1}, the proportion depending upon the ratio of the marginal activity contribution of x_k and x_{k+1}, that is, $(\partial \gamma_i / \partial x_k)/(\partial \gamma_i / \partial x_{k+1})$.

If the commodities have some general characteristics, the preceding results are vitiated to some extent. For example, suppose initially that x_j is a purely general good and furthermore that max $x_j^i = x_j^1$. If a change in the knowledge set occurs for, say, $w_h = \gamma_h(x_1, \ldots, x_k)$, $h \neq 1$ such that for S^* the maximum level of drive reduction attainable after the change in knowledge set max$_i$, $x_j^i = x_j^1$ (that is, the amount of x_j needed) is unchanged, then even though the equilibrium level of S^* had increased due to a change in knowledge, there would be no effect on the demand for x_j.

In general if x_j is not a purely divisible good and a change in knowledge occurs such that $S^* = \phi(w_1^*, \ldots, w_n^*, \omega_1^*, \ldots, \omega_m^*)$ changes to $S^{**} = \phi(w_1^*, \ldots, w_h^* + \delta w_h, \ldots, w_n^*, \omega_1^*, \ldots, \omega_m^*)$, where $\delta w_h > 0$ and $\delta w_h = \gamma_h(\delta x_1, \ldots, \delta x_j, \ldots, \delta x_k)$, then δx_j would not be equivalent to the change in demand for x_j. The change in demand would depend upon the degree of general usage of x_j and the specific characteristics of the maximizing S^{**} solution of the individual calculus.

Type 2. This type of a change in the individual's knowledge set is a situation where the same amount of goods will fulfill a greater number of activity units. In activity $w_i = \gamma_i(x_1, \ldots, x_n)$ the function γ_i changes such that for some given level of inputs $(x_1, \ldots, x_n)$, w_i' is greater than w_i, where w_i' is the activity level after change. This could be construed as disembodied knowledge change from the point of view of the consumer, whereas type 1 could be thought of as embodied. Type 1 is associated directly with a change in knowledge of a particular commodity, and type 2 represents a changed use of existing commodities.

As an illustration, suppose that w_2 in Figure 3.21 is affected by a type 2 change so that the point d is shifted back to d' (d and d' are the identical number of units of activity w_2 before and after knowledge change). After some learning process has altered the knowledge set, the new feasible activity set in Figure 3.21 would be $0a''bc$, and in terms of Figure 3.21 the induced budget restriction $c'a'$ would appear to shift backward to $c'a'''$.

This, however, is not the case, since the unit measure of the w_2 ray has changed. Therefore, in Figure 3.22 the same increased knowledge is represented with the unit measure of the activity held constant. The induced budget condition on $w_1 w_2$, $c'a'$, shifts out to $c'a'''$ and, although prices remain fixed, the isocost curves also shift outward, for example, fa' shifts out to fg. C_0^* (or fg) and C_0 (or fa') represent the same amounts of money and prices, but C_0 is before

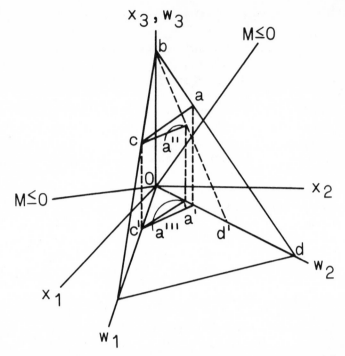

Fig. 3.21. Change in the efficacy of a commodity in servicing an activity, shown
in three dimensions. (This figure assumes that the homogeneity of γ_i
is unaffected, although in general the degree of homogeneity may or
may not be affected. If the homogeneity of γ_i were affected, the optimal, cost-minimizing activity expansion paths would shift and in
general become nonlinear.)

knowledge change and C_o^* is after the improvement. It should be
clear that prices of products remain constant, but prices of activities
change, as shown by the shifting curves in Figure 3.22. Clearly then,
the Slutsky analysis of type 2 is identical with type 1 as the altered
knowledge manifests itself as a change in the price of activities. It
should be reiterated that the price of an activity differs among individuals, even though they service the activity with identical commodities, in that a component of the activity price is an opportunity
cost.

Type 3. This type of knowledge set alteration is also disembodied in that there is a change in ψ such that for any T (time used)
there is a greater amount of $(w_1, \ldots, w_n)$ now feasible. This is perhaps best interpreted intuitively as the smoothing of frictions in the
economy or a change which permits activities to be carried on more
intensively.

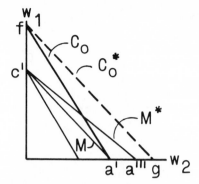

Fig. 3.22. Change in the efficacy of a commodity in servicing an activity, shown on a two-dimensional activity plane.

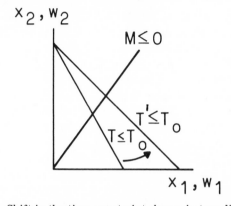

Fig. 3.23. Shift in the time constraint shown in two dimensions.

In the graphical interpretation (Fig. 3.23) the time constraint shifts outward as the measures of w_1, x_1 are held constant. In this case the change in the knowledge set results in a change in the price of activities. However, in this case the change in the price of an activity is due solely to the shadow price component, the opportunity cost of time. Formally, however, the Slutsky analysis is unchanged from type 1 as, analytically, the result is a change in activity price, dPw.

Type 4. Type 4 knowledge enhancement is represented by a change in the known activity set. For example, known activities might change from

$$(w_1, \ldots, w_n, \omega_1, \ldots, \omega_m)$$

to

$$(w_1, \ldots, w_n, w_{n+1}, \omega_1, \ldots, \omega_m, \omega_{m+1})$$

The analysis heretofore has assumed that changes in knowledge increase the known activity set. That is, presumably knowledge change does not destroy old activities, although it may very well make old activities inefficient.

With types 1–3 it was assumed that the maximum value of S after the increase in knowledge was greater than or equal to the maximum S before change. That is, if the change in known relations is relevant to the state of drive reduction of the individual, it must be such that the feasible maximum is increased. However, with types 4 and 5 this postulate is not as likely to hold true. Since the general intuitive interpretation of a change in the known activity set is any change in ideas, it is quite conceivable that such a new idea would create a host of fears and thus reduce the maximum drive reduction attainable. It could be argued that the development of nuclear energy and the atomic bomb opened up a range of additional new activities. As the people of the world learned of these new ideas, the drive for security increased; and the result was a lowering of the maximum drive reduction immediately available. This leads to an entire complex of new activities, such as bomb shelters in the 1950s and a gradual but radical and necessary metamorphosis of foreign policy of the major powers from the early 1940s to the late 1960s. This is probably the exception rather than the rule, at least in the early stages of new technology. Ostensibly, the driving force behind invention and innovation is further drive reduction. Even in the case of the atomic bomb the initial purpose was the winning of World War II and increased immediate security.

From the postulates associated with Model 3.2 the new maximum value of drive reduction and the corresponding constrained optimal activity mix after a change in the knowledge set need not be in any particular correspondence with the activity mix selected before knowledge increases.

Formally, let

$$\max \ \{S = \phi(w_1, \ldots, w_n, \omega_1, \ldots, \omega_m)\} = S^*$$
$$= \phi(w_1^*, \ldots, w_n^*, \omega_1^*, \ldots, \omega_m^*)$$
$$\max \ \{S = \phi(w_1, \ldots, w_n, w_{n+1}, \omega_1, \ldots, \omega_m, \omega_{m+1})\} = S^{**}$$
$$= \phi(w^{**}, \ldots, w_{n+1}^{**}, \omega_1^*, \ldots, \omega_{m+1}^{**})$$

Without recourse to further information such as the specific delineation of the drive set and to the degree of substitutability of the newly learned activity and old activities or information as to the nature of the learning process itself, no comparison is possible between activities selected under the old maximum $S*$ and activities under the new maximum $S**$.

If the analysis is limited to expanding the known activity set from one activity to two, the decrease in the old activity will be proportional to the increase in the newly discovered activity, the proportion depending upon the ratio of the marginal drive reduction of the two activities. This is, of course, assuming the individual is not affected by change in the knowledge sets of others with respect to this new activity and it is a relevant activity to his optimal activity selection.

Type 5. In this situation the analysis is quite similar to type 4. Here the known activity set is constant while the functional relation between drives and activities is altered. While in general there is no conclusive hypotheses as to the relative nature of the two sets of activity selection, some analysis is possible. As contrasted to type 4 knowledge change it is possible that the new equilibrium could leave the selected activity mix unchanged, and consequently, there would be no change in commodity demand. Additional information on the learning process could provide data as to specific changes in the functional relation between activities and drives. For example, the change in the knowledge set could be limited to some subset of the total available activities. In essence this amounts to a parametric change in the objective function of the individual, and some work has been done with this type of analysis. A further discussion of this area of application is presented in Chapter 11.

As one can quickly ascertain from the graphical presentation of the types of technical change, there is no completely accurate objective method for measuring the value of a change in knowledge, given the present data available.

If the S function is assumed to have meaningful cardinal properties and is an accurate measure of what is meant by personal welfare, the criterion of improvement would be the change in drive reduction available (for example, $S^1 - S^o$ in Fig. 3.20). For the information to be empirically useful, one would have to measure drive reduction over the period in which the activity lasts. Even if this could be done for a single individual, many reservations would be forthcoming as to the meaning of aggregating over different individuals to ascertain the total value of the improvement. Any such social welfare criterion is sure to be an arbitrary value judgment.

The traditional method of calculating the cost reduction of an activity which has been affected by a change in knowledge fails to account for the marginal evaluation of the increased activity feasibility. This procedure has been one of calculating the costsaving and allowing others to interpret the psychological welfare equivalents of such a change. However, for types 3, 4, and 5 there is no change in cost whatsoever, while in general there would be a change in the optimal outlay for activities.

Figure 3.24 gives the graphical presentation of a type 1 or type 2

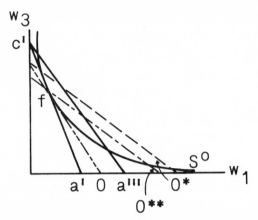

Fig. 3.24. Change in outlays for economic activities due to a change in the knowledge set.

improvement. After the knowledge set is altered, the original activity mix (the tangency at point f of S^o and the original budget line $c'a'$) can be purchased by an amount O^{**}, which is less than the original cost. The knowledge advance has caused an outward shift in the original budget line $c'a'$ to $c'a'''$ and an accompanying change in the relative prices of the activities w_1 and w_3. This is pictured by the fact that the original outlay O shifts out to O^* after the improvement in knowledge. Only under very restrictive conditions would the difference in costs $O^* - O^{**}$ be an indicator of increased personal welfare.

This criterion is clearly not applicable if type 3 occurs. The amount of outlay for the activity mix both before and after the change is the same. However, the increased capacity for activity selection does occur, and thus there is some element of increased welfare present. As shown in Figures 3.25 and 3.26, the outlay line O is the same both before and after the budget shift.

For type 3 a third objective empirical measure presents itself as a possible measure of increased welfare and the value of increased knowledge, namely, the change in the maximum amounts of an activity feasible after the improvement. This criterion is also applicable to types 1 and 2 as well as 3.

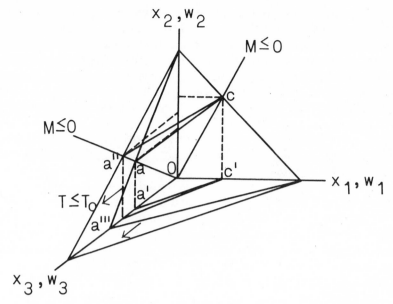

Fig. 3.25. Shift in the time constraint, shown in three dimensions.

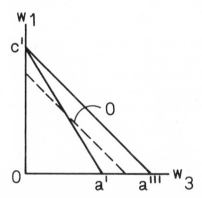

Fig. 3.26. Shift in the induced budget constraint due to a shift in the time constraint, shown in two dimensions.

Since types 1–3 result in some shift in the induced budget line, as depicted in Figures 3.20, 3.24, and 3.26, the value would be $0a''' - 0a'$. In the cases where the increased efficacy of products or activities results in an increase in the maximum amounts of several activities, the criterion might be $\Sigma w_i^* - \Sigma \overline{w}_i$, where w_i^* is the maximum feasible activity w_i after technical change, and $\overline{w}_i$ is the maximum w_i feasible previous to the improved conditions. However, it is quite questionable just what it means to add up activities. When the feasible maximum of only one activity is affected, the criterion obviously fails to take account of the (assumed) diminishing marginal values of such increases. When more than one activity is affected, the problem is compounded. Not only should the marginal effects be considered but also the "interactivity tradeoff" or rate of substitution between activities would make a great deal of difference in the value of the improvement. For example, does it make a difference whether an hour's increased time availability can be manifested in sexual acts or eating? Only with information about the drive reduction effect of this increased activity feasibility can anything clearly be established. Again interpreting drives as representing the meaning of welfare is implicit. Speculation as to how increased time availability or decreased costs of an activity will be used and their consequent benefits to an individual cannot be much more than just speculation without a more objective criterion such as drive reduction. Solving the problems associated with the evaluation of technical change (a special case of the more general analysis of knowledge change) is central to a more relevant evaluation of welfare and efficiency.

THE VALUE OF KNOWLEDGE CHANGE WHEN LEARNING IS COSTLY

The foregoing preliminary discussion of knowledge change has ignored the cost of learning associated with the change in the constrained maximum drive reduction available. Suppose that a change in technology occurs so that for the individual a higher level of drive reduction is now feasible if the requisite learning alters the knowledge set. The cost of learning may play an important role.

In the implicit analysis of technical change as given above, technology is assumed not to affect activities, and the cost of learning about new availabilities is equal to zero. The usefulness of the assumption that costs of learning are insignificant is that, relative to the amount of use from the technological change, these learning costs only occur once, while the altered commodity may be used several times; that is, adapting to technical change is an investment as durable as the technical change.

This brings up a slight digression on the resistance to change by those meshed in an obsolete technology. Essentially this can be compared to the difference between a local maximum and a global maximum. Beginning from a state of ignorance the best (in terms of costs and the current state of the arts) functional relations upon which to base one's individual calculus are attained as a result of the experiences one goes through. As technology progresses, new experiences are available; and for those starting from a position of ignorance, a different functional relation would be adjudged better in general than the ones selected before the change occurred. However, it may very well be that the costs associated with unlearning old habits and forming new ones would be greater than the benefits which might occur. Thus technical changes alter some people's opinions while not changing others. Also, since learning is an investment with respect to technical change, those who are younger and expect the benefits to accrue over a longer period would have more incentive to adapt.

The only consistent, unambiguous measure of technical change (or any knowledge change) in terms of the models developed here is one based upon drive reduction. The only alteration that the learning process places on those comparative static conclusions is one of a time lag or an opportunity cost. That is, after the technical change occurs with respect to a product set, $S* > S$ becomes attainable. The transition by the individual to this greater level of drive reduction will depend upon the speed of the learning process. This can be simplified and approached as a problem in the calculus of variations. Let

$S*$ = maximum available drive reduction available after technological change

$S(t)$ = actual drive reduction at time t

$K(t)$ = the knowledge set, that is, the set of functions used at time t in the calculus process

w = learning activity

Assume:

$$dK/dt = f(w), \qquad w = f^{-1}(dK/dt)$$

Drive reduction can now be viewed as a function of the knowledge set K and the learning activity $S = S(K, w)$. The conditions for a maximum, assuming continuous functions, can be derived as follows:

$$\max \int_0^\infty S[K(t), w] \, dt = \max \int_0^\infty S[K(t), dK/dt] \, dt \qquad (3.21)$$

Euler-Lagrange conditions for a maximum are

$$\partial S^o/\partial K = (d/dt)(\partial S^o/\partial K'), \text{ where } K' = dK/dt = f(w) \qquad (3.22)$$

Assume:

1. $\partial S/\partial K > 0$, that drive reduction increases as the knowledge set increases

2. $[d(dK/dt)]/dw > 0$, the more of the learning activity which is undertaken, the faster the knowledge set increases

3. $dS/dw < 0$, learning causes drive reduction to decline

4. $d^2 S/dw^2 < 0$, the rate at which learning causes drive reduction to decrease is increasing

    With the assumption of continuity and the assumptions given by items 1–4, Equation 3.22 says that the optimal learning path starts off with a relatively large amount of learning and slows down as $S[K(t)]$ approaches S^*. Discontinuities in the various functions would imply that the level of learning activity would proceed in jumps rather than a smooth decline, but the general notion of the optimal path is the same. Also it should be noted that item 3 does not necessarily imply that learning in itself is drive enhancing. It may very well be drive reducing; however, the equilibrium total drive reduction is less with learning included than without; that is, learning is not as effective in reducing drives as other activities available.

    The value of any type of technical change in terms of the additional drive reduction is

$$V = \int_0^\infty S(t) - S \, dt \qquad (3.23)$$

where S is equal to maximum drive reduction available before the technological change and where $S(t) < S^*$ which is the maximum drive reduction available after the technical change. (It is also assumed that for the evaluation at any point in time, current, present, and past units of drive reduction are expressed in a common denomination.) Graphically this is shown in Figures 3.27 and 3.28.

    In Figure 3.27 the optimal path from S to S^* does not involve

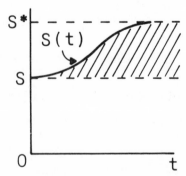

Fig. 3.27. Learning which causes no loss in drive reduction.

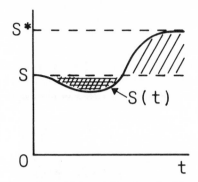

Fig. 3.28. Learning which entails a loss in drive reduction.

any immediate loss in satisfaction, since the immediate returns from learning sufficiently offset the losses from the learning activity. In Figure 3.28 the total value of the technical changes is the lined area minus the cross-hatched area. Of course it is possible that the value in cases such as Figure 3.28 would be negative. If the individual has a choice between following $S(t)$ and remaining along S, he would choose $S(t)$ only if the total value were positive. This is the argument presented earlier; for some the value of the new technological adaptation would be negative, while for others it would be positive. Any value of technical change for the individual depends upon where the individual starts, that is, his initial knowledge set, the ease of learning or the effect of learning on his drive state, and so forth.

Equation 3.23 expresses the value of the technical change to one individual. Any aggregation over various individuals is a problem associated with any social welfare criteria—how to compare individuals. Of course any such criteria is arbitrary, but given some weighting for the various affected individuals of society, an aggregate value could be derived.

SUMMARY

This chapter discusses the aspects of a generalized static model of individual choice of activities—both economic and noneconomic. This choice is construed as a general mathematical programming problem subject to constraints. In general, the constraints include every physical and social restriction which is effective on the individual's decision calculus. For didactic purposes, the discussion here has been limited to two constraints—a time and a budget constraint. With this model, several types of knowledge change have been analyzed using comparative statics. In the next chapter, the process of knowledge change is specified.

chapter 4

The Process of
Knowledge Change

IN THIS CHAPTER the model is further generalized by delineating a specific and rigorous method for the generation and alteration of preferences. The assumptions employed to facilitate handling of any such complex operation are designed to extract the meaningful and relevant forces. As such, the models created should yield a theoretical structure which provides further insight into the problems of a dynamic society and also through which more meaningful questions can be raised as to the nature of welfare, efficiency, and optimality.

THE EXTENT OF THE KNOWLEDGE SET

Heretofore it has been assumed that the initial knowledge set is given. In Chapter 3 the individual was viewed as having a given set of knowledge about the various relations which were relevant to his decision-making process—the product-activity relations, the activity-drive relations, the activity-time-use relations, the constraints, and the extent that various activities and products were available or "known." In addition, an arbitrary change in the knowledge set was analyzed in the comparative static sense. However, each of these aspects of the individual's knowledge set is somehow generated by the individual and in general is also revised and altered as time passes. Each restructuring of the individual's set of beliefs comes about by some process. Old relations have to be replaced by newer, improved ones. If the calculus process of maximizing drive reduction is sufficiently important for the individual to carry it out, he must continually decide upon which functional relations, product sets, and activity sets are correct, or most nearly correct, or most useful. As with the statistician, physicist, or whatever, each person must also estimate the relevancy and the extent of the various forces operating in his environment. The question is, How can this behavioral aspect of individuals best be analyzed?

The following analysis of the way in which the knowledge set changes is a general view of a subset of what is usually termed learning. Learning can be classified into two types: the acquisition of knowledge or the ascertainment of truth by the individual and the acquisition of skills through instruction or study. In this chapter we are almost solely concerned with the first meaning. The second meaning, the acquisition of skills or technical acumen, can be thought of as obtaining a stock X_j which will produce a flow of output x_j over future time periods. Obtaining this stock of skills requires resources and thus has a price, while the output has some expected discounted price for which it can be sold. Thus this second type of learning can be analyzed as carrying out a particular economic activity without a change in the knowledge set. In the following, change in the knowledge set itself is the primary interest.

A SUBJECTIVE PROBABILITY APPROACH

A first approach toward simplifying the process of preference formation and change is to view the individual as having a probability distribution over all possible product-activity relations as well as over all possible activity-drive relations.

The sets W^* and X^* are defined as all possible activities and all possible goods and services respectively. In cases where a good has not yet come into existence or is no longer produced, the individual would assign a probability of zero (or near zero) to the expectation of that particular good servicing an activity. The probability of drive reduction being produced by activities which are unknown or no longer available to the individual is similarly zero or near zero.

A probability distribution over commodity-activity relations and activity-drive relations corresponds objectively and theoretically to the subjective set of beliefs which the individual has at any point in time. Even though probabilistic utility functions have often been used to test and explain stochastic behavior in various psychological experiments,[1] this interpretation of probability is certainly not the only one nor is it the one which will be followed here.

In the theoretical models developed below, the goal is to extract and simplify the most important aspects of the learning process.

1. For example, Luce (1959) and others.

Thus there is a distinct methodological question to be answered at this point which concerns the concept of probability. What is *probability* and what are *random* events? It can be argued that no probability is objective in the pure sense of the word since every process is deterministic, given a sufficient amount of information. The flip of a coin is often described as a random process with the probability of a head facing up being one-half. But if one knew the force of the muscle, the wind conditions, the side of the coin which was initially facing up, the weight of the coin, the difference in levels at which the coin was flipped and caught, and so forth, one could determine precisely whether heads or tails would come up.

Clearly, then, the question is, What is the best way to characterize real-world phenomena which will provide sufficient simplicity for understanding and predicting and controlling aspects of that environment? Thus a *random process* is a description of the potential consequences of either partially unknown or uncontrollable forces or of those which it is not worthwhile to further understand or control. *Objective probability* of various outcomes merely serves as a substitute for a finer specification of the actual forces in operation.

On the other hand, *subjective probability* is a degree of belief. It specifically recognizes the absence of complete and accurate information and as such represents a subjective evaluation or weighting of the bits of evidence available. Consequently, whenever one substitutes a probability distribution for a more complex aggregate of data, one is actually applying a subjective weighting of the available or usable evidence. To return to the coin-flipping example—when one says that the outcome is distributed binomially with a parameter equal to 1/2 if the coin is unbiased, he is saying that the relative frequency of placing, force of flipping, and so forth, is such that the outcome of heads will approximately equal the outcome of tails. He is subjectively weighting the evidence that the various forces affecting the outcome will balance out to an even long-run relative frequency.

Thus methods used to simplify and explain in a theoretical structure are generally different from those employed when analyzing specific experimental data. Empirical phenomena which impinge upon the individual within his environment can be usefully and arbitrarily classified into processes which yield specific outcomes and those which yield random or variable outcomes (obviously, there is an arbitrary line separating these two sets.) Pounding a stake with a sledgehammer with a specified force through soil of a given density could yield a deterministic outcome. On the other hand, the process of flipping a coin is best characterized as a variable outcome of heads or tails depending upon the bias of the coin. The first classification is the idealized situation of no random elements entering the process (all forces are known and specified), while the second would tend to be more useful in any actual application. Both types of processes will be considered and their degree of variability specifically included.

Individual actions based upon the decision calculus can be similarly classified. That is, there can be decisions which specify a fixed set of activities to be undertaken and those which specify some set of activities to be carried out at random. Once the specific activity process is analyzed, the random activity process follows with a slight theoretical extension. Therefore it will be assumed initially that the calculus process results in deterministic behavior even though the beliefs of the individual are not known to him with certainty.

The subjective probability of a particular aspect of the knowledge set is defined as the degree of belief in that particular facet. Having experienced empirical evidence (observations of real-world phenomena) the individual will form opinions as to what in fact is happening. From a complex of perceptions the individual must separate the "noise" or the irrelevant aspects from the important, determining forces in the environment. Given this information, he will formulate subjective probabilities as to what empirical relations are true, nearly true, false, or simply unimportant. With the advent of additional evidence these subjective probability distributions are postulated as being altered in a manner consistent with Bayesian probability theory.[2]

It should be stressed that these subjective probabilities need not conform to an objective definition based on frequency. As stated by Jeffreys:

> The essence is that no probability, direct, prior, or posterior, is simply a frequency. The fundamental index is that of a reasonable degree of belief, which satisfies certain rules of consistency and can in consequence of these rules be formally expressed by numbers by means of the addition rule, which in itself is a convention. . . . In many cases the numerical assessment is the same as that of a corresponding frequency, but that does not say that the probability and frequency are the same thing even in these cases. The equations of heat conduction and diffusion have the same forms, but that does not make heat a vapor.[3]

2. General literature on Bayesian statistics would include among others Savage (1954), Schlaifer (1959), Jeffreys (1961), Kyburg and Smokler (1964), and Fellner (1965). See especially Fellner for a review of the development of Bayesian probability theory from Keynes and Ramsey to the present along with his own application and analysis of the maximization process. For more recent developments of Bayesian probability theory see Good (1965) and Raiffa and Schlaifer (1968).

3. Jeffreys (1961), p. 372.

AXIOMS OF PREFERENCE CHANGE

The following axioms of learning and preference behavior imply that a probability distribution exists and also specify how it changes. If a person at time t believes A more strongly than he believes B, this belief can be formalized in the following way.

Define the following symbols as:

A = a proposition
$\widetilde{A}$ = not A
$A \cap B$ = A and B both
$A \cup B$ = either A or B or both
$\{A_i\}$ = a collection of propositions
$\{A_i\}$ = a propositional range if and only if exactly one of A_i is true
$\geqslant$ = is believed to be at least as likely as

The following properties are assumed to guide rational behavior:

1. Beliefs are transitive: $A \geqslant B$, $B \geqslant C$ implies $A \geqslant C$
2. $A \geqslant B$ implies $\widetilde{B} \geqslant \widetilde{A}$
3. There exist upper and lower bounds T and F to degrees of belief: $T \geqslant A \geqslant F$
4. If $A \cap C = \phi$ = false set (that is, if A and C cannot both occur), if $B \cap C = \phi$, and if $A \geqslant B$, then $A \cup C \geqslant B \cup C$
5. Additivity: If $A \cap B = \phi$, then $P(A \cup B) = P(A) + P(B)$, where $P(A) + P(\widetilde{A}) = 1$, and $P(A) \geqslant 0$. P is a function which maps the proposition into the set of real numbers $[0, 1]$ and has the property that $P(A_i) \geqslant P(A_j)$ if and only if $A_i \geqslant A_j$.
6. Inference or the implementation of new evidence:

$$P(A/B) = [P(A \cap B)]/[P(B)]$$

Item 6 is interpreted graphically in Figure 4.1. Given that B is true,

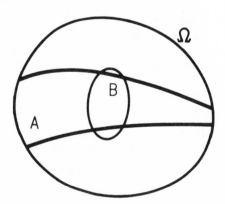

Fig. 4.1. Graphical representation of inference.

the individual's beliefs can be reduced from Ω to inside the set where B is true.

In Model 4.1 which follows, these axioms will be applied to consumer behavior. The individual is viewed as a hypothesis tester, specifically forming his set of beliefs (or the probabilities which he attaches to the proposition that an activity will fulfill a particular drive or that a product will fulfill an activity) according to his past experiences. It will also be assumed that the individual selects some criteria (also dependent upon past experiences) as to whether he will carry out an activity and the associated commodity exchanges or whether he will gather more information before doing anything. These criteria are of course subject to the various constraints and exigencies under which he is operating.

For a propositional range $\{A_i\}$, the individual will act on the basis of A_i only if $P(A_i) \geqslant P_o$, where P_o is the criterion of sufficient information. If for all i, $P(A_i) < P_o$, the decision criteria would specify that no action with respect to the propositional range be undertaken until for some i, $P(A_i) \geqslant P_o$. The specific criteria level P_o depends upon past experiences with decision making and also on the importance and relevance of the propositional range in question.

The individual will create decision criteria for each propositional range. When the subjective belief of a proposition is less than certainty, these decision criteria determine whether or not a functional relation from a propositional range will be included in the felicific calculus, the concomitant amount of further search activities, and so forth. Thus simple action spaces and complex action spaces associated with decision criteria can be distinguished. A simple action-space decision criterion will be defined as one where there is only one probability decision point P_o for a propositional range. If any proposition has an associated subjective probability greater than P_o, it is included in the maximization decision calculus. If all propositions are less than P_o, no proposition from the given propositional range is included, nor are any other activities (such as search) included in the calculus process, specifically as a consequence of the low subjectivity probability levels of the propositions in the range. Either simple action space includes a single proposition in the calculus or no proposition from that range, or consequent search activity, is included.

A complex action decision criterion is defined as one where the functional relations included in the decision process depend upon more than one subjective probability level. A complex action decision criterion might be one which specified that if $P(A_i) > P_1$, $A_i \epsilon (A_1, \ldots, A_n)$ then include search activity S_j in the decision calculus. If $P(A_i) > P_o > P_1$, include A_i in the decision calculus and terminate search activity in this area. Clearly, the stages associated with any complex action decision criterion could be any number greater than one, and the associated activities with these stages could be of any degree of complexity as well as continuous or discontinuous.

However, a cursory examination of the model will show that the concept of complex action spaces can be eliminated as superfluous. Specifically, a search activity is included in the calculus in precisely the same manner as any other proposition. Thus the inclusion, and hence the subjective weighting, of an information-gathering activity results after consideration of subjective probability distributions over all propositional ranges. Consequently, while a complex action decision criterion may be a useful intuitive concept, it can be ignored or, more precisely, subsumed in the model.

For mathematical clarity and without loss in generality, it will be assumed that $\Sigma_{i=1}^{n} P(A_i) = 1$ for each propositional range of possible product-activity relations (or activity-drive) relations. The range is represented by $\{A_1, \ldots, A_n\}$, where A_i is the proposition that $w_i(X_s)$ [or $\phi_i(W)$] is a true relation between a product set X_s (or activity set W) and activity w_i (or drive reduction S). This simply normalizes the various probabilities. Intuitively, the propositions A_j can be thought of as any collection of particular functions. For example, A_1 could represent the proposition that the relation between w_i and x_i is linear with slope equal to α and intercept equal to zero, while A_2 could represent the class of all other linear functions with the parameters not equal to α and zero, while A_3 represents the class of all quadratic functions, and A_4 all other possible functions.

Another interpretation is that each A_i represents a class of functions. That is, each A_i is equivalent to another propositional range $A_i = \{A_{io}, \ldots, A_{iM_o}\}$, $i = 1, \ldots, n$ such that the function A_{ij} is more general than A_{ij+1}. If $P(A_i) > P_o$, the specific form selected from the general class $\{A_{ij}\}$ might be A_{im} where $1 \leqslant m \leqslant M_o$ and $(m + 1)/M_o > P(A_i) - P_o \geqslant [m(1 - P_o)]/M_o$. This formation has the property that the nearer $P(A_i)$ is to one, the more specifically A_i is known and if $P(A_i) = 1$, then A_i is known in its most specific form A_{iM_o}. Or in other words, as a particular relation is known with greater certainty, it is also known in greater detail.

Graphically, an individual's state of belief in the case of a three-element propositional range can be represented as a point in an equilateral triangle where the perpendicular distance from the point to each of the bases of the triangle is equivalent to the probability that each proposition is true. If the point representing the state of belief is in any vertex, one proposition is known with certainty to be true while all others are known with certainty to be false. Similarly, if the point lies along any of the bases, the probability of one proposition being true is equal to zero while the sum of the other two equals one.

In Figure 4.2 such a situation is presented, where point x repre-

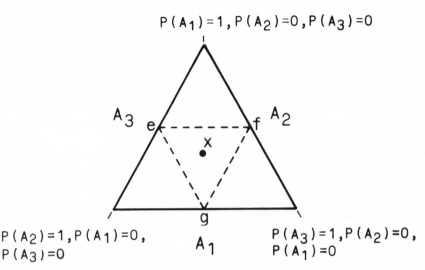

$$P(A_1) = 1, P(A_2) = 0, P(A_3) = 0$$

$$P(A_2) = 1, P(A_1) = 0, \quad A_1 \quad P(A_3) = 1, P(A_2) = 0,$$
$$P(A_3) = 0 \qquad\qquad\qquad\qquad P(A_1) = 0$$

Fig. 4.2. Graphical representation of all possible probability mixtures among three propositions.

sents the case where $P(A_1) = P(A_2) = P(A_3) = 1/n = 1/3$. The dashed lines represent a decision criterion of $1/2$. If the decision criterion P_o is equal to $1/2$, the point representing the state of belief must be outside the dashed triangle efg.

From this graphical representation it is obvious that any experience vector must be symmetric (where it is a vector of empirical data which alters the individual's state of belief). If the probability of A_i increases from $1/n$ then $P(A_i) < 1/n$ or at least one i. Likewise if $P(A_i) > 1/2$, the $P(A_j) < 1/2$ for all $j \neq i$ since $\Sigma_{j \neq i} P(A_j) = 1 - P(A_i)$.

The theoretical structure of Model 4.1 in mathematical symbols is nearly identical to Model 3.2 with the addition of how functional relations are selected. For simplicity, Model 4.1 assumes that the decision criterion in Equations 4.3 and 4.4 is the same. This could be easily generalized.

MODEL 4.1

Maximize

$$S = \phi(W) \tag{4.1}$$

where

$$W = \gamma(X)$$
$$W = (w_1, \ldots, w_n)$$
$$w_i = \gamma_i(X), \qquad i = 1, \ldots, n$$

subject to

$$M = \sum_{i=1}^{k} p_i x_i \leqslant 0$$

$$T = \psi(W) \leqslant T_o$$
$$g_1(W) \geqslant 0$$
$$\vdots$$
$$\qquad\qquad\qquad\qquad \text{or } g(W) \geqslant 0 \qquad (4.2)$$
$$\vdots$$
$$g_m(W) \geqslant 0$$
$$w_i \geqslant 0, \qquad i = 1, \ldots, n$$
$$x_j \geqslant 0, \qquad j = 1, \ldots, k$$

The functional relations are selected as follows:

Let E be an n-dimensional vector which adequately describes an individual's past experiences. This would include, for example, past commodities selected, the resulting level of activities, and the consequent drive reduction. Presumably E would also describe all imaginary experiences as well, such as imagining the status that a diamond would provide.

$P[\phi(W)/E]$ = degree of belief that $\phi(W)$ is true given past experience E

$P[\gamma(X)/E]$ = degree of belief that $\gamma(X)$ is true given past experience E

$P[E_s/\phi(W)]$ = degree of belief that experiences of drive reduction as described by E_s could have occurred given that $\phi(W)$ is true

$P[E_w/\gamma(X)]$ = degree of belief that experiences of activities could have occurred given that $\gamma(X)$ is true

$$P[\phi(W)/E] \geqslant P_o \qquad (4.3)$$

$$P[\gamma_i(X)/E] \geqslant P_o \qquad (4.4)$$

From Bayes's theorem, the new degree of belief in $\phi(W)$ after an experience is given by Equation 4.5 where P' is posterior probability or the postexperience degree of belief. (Bayes's theorem is really nothing more than the mathematical statement of conditional probability as illustrated in Figure 4.1.)

$$P'[\phi(W)] = \frac{P[E/\phi(W)] \cdot P[\phi(W)]}{\displaystyle\int_{-\infty}^{\infty} P[E/\phi(W)] \cdot P[\phi(W)] d\phi(W)} \tag{4.5}$$

Similarly, the posterior probability attached to $\gamma(x)$ depends upon past experiences as given in Equation 4.6.

$$P'[\gamma(X)] = \frac{P[E/\gamma(X)] \cdot P[\gamma(X)]}{\displaystyle\int_{-\infty}^{\infty} P[E/\gamma(X)] \cdot P[\gamma(X)] d\gamma(X)} \tag{4.6}$$

In Model 4.1, $\phi(W)$ and $\gamma(X)$ are to be interpreted as propositions. $\phi(W)$ is the proposition that the "true" (meaning the rational perception of phenomena given all information, or what is termed perfect knowledge) relationship between activities and drives is expressed by the functional form ϕ. Likewise, $\gamma(X)$ is the proposition that the true relationship between products and activities is expressed by the functional form γ.

SOME EXAMPLES OF KNOWLEDGE GENERATION

As an example, consider a typical Bayesian problem interpreted in learning terms. Suppose that the flipping of a coin is defined as an activity w. Satisfaction or drive reduction results when a head appears. Therefore the relation between S and w is dependent upon λ, where λ is the parameter of the coin and is unknown. If the coin were a fair one, $\lambda = 1/2$; but all that is known for certain is that $0 \leqslant \lambda \leqslant 1$ and that $\int_0^1 P(\lambda)d\lambda = 1$.

Suppose E, or experience, is composed of m heads and n tails out of $m + n$ trials. Therefore, $P(E/\lambda) = \lambda^m (1 - \lambda)^n$.

By Bayes's theorem the individual will have a different probability distribution over the possible values of λ given by

$$P'(\lambda/E) = \frac{P(E/\lambda) \cdot P(\lambda)}{\displaystyle\int_0^1 P(\lambda) \cdot P(E/\lambda)d\lambda}$$

Since the individual has no other experience to bias his estimation of $P(\lambda)$, assume that as λ varies from 0 to 1, $P(\lambda)$ is constant, then

$$P'(\lambda/E) = \frac{P(E/\lambda) \cdot P(\lambda)}{P(\lambda) \displaystyle\int_0^1 P(E/\lambda) \cdot d\lambda} = \frac{P(E/\lambda)}{\displaystyle\int_0^1 P(E/\lambda)d\lambda}$$

(For greater detail of this implementation of the Bayes postulate see Appendix C.) Since $P(E/\lambda) = \lambda^m (1 - \lambda)^n$, then

$$P'(\lambda/E) = \frac{\lambda^m (1 - \lambda)^n}{\displaystyle\int_0^1 (1 - \lambda)^n d\lambda}$$

The a posteriori expected value of the parameter is

$$P'(\text{head}) = \int_0^1 \lambda P'(\lambda) d\lambda = \frac{\displaystyle\int_0^1 \lambda^{m+1} (1 - \lambda)^n d\lambda}{\displaystyle\int_0^1 \lambda^m (1 - \lambda)^n d\lambda}$$

$$= \frac{B(m + 2, n + 1)}{B(m + 1, n + 1)}, \text{ where } B(m,n) \text{ is a beta function}$$

Since

$$B(m,n) = \frac{\Gamma(m)\Gamma(n)}{\Gamma(m + n)}, \text{ where } \Gamma(m) \text{ is a gamma function}$$

and $\Gamma(m) = (m - 1)!$ if m is an integer > 1, then

$$P'(\text{head}) = \frac{[(m + 1)!n!/(m + n + 2)!]}{(m!n!)/[(m + n + 1)!]} = \frac{m + 1}{m + n + 2}$$

regardless of the actual value of λ. From this result several interesting observations can be noted. First, if m is thought of as the number of successes out of $m + n$ trials, the expected value of a success converges to the frequency of successes out of the total number of trials. Second, if two people agree as to the number of successes versus failures, their estimates of the probability distribution of the parameter will converge regardless of how their initial or prior probability estimates differed. Third, even though the above example is of a specific random process (that is, even if the parameter of the coin is known with certainty, the outcome is still variable) the mathematical analysis will apply to other processes as well. This will be further developed below.

As another example of the learning process and its effects on the calculus of the individual, suppose there is one activity W and the individual is indifferent in his beliefs about three functional relationships ϕ_1, ϕ_2, ϕ_3 and also feels certain that all other possible functional forms are not correct relations or are irrelevant. Thus his a priori beliefs would be written as

$$P[\phi_1(W)] = 1/3$$
$$P[\phi_2(W)] = 1/3$$
$$P[\phi_3(W)] = 1/3$$
$$P[\phi_i(W)] = 0, \quad i > 3$$

Also assume that he believes that W will provide one unit of drive reduction to the extent that

$$P[E_s/\phi_1(W)] = 1/2$$
$$P[E_s/\phi_2(W)] = 1/3$$
$$P[E_s/\phi_3(W)] = 1/4$$

Subsequent to selecting one unit of activity W the individual finds that $E_s = 2$ or that two units of drive reduction occurred, then this new degree of belief in $\phi_1(W)$ is found by Bayes's formula:

$$P'[\phi_1(W)] = \frac{(1/2)^2 \cdot 1/3}{(1/2)^2 \cdot 1/3 + (1/3)^2 \cdot 1/3 + (1/4)^2 \cdot 1/3} = 36/61$$

Similarly, for

$$P'[\phi_2(W)] = \frac{(1/3)^2 \cdot 1/3}{(1/2)^2 \cdot 1/3 + (1/3)^2 \cdot 1/3 + (1/4)^2 \cdot 1/3} = 16/61$$

$$P'[\phi_3(W)] = \frac{(1/4)^2 \cdot 1/3}{(1/2)^2 \cdot 1/3 + (1/3)^2 \cdot 1/3 + (1/4)^2 \cdot 1/3} = 9/61$$

In general, then, it is possible to view the decision-making process in the following manner. For each relation to be determined for use in the personal calculus process, assume that the individual selects one function from a given propositional range. For exemplary purposes consider the selection of a function γ for an economic activity w_j.

From the propositional range

$$\{\gamma_1(X_{s_1}), \gamma_2(X_{s_2}), \ldots, \gamma_m(X_{s_m})\}$$

where $s_i \subset \{1, \ldots, k\}$, for all i (thus X_{s_i} represents a particular bundle of commodities) the individual must select one γ in order to plan on undertaking activity w_i. Since by definition one of the propositions in the above propositional range can be true, at most, the individual's degree of belief in each $\gamma_i(X_{s_i})$ can be expressed as

$$P[\gamma_i(X_{s_i})] = \xi_i, \quad i = 1, \ldots, m$$

$$\xi_i \geqslant 0, \sum_{i=1}^{m} \xi_i = 1$$

$$P[E/\gamma_i(X_{s_i})] = \mu_i, \qquad i = 1, \ldots, m$$

Thus ξ_i is equal to the degree of belief in the s_i combination of goods providing activity output according to the parameters of γ_i where i ranges over all possible functional forms; and μ_i is equal to the degree of belief that an experience, as defined by E, will result given that $\gamma_i(X_s)$ is in fact true and in consideration of the vicissitudes of nature and the capriciousness of the human sensory processes.

For each experience vector E there would be in general a different μ_i for each $\gamma_i(X_{s_i})$. Thus interpreted, ξ_i can be thought of as the probability that $\gamma_i(X_{s_i})$ is true and $(1 - \xi_i)$ is the probability that $\gamma_i(X_{s_i})$ is false. On the other hand, μ_i could be intuitively thought of (although not necessarily) as the frequency with which E will result if $\gamma_i(X_{s_i})$ is true, or as how often an individual will perceive E if $\gamma_i(X_{s_i})$ is true. If the individual suffers from no changes or variability in perceptive powers, $P[E/\gamma_i(X_{s_i})] = \mu_i = 1$. If this is the case and $P[\gamma_i(X_{s_i})] = P[\gamma_j(X_{s_j})]$ for all i and j, the individual will never alter his beliefs.

In general, starting from a condition of ignorance, that is,

$$P[\gamma_i(X_{s_i})] = P[\gamma_j(X_s)]$$

for all i and j and where $P[E_j/\gamma_i(X_s)] = \mu_i^j \leqslant 1$, with the strict inequality holding for at least one i and assuming a finite number of discrete possible γ_i's (perhaps corresponding to the psychologist's just noticeable difference (j.n.d.) if the range of each of the γ functions is continuous), then

$$P'[\gamma_i(X_s)/E_j] = \mu_i^j \bigg/ \sum_{i=1}^{n} \mu_i^j \qquad (4.7)$$

With further experience E_{j+1} the degrees of belief are altered further.

$$P''[\gamma_i(X_s)/E_{j+1}] = \frac{\mu_i^{j+1}\left(\mu_i^j \bigg/ \sum_{i=1}^{n} \mu_i^j\right)}{\sum_{i=1}^{n} \mu_i^{j+1}\left(\mu_i^j \bigg/ \sum_{i=1}^{n} \mu_i^j\right)} = \frac{\mu_i^{j+1}\,\mu_i^j}{\sum_{i=1}^{n} \mu_i^{j+1}\,\mu_i^j} \qquad (4.8)$$

or for m experiences

$$P^m\,[\gamma_i(X_s)/E_{j+m}] = \frac{\prod\limits_{k=1}^{m}\mu_i^{j+k}}{\sum\limits_{i=1}^{n}\prod\limits_{k=1}^{m}\mu_i^{j+k}} \qquad (4.9)$$

Over time the process of learning can be pictured as in Figure 4.3,

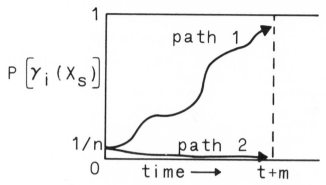

Fig. 4.3. Paths of the probability of a function over time.

where $\gamma_i(X_s)$ is the true relation and the learning process is consistent. The path of the degree of belief in the true relation, path 1, approaches the certainty axis, where $P[\gamma_i(X_s)] = 1$, depending upon the nature of the μ_i's, while the belief in all other relations approaches $P[\gamma_j(X_s)] = 0$, or a path similar to path 2.

The subjective determination of the μ_i's of each experience depend upon the individual's estimation process and, to some extent, the degree of analogizing he does between one particular activity-product relation and other relations in his environment. Suppose that the individual used several actual observations to run a mental linear least squares regression. Given the estimated parameters for the linear equation and their associated standard deviations, he could then evaluate the probability of any further observation being predicted by the model. Suppose his linear regression gives

$$w = a + bx + \epsilon, \qquad \epsilon \sim N(0,\sigma^2)$$

Using $w = a + bx$ in the calculus process, x^* was purchased and w^* was the activity level which resulted, where

$$w^* = a + bx^* + \epsilon^*$$

Dividing ϵ^* by the standard deviation estimate for σ, the probability of ϵ^* is easily obtained from standard normal probability tables.

In fact, for each $\gamma_i(X_s)$ relation in the propositional range which has an assumed random element ϵ_i distributed normally with mean 0 and variance σ_i^2, if $\overline{\gamma}_i(X_s)$ represents the deterministic portion of $\gamma_i(X_s)$, the experience E_j is

$$w^* = \gamma_i(x^*) = \overline{\gamma}_i(w^*) + \epsilon_i^*$$

Therefore,

$$P[E_j/\gamma_i(X_s)] = \mu_i^j = 1 - 2(2\pi)^{-1/2} \int_0^{\epsilon_i^*/\sigma_i} \exp(x^2/2)\, dx$$

Clearly, if $\epsilon^* = 0$, that is, if the results of a purchased bundle of commodities were exactly as expected, $\mu_i^j = 1$. In general however, experience would not be limited to actual observations only but would include "imagined" observations which result from reading books, talking to others, advertising, and so forth. Also, it would seem reasonable that the individual would weigh these observations differently. An actual observation would perhaps carry more weight in the estimation process than an imagined experience.

In addition, the estimation procedure for any single individual would necessarily be a rough approximation to the above discussion. The estimates could be linear, quadratic, exponential, or whatever. The assumption is that each experience E_j can be evaluated subjectively by the individual as to the probability that it resulted from a given function in the propositional range.

Suppose that μ^j is constant in Equation 4.9, as k goes from 1 to m. In other words, suppose each experience is the same and the individual associated the same probability with each respective function after each successive experience.

Then Equation 4.9 simplifies to Equation 4.10,

$$P^m\left[\gamma_i(X_s)/E_{j+m}\right] = \frac{(\mu_i^j)^m}{\sum_{i=1}^{n}(\mu_i^j)^m} = \frac{1}{(\mu_1^j/\mu_i^j)^m + \ldots + 1 + \ldots + (\mu_n^j/\mu_i^j)^m}$$

$$(4.10)$$

In addition to the standard regression techniques of estimating the probability of a particular experience, there are many other ways in which this could be derived. Suppose that each proposition in the propositional range is in a deterministic form and is viewed as being controlled by a parameter λ_i as to whether it is a correct relation. In other words, λ_i could be thought of as the frequency with which proposition i is the correct one. (Further discussion of this approach is given in Appendix C.)

If the individual can classify every experience E_j as containing t_j units of successes and r_j units of failures with respect to $\gamma_i(X_s)$, then μ_i^j for experience E_j is equal to $\lambda_i^{t_j} (1 - \lambda_i)^{r_j}$. Further, from Equation 4.9 then,

$$P^m[\gamma_i(X_s)/E_{j+m}] = \frac{\prod_{k=1}^{n} [\lambda_i^{t_{j+k}} (1 - \lambda_i)^{r_{j+k}}]}{\sum_{i=1}^{n} \prod_{k=1}^{m} [\lambda_i^{t_{j+k}} (1 - \lambda_i)^{r_{j+k}}]}$$

Also if the λ_i are constant as k goes from 1 to m, the above reduces to a form similar to the coin-tossing case, where

$$P[\gamma_i(X_s)/E] = \frac{\lambda_i^\alpha (1 - \lambda_i)^\beta}{\sum_{i=1}^{n} \lambda_i^\alpha (1 - \lambda_i)^\beta}, \qquad \alpha = \sum_{k=1}^{m} t_{j+k}, \qquad \beta = \sum_{k=1}^{m} r_{j+k}$$

or that α is equal to the total number of successes over all experiences and β is equal to the total number of failures over all experiences.

With the individual as with the scientist, it is often not necessary to establish the exact functional relation between goods and activities or between activities and drives. All that is necessary is a sufficient approximation considering the costs of establishing the form and parameters of functional relations more precisely.

Since each functional relation predicts an outcome (that is, if $\gamma_i(X_s)$ is $w_i = ax_1 + bx_2$, for some quantities $\overset{*}{x}_1$, $\overset{*}{x}_2$ a definite level of w_i is determined), the actual outcome can be evaluated in terms of units of success and units of failure as to how closely the postulated $\gamma_i(X_s)$ predicted it. Evaluating an experience in terms of relative successes and failures is a proxy for a more detailed and sophisticated form of estimation of μ_j. Essentially, this describes the estimation process as analogous to the ascertainment of the parameter of a coin.

In general the level of P_o upon which the decision criteria are based would depend upon the difficulty associated with the calculation of $\gamma_i(X_s)$ as well as the additional value of a more finely tuned approximation to reality. There is a tradeoff between the drive enhancement associated with more intricate calculation and the drive reduction associated with a function which has a greater degree of belief. For example, a linear function may be acceptable at a lower degree of belief than a third-degree polynomial.

However, for purposes of simplicity and clarity it will be assumed that the drive enhancement of calculating the various relevant functions is the same. This allows the decision criterion to be based solely upon the degree of belief of a function. Also it will be assumed again that there is some acceptable level of belief below which no functional relationship will be selected, namely, P_o.

Previously, it was postulated that the individual selects a decision criterion on the basis of past experiences. Or, if $P[\gamma_i(X_s)/E] \geq P_o$, the individual "acts as if" $P[\gamma_i(X_s)/E] = 1$. If $\gamma_i(X_s)$ is in fact true and $P[\gamma_i(X_s)/E] \geq P_o$, then further understanding the relations of the real world (under the first interpretation of the propositional range) is not relevant to the welfare of the individual aside from aesthetic or academic values. This of course assumes that the worldly environment is unchanging or that the true relation $\gamma_i(X_s)$ is static. While this may be a reasonable approximation to many aspects of the real world, especially since γ_i refers to a specific bundle of goods X_s and this degree of constancy can be arbitrarily finely delineated, many other relationships are in a continual state of flux.

However, under the second interpretation of the nature of the propositional range,[4] further increases in the probability of an accepted functional relation imply a better, finer understanding of this relation. As the individual gains more and more experience, the probability that $\gamma_i(X_s) = w_i$, say, is true becomes higher and higher. Concomitantly, the precision of $\gamma_i(X_s)$ is known in greater and finer detail. This formulation would be consistent with the development of skilled labor or any similar "learning by doing" aspects of the environment. Another example would be the development of a wine taster's discerning palate. With little experience, a general relation between wines and the activity of drinking and tasting wine is recognized. As experience increases, these relations are not only held more firmly in the gourmet's mind but he is able to discern the bouquet and aftertaste to various degrees.

AN ALLOWANCE FOR FORGETTING

This development of skills (a greater and finer ability) over time can be brought out more clearly if Equation 4.11,

$$P'(\gamma) = \frac{P(E/\gamma) \cdot P(\gamma)}{\int_{-\infty}^{\infty} P(E/\gamma) \cdot P(\gamma)d\gamma} \tag{4.11}$$

4. Cf. pp. 74–75.

is generalized in the following fashion. Since Equation 4.11 states that posterior probability $P'(\gamma)$ depends upon prior probabilities, one could replace prior and posterior by a specific time notation. That is, let $P_T(\gamma)$ equal the probability at time T, then Equation 4.5 becomes

$$P_T(\gamma) = \frac{\displaystyle\prod_{t=0}^{T} P[E(t)/\gamma]\, P_1(\gamma)}{\displaystyle\int_{-\infty}^{\infty} \prod_{t=0}^{T} P[E(t)/\gamma]\, P_o(\gamma)\, d\gamma} \qquad (4.12)$$

Thus Equation 4.12 gives the probability of γ_i at any point in time $T > 0$ as a function of experiences up to that time $E(t)$. Taking the logarithm of both sides of Equation 4.12, we have

$$\log P_T(\gamma) = \sum_{t=0}^{T} \log P[E(t)/\gamma] + \log P_o(\gamma)$$

$$- \log \int_{-\infty}^{\infty} \left\{ \prod_{t=0}^{T} P[E(t)/\gamma] \right\} P_o(\gamma)\, d\gamma \qquad (4.13)$$

Forgetting can now be introduced in the calculus of the individual. Specifically, a forgetting rate $\epsilon(t)$ could be added such that if experiences associated with γ are zero, the probability of γ falls at the rate $\epsilon(t)$. This also implies that the individual loses his acuity and the like if experiences do not keep occurring. Equation 4.14 states this formally:

$$\log P_T(\gamma) = \log \frac{\left\{ \displaystyle\prod_{t=0}^{T} P[E(t)/\gamma] \right\} P_o(\gamma)}{\displaystyle\int_{-\infty}^{\infty} \left\{ \prod_{t=0}^{T} P[E(t)/\gamma] \right\} P_o(\gamma)\, d\gamma} - \int_{0}^{T} \epsilon(t)\, dt \qquad (4.14)$$

Therefore, if $E(T) = 0$, then $P[E(T)/\gamma] = P[E(T-1)/\gamma]$ for all γ, and thus

$$\frac{d \log P_T(\gamma)}{dt} = \frac{dP_T(\gamma)}{P_T(\gamma)dt} = -\epsilon(T) \qquad (4.15)$$

CALCULATING THE EXPERIENCES NECESSARY
TO CHANGE KNOWLEDGE

In the remainder of the chapter two types of knowledge change will be discussed: (1) the forming of an opinion and (2) the altering of an opinion. In type 1 the problem is to get one relation $\gamma_i(X_s)$ into the position where $P[\gamma_i(X_s)/E] \geq P_o$. In type 2 the process is one of moving from where $P[\gamma_j(X_s)/E_o] \geq P_o$, and $P[\gamma_i(X_s)/E_o] < P_o$, for $i \neq j$, to where $P[\gamma_j(X_s)/E_1] < P_o$ and $P[\gamma_i(X_s)/E_1] \geq P_o$. These types of change in the knowledge set will be analyzed by two methods: (I) the more general analysis where μ_j is given by any manner and (II) where μ_j is determined by the relative amounts of successes and failures associated with each experience. By concentrating on changes in functional relations, all changes in the knowledge set can be considered. Estimation of the functional relations necessarily includes the estimation of not only the form but also the parameters and thus the range of commodities and activities which are available.

In cases I.2 and II.2 it will be assumed that the individual begins with a wrong opinion, that is, $P[\gamma_i(X_s)/E_o] \geq P_o$, and the subsequent experiences are consistent in lowering $P[\gamma_j(X_s)]$ and in increasing the value of $P[\gamma_i(X_s)]$ so that after some period of time $\gamma_j(X_s)$ is replaced in the knowledge set with $\gamma_i(X_s)$. The speed and efficiency of this process will depend in part upon the resources utilized in the learning process and the "perfectness" of each experience. A perfect experience in cases I.1 and I.2 will be defined as $\mu_j = 1$ for $\gamma_j(X_{s_j})$, while a perfect experience in cases II.1 and II.2 will be defined as one where if r is the number of units of success and t is the number of units of failure in an experience, $t = 0$ and r, $r > 0$ corresponds to something which might be called the intensity of the experience. In addition it is assumed that P_o is fixed by a wealth of other experience and remains constant throughout the learning process with respect to $\gamma_i(X_s)$.

In cases I.1 and I.2 the posterior probability of each γ_j can be directly determined, once the μ_j's and the prior densities are known. In cases II.1 and II.2 the estimation process gives the entire distribution of the parameter λ_i. The expected value of each λ_i will determine whether or not γ_i is used in the decision-making process. Although basing a decision criterion on the expected value of λ_i rather than on other parameters (for example, the variance) seems to be a bit restrictive, in this simplified case it is not since the variance is inversely related to the mean. That is, for any total number of successes and failures, the closer the expected value is to one, the lower is the variance.

r units of success and t units of failure from a condition of ignorance give an expected value for λ of $(r + 1)/(r + t + 2)$. The variance σ^2 is

$$\sigma^2 = E_x(\lambda^2) - E_x(\lambda)^2 = \frac{\displaystyle\int_0^1 \lambda^{r+2}(1-\lambda)^t \, d\lambda}{\displaystyle\int_0^1 \lambda^r(1-\lambda)^t \, d\lambda} - \left(\frac{r+1}{r+t+2}\right)^2$$

$$E_x(\lambda^2) = \frac{[\Gamma(r+3)\Gamma(t+1)]/[\Gamma(r+t+4)]}{[\Gamma(r+1)\Gamma(t+1)]/[\Gamma(r+t+2)]}$$

$$= \frac{[(r+2)!t!]/[(r+t+3)!]}{(r!t!)/[(r+t+1)!]}$$

$$= \frac{(r+1)(r+2)}{(r+t+3)(r+t+2)}$$

therefore,

$$\sigma^2 = \frac{(r+1)(r+2)}{(r+t+3)(r+t+2)} - \frac{(r+1)^2}{(r+t+2)^2} = \frac{(r+1)(t+1)}{(r+t+2)^2(r+t+3)}$$

The limit of σ^2 as the expected value of λ approaches one is

$$\lim_{(t/r)\to 0} \frac{(r+1)(t+1)}{(r+t+2)^2(r+t+3)} = 0$$

Case I.1: The forming of a general opinion
From Equation 4.10, m experiences result in

$$P^m[\gamma_i(X_s)/E_{j+m}] = \frac{(\mu_i^j)^m}{\displaystyle\sum_{i=1}^n (\mu_i^j)^m}, \qquad \text{for } i = 1, \ldots, n$$

when it is assumed that the individual starts from a condition of ignorance, defined as $P(\gamma_i) = P(\gamma_j) = 1/n$, for all $i, j = 1, \ldots, n$, and each of the m experiences are equal and result in μ_i^j as the evaluation of E_j with respect to the function γ_i.

With this information one can determine the number m of experiences necessary for $\gamma_i(X_s)$ to be included in the calculus process, that is, $P^m[\gamma_i(X_s)/E_{j+m}] \geq P_o$ is equal to the minimum probability level for $\gamma_i(X_s)$ to be included in the knowledge set. Therefore,

$$(\mu_i^j)^m \bigg/ \sum_{i=1}^n (\mu_i^j)^m$$

must be greater than or equal to P_o which is equivalent to requiring

$$(1 - P_o)/P_o \geqslant \sum_{\substack{k=1 \\ k \neq i}}^{n} (\mu_k^j / \mu_i^j)^m$$

Numerically, let $P_o = .9$, $k = 2$, $\mu_1 = .9$, and $\mu_2 = .8$. Then for γ_1 to be selected and used over γ_2, it is necessary that $.1/.9 \geqslant (.8/.9)^m$ or $m \geqslant 18.7$. Thus after 19 experiences of quality μ_i^j, γ_1 would be part of the knowledge set since $P^{19}[\gamma_1(X_s)] = .903 \geqslant .9 = P_o$.

If the successive experiences are such that the probability μ_k^j varies, the algebraic manipulation is more complex but the result is analogous. The total number of experiences required would vary directly as the probability μ_k^j varied.

Case II.1:   The forming of an opinion by successes and failures
    Assume $\gamma_i(X_s)$ is true and $P[\gamma_j(X_s)] < P_o$, for all γ.

Suppose each $\gamma_j(X_s)$ has some associated degree of belief. Then starting from a position where for each function the parameter λ_j is unknown, we know by definition that $0 \leqslant \lambda_j \leqslant 1$, and

$$\int_0^1 P(\lambda_j)d\lambda_j = 1$$

Further, assume a rectangular distribution over each parameter λ_j.

After an initial arbitrary experience, for each $\gamma_j(X_s)$, $j = 1, \ldots, n$, the individual can define r_j and t_j as the degree of success with which the actual experience fulfills the expected experience as dictated by the function $\gamma_j(X_s)$.

Since $\gamma_i(X_s)$ is to be the true relation and assuming the effort involved in calculating $\gamma_j(X_s)$ is equal for all j, then $r_i > r_j$, $j \neq i$, and $t_i < t_j$, $j \neq i$. Thus $\lambda_i > \lambda_j$, $j \neq i$.

To attain P_o, the desired criterion level, the fraction

$$(r + 1)/(r + t + 2)$$

must be greater than P_o. If it is not, no decision is made until additional information is obtained. Let r_2 and t_2 be the second experience vector and P' be equal to the probability after the first experience, P'' be equal to the probability after the second experience, and so forth. Since

$$P'(\lambda/E) = \frac{P(E/\lambda) \cdot P(\lambda)}{\displaystyle\int_0^1 P(E/\lambda) \cdot P(\lambda)d\lambda}$$

then

$$P''(\lambda/E) = \frac{\lambda^{r_2}(1-\lambda)^{t_2}\,[\lambda^{r_1}(1-\lambda)^{t_1}]\Big/\Big[\int_0^1 \lambda^{r_1}(1-\lambda)^{t_1}\,d\lambda\Big]}{\int_0^1 \Big[\lambda^{r_2}(1-\lambda)^{t_2}\,\dfrac{\lambda^{r_1}(1-\lambda)^{t_1}}{\int_0^1 \lambda^{r_1}(1-\lambda)^{t_1}\,d\lambda}\Big]\,d\lambda}$$

or

$$P''(\lambda/E) = \frac{\lambda^{r_1}(1-\lambda)^{t_1}\cdot\lambda^{r_2}(1-\lambda)^{t_2}}{\int_0^1 \lambda^{r_2}(1-\lambda)^{t_2}\lambda^{r_1}(1-\lambda)^{t_1}\,d\lambda}$$

$$= \frac{\lambda^{r_1+r_2}(1-\lambda)^{t_1+t_2}}{\int_0^1 \lambda^{r_2+r_1}(1-\lambda)^{t_1+t_2}\,d\lambda}$$

The expected value of λ after two experiences is

$$E_x(\lambda) = (r_1 + r_2 + 1)/(t_1 + t_2 + r_1 + r_2 + 2)$$

which is the same form as the expected value of λ after one experience in that the expected value depends only upon the relative amounts of successes versus failures. For example, since

$$r + 1 \geqslant P_o(r + t + 2)$$

is a necessary condition for a decision, suppose $P_o = .9$, then

$$r + 1 \geqslant .9r + .9t + 1.8; \;\; .1r \geqslant .9t + .8;$$

or r must be greater than $9t + 8$.

The conclusion of case II.1 is that the degree of success relative to the degree of failure must be as in Equation 4.16 below for the decision to be implemented.

$$m \geqslant [P_o(n + 2) - 1]/(1 - P_o)$$

m = total number of successes

n = total number of failures

(4.16)

Thus for the decision criteria to be reached if r_j and t_j are constant for each experience,

$$r_j > (P_o t_j)/(1 - P_o) \qquad (4.17)$$

Only if Equation 4.17 holds for each experience j will the learning process surpass the decision criterion P_o in a monotonic manner. For example, if P_o = .9 then r_j must be greater than $9t_j$.

Case I.2:   Altering a general opinion
Assume:

1. $\gamma_1(X_s)$ is true
2. There exist n relevant functions which the individual feels may be true, $\gamma_k(X_s)$, $k = 1, \ldots, n$
3. Initially,

$$P[\gamma_2(X_s)] = P_o > 1/2$$

$$P[\gamma_k(X_s)] < P_o k = 1, \ldots, n; k \neq 2$$

4. The wrong opinion, $[\gamma_2(X_s)]$, was generated as in case I.1. Therefore,

$$(1 - P_o)/P_o = \sum_{\substack{k=1 \\ k \neq 2}}^{n} (\mu_k^j/\mu_2^j)^m$$

where m is equal to the number of constant previous experiences E_j. And also,

$$P^m[\gamma_1(X_s)] = (\mu_1^j)^m \bigg/ \sum_{k=1}^{n} (\mu_k^j)^m$$

In order for $\gamma_2(X_s)$ to be replaced by $\gamma_1(X_s)$ it is necessary that $P^{m+r}[\gamma_1(X_s)] \geqslant P_o$ and $P^{m+r}[\gamma_2(X_s)] < P_o$. Therefore, if a new experience occurs, E_h, where $\mu_1^h > \mu_2^h$ and if E_h is constant for several iterations, the number of experiences necessary to replace $\gamma_2(X_s)$ with $\gamma_1(X_s)$ can be determined.

After one new experience E_h the probability of $\gamma_1(X_s)$ being true is

$$P^{m+1}[\gamma_1(X_s)] = \frac{\mu_1^h(\mu_1^j)^m}{\sum_{k=1}^{n} \mu_k^h(\mu_k^j)^m}$$

Therefore, if

$$P^{m+r}[\gamma_1(X_s)] = \frac{(\mu_1^h)^r(\mu_1^j)^m}{\sum_{k=1}^{n} (\mu_k^h)^r(\mu_k^j)^m} \geqslant P_o$$

it follows that

$$(1 - P_o)/P_o \geqslant \sum_{k=2}^{n} \frac{(\mu_k^h)^r (\mu_k^j)^m}{(\mu_1^h)^r (\mu_1^j)^m}$$

As a numerical example which is similar to case I.1 let $P_o = .9$, $k = 2$, $m = 19$, $\mu_2^j = .9$, $\mu_1^j = .8$, then

$$P^{19}(\gamma_2) = .903$$

and

$$P^{19}(\gamma_1) = .097$$

If E_h is such that $\mu(h/2) = .6$, $\mu(h/1) = .9$, then

$$(1 - P_o)/P_o \geqslant [(.9)^{19}(.6)^r]/[(.8)^{19}(.9)^r]$$

The solution is $r \geqslant 10.9$, or after 11 new experiences, $\gamma_2(X_s)$ will be replaced in the calculus process by $\gamma_1(X_s)$. From the results of case I.1 one would expect if E_h just reversed the values of μ_1^j and μ_2^j such that $\mu_1^h = .9$ and $\mu_2^h = .8$, that $r \geqslant 38$, that is, it would take 19 E_h experiences to reduce things to the original level of ignorance and 19 more to make $P[\gamma_1(X_s)] \geqslant P_o$ and in fact that is the case.

Although the assumptions of the cases presented above simplify the problem considerably, the basic forces and intuitive ideas remain. That is, similar and analogous results could be derived if one were to relax the assumption that the $P[E_j/\gamma_i(X_s)]$ were constant and that E_j was also. However, the algebraic conditions and numerical example would be more complex but easily worked with no change in the essence of the argument.

Case II.2: Altering an opinion by successes and failures
Assume:

1. $\gamma_i(X_s)$ is true
2. There exist n relevant functions which the individual feels may be true,

$$\gamma_k(X_s), \qquad k = 1, \ldots, n$$

3. Initially for each k, γ_k is unknown for certain but,

$$E_x(\lambda_j) = \int_0^1 \lambda_j P[\gamma_j(X_s)] \, d\lambda_j = P_o$$

$$E_x(\lambda_k) = \int_0^1 \lambda_k P[\gamma_k(X_s)] \, d\lambda_k < P_o, \qquad k = 1, \ldots, n; k \neq j$$

If this information were originally formed as in case I.2, then

$$r_j = [P_o(t_j + 2) - 1]/(1 - P_o)$$

and

$$r_k < [P_o(t_k + 2) - 1]/(1 - P_o)$$

For a change in knowledge, it is necessary that the equality become an inequality, that is,

$$r_j^* < [P_o(t_j^* + 2) - 1]/(1 - P_o)$$

for the ith relation,

$$r_i^* \geqslant [P_o(t_i^* + 2) - 1]/(1 - P_o)$$

and

$$r_k^* < [P_o(t_k^* + 2) - 1]/(1 - P_o)$$

for all $k \neq i, j$, where r^*, t^* represent accumulated experience.

The learning process will smoothly converge to the correct relationship after a sufficient number of experiences as long as

$$r_i^T > (P_o t_i^T)/(1 - P_o)$$

for each T, and $r_j^T \leqslant [P_o(t_j^T + 2) - 1]/(1 - P_o)$ for each T, with the strict inequality holding for at least one $T \leqslant n$, which is the number of experiences necessary for $r_i^* \geqslant [P_o(t_i^* + 2) - 1]/(1 - P_o)$.

The theory of learning developed here is quite compatible with much empirical work which has been done in psychology. For example, the approaches used in experimental psychology (which entail a learning model that postulates that the empirical observation of a subject moving from, say, an unconditioned state to a conditioned state is based on some probability) are perfectly conformable to the above theory.[5] In this form of experimental empiricism, the "correct" versus "incorrect" responses are assumed known by the observers, while here the correctness of any set of beliefs depends solely upon the individual.

Cases I.1, I.2, II.1, and II.2 demonstrate the selection of various product-activity relations utilized in the individual's calculus process. Similar arguments would hold for the other relations in the knowledge set, except that rather than a decision criterion P_o, the individual would simply select the best relation, that is, the one with the highest probability.

5. For examples see Suppes and Ginsberg (1963), Atkinson and Estes in Luce, Bush, and Galanter (1964) vol. II, Myers and Atkinson (1964), and Kraemer (1964).

In Model 4.1 the felicific calculus process and the learning process are segregated. Given an initial set of relations in the knowledge set, the individual maximizes drive reduction for the next period t by carrying out a set of activities (W_t). These activities become experiences which are evaluated as to their success or failure to meet his expectations. This additional information alters the degree of belief in the various relations, and subsequent calculations are performed in view of these altered relations and other changed parameters in the environment (such as prices). Again $S = \phi(w_1, \ldots, w_m)$ is a surrogate for the overall calculus $\int_0^\infty S(t)dt$, and the drive reduction associated with the various activities is discounted to present value.

This variable preference model is in a sense a two-stage process. At any time the calculus process is carried out with the best estimate of ϕ and the best estimate of activity-product relations which meet the decision criteria. If learning takes place, a subsequent maximizing calculation will use either a different ϕ function, different γ functions, or a different ψ function.

AN EXPLICIT SEARCH ACTIVITY MODEL

Model 4.2 will consider explicitly the presence of a search activity w_s which is a known activity to the individual, that is,

$$P[\gamma_s(X_{s_s})/E] \geqslant P_o$$

The individual "knows" the relation between commodities and time used in the search activity w_s, namely, $\gamma_s(X_s)$ and $\psi(w_s)$, in precisely the same way he "knows" any other relation used in the calculus process. Let the direct effects of the search activity on drives be zero.

$\phi(\overline{w}_s) = 0$, where $\overline{w}_s$ = direct effects of search on drives, then

$$\phi(w_s) = \phi(w_{n+1}^f, \ldots, w_{n+t}^f, \omega_{m+1}^f, \ldots, \omega_{m+r}^f)$$

where w_{n+1}^f is the present effect of future activities and, currently,

$$P[\gamma_{n+i}(X_{s_i}^f)] < P_o, \qquad i = 1, \ldots, t$$

$$P[\gamma_{i \leqslant n}(X_{s_i}^f)] \geqslant P_o$$

Thus $\phi(w_s) = \phi(w_{n+1}^f, \ldots, \omega_{m+r}^f)$ is what the individual assumes will be the effect of w_s on his knowledge set. That is, each level of w_s is equivalent to some experience. After a sufficient amount of experience more activities will become known and can be included in the calculus process. This adds to the total level of drive reduction. Therefore, at any point in time the model becomes as Model 4.2.

MODEL 4.2

Maximize

$$S = \phi(w_1, \ldots, w_n, w^f_{n+1}, \ldots, w^f_{n+t}, \omega_1, \ldots, \omega_m,$$
$$\omega^f_{m+1}, \ldots, \omega^f_{m+r})$$

subject to

$$\sum_{i=1}^{k} P_i x_i \leqslant 0$$

$$w^f_{n+i} = K_{n+i}(w_s), \quad i = 1, \ldots, t$$

$$\psi(w_1, \ldots, w_s, \ldots, w_n, \omega_1, \ldots, \omega_m) \leqslant T_o$$

$$g_1(w_1, \ldots, w_s, \ldots, w_n, \omega_1, \ldots, \omega_m) \geqslant 0$$

$$\vdots$$

$$g_o(w_1, \ldots, w_s, \ldots, w_n, \omega_1, \ldots, \omega_m) \geqslant 0$$

$$w_i, x_i, \omega_1, \geqslant 0, \text{ for all } i$$

If S^* is a constrained maximum with $w^*_s > 0$, the search activity will be undertaken until sufficient additional experience alters Model 4.2. It is possible that additional experience would amount to no information, which would also alter $\gamma_s(X_s)$. The result might be to terminate the search activity w_s. On the other hand, the information could be such that the search activity was much more lucrative than originally perceived, and the next maximizing solution would include a higher level of search activity w_s.

SUMMARY

This chapter develops a learning process which bases preference change on the experiences of the individual. From the generality of Model 4.1, several specific applications can be made. Some examples discussed here were the inclusion of a forgetting rate and the specification of a specific search activity. With this basis of individual choice and knowledge change, we next consider the effects of personal interaction and the formation of groups.

Generalization to Personal Interaction and Group Formation

THE ANALYSIS thus far has ignored the effects of both the individual on his environment and, for the most part, the effects of the environment on the individual. The latter has been included only in the form of parameters and constraints. Social restrictions and rewards were implicitly included as one form of constraint the individual must obey or as part of the drive reduction associated with the various activities available to the individual. But there has been very little consideration of direct effects of one individual on another. In this chapter the analysis is expanded by permitting interpersonal interaction. Some of the parameters which have been held constant will now be allowed to vary and the consequences will be explored.

FORMAL STATEMENT OF INTERACTION

Define the following terms as:

S^i = drive reduction of ith individual,

w_j^i = activity j undertaken by individual i,

    if $j = 1, \ldots, n$; w_j^i is an economic activity

    if $j = n + 1, \ldots, m$; w_j^i is a noneconomic activity

$G = \{1, 2, \ldots, p\}$ = the index of those in the group

The concept of a "group" includes all individuals who interact with one another, as given by Equation 5.1 below. If the drive reduction of i is affected by individual j, activities carried out by individual j would be included in the functional relation between i's activities and i's drive reduction S^i.

Parts of this chapter are very similar to Roberts (1971).

$$S^i = \phi^i \, (w_1^1, \ldots, w_m^1, w_1^2, \ldots, w_m^2, \ldots, w_1^p, \ldots, w_m^p) \quad (5.1)$$

Social interaction will be defined when the various activities undertaken by g are affected by those of individual i, that is,

$$w_j^g = w_j^g \, (w_1^i, \ldots, w_m^i), \quad g \neq i; \, i, g \epsilon G$$

Which is to say that social interaction is explicitly designated when the others' activities affect individual i but only insofar as individual i can influence activities of others. Activities of others which the individual cannot influence are treated the same as other environmental parameters. They are not, however, part of social interaction. Each activity carried out by individual i is potentially composed of "direct" and "indirect" effects, thus Equation 5.1 can be written more simply as:

$$S^i = \phi^i \, [\phi^{*i}(W_j^i), \, W_k^g(W_j^i)], \quad \begin{matrix} j = 1, \ldots, m \\ g = 1, \ldots, p \\ k = 1, \ldots, m \end{matrix} \quad (5.2)$$

Suppose that w_j^i is the activity of telling funny stories. If the individual gets increased satisfaction "directly" from this activity, $(\partial\phi^i/\partial\phi^{*i})(\partial\phi^{*i}/\partial w_j^i) > 0$. This would be the marginal satisfaction from, say, telling a joke to himself in a closed room. If the telling of the story caused another person to laugh and this gave the joketeller increased satisfaction, the "indirect" effect is $(\partial\phi^i/\partial w_k^g)(\partial w_k^g/\partial w_j^i) > 0$, where w_k^g is laughing by the other individual and w_j^i is the telling of the joke by i.

As another example, let w_j^i be interpreted as individual i acting very belligerent and assume this gives him a sense of independence, then $(\partial\phi^i/\partial\phi^{*i})(\partial\phi^{*i}/\partial w_j^i) > 0$; that is, the "direct" effects are positive. However in the presence of another, i's belligerence causes the other individual to be belligerent as well. This, in turn, reduces i's drive reduction, as he is annoyed and irritated; that is,

$$(\partial\phi^i/\partial w_k^g)(\partial w_k^g/\partial w_j^i) < 0$$

Here the "indirect" effects would be negative.

Three types of activities can be distinguished as to their effects on drive reduction in some arbitrary area near the maximizing solution.

1. Independent activities:

$(\partial\phi^i/\partial\phi^{*i})(\partial\phi^{*i}/\partial w^i) \geqslant 0 \; (\partial\phi^i/\partial w_j^g)(\partial w_j^g/\partial w^i) = 0$, for all g and j

(The strict equality would hold only if either all the constraint shadow prices were zero or if the activity were carried out at a zero level near the optimal solution. Therefore, if we exclude activities at the zero level as being irrelevant and assume nonsatiation—that is, at least one shadow price is positive—the strict inequality must hold.) For an independent activity, the "direct" effects are nonnegative, while the "indirect" effects are nil.

2. (a) Socially reinforced activities:

$$(\partial\phi^i/\partial\phi^{*i})(\partial\phi^{*i}/\partial w^i) > 0, \sum_{g=1}^{p} \sum_{j=1}^{m} (\partial\phi^i/\partial w_j^g)(\partial w_j^g/\partial w^i) > 0$$

(b) Socially inhibited activities:

$$\sum_{g=1}^{p} \sum_{j=1}^{m} (\partial\phi^i/\partial w_j^g)(\partial w_j^g/\partial w^i) < 0$$

A socially reinforced activity has positive direct effects and positive indirect effects; while for a socially inhibited activity, the indirect effects are negative.

3. Purely social activities:

$$(\partial\phi^i/\partial\phi^{*i})(\partial\phi^{*i}/\partial w^i) \leqslant 0, \sum_{g=1}^{p} \sum_{j=1}^{m} (\partial\phi^i/\partial w_j^g)(\partial w_j^g/\partial w^i) > 0$$

Purely social activities have negative direct effects and positive indirect effects. The remaining possibility is where both the direct effects and the indirect effects are negative and would never be carried out.

The classifications can be contrasted to a Robinson Crusoe (RC) solution, which is defined as the mix of activities the individual would choose if he were the total social group, that is, if he were in isolation or stranded on a desert island. The Robinson Crusoe solution could be of types 1, 2a, or 2b—never 3.

The maximizing solution when an individual is in a social group rather than in isolation would potentially include activities of all types. Assuming that an RC solution activity is not replaced in the optimal solution for the social group case (SG) (for very small changes in the maximum value of the objective function such that no activity in the original RC solution is reduced to zero), type 1 is affected only by the changes in the shadow prices of the constraints; the aggregate of type 2a activities is at a level higher in SG than RC. Those of type 3 would increase from zero level in RC to a positive level in SG if they were in the optimal SG solution.

SOME EXAMPLES OF TYPES OF ACTIVITIES

While particular activities included in each type would vary from person to person and social group to social group, the following might be included in each type.

Type 1	Type 2a	Type 2b	Type 3
eating	joketelling	being belligerent	back scratching
breathing	bathing	masturbating	working for others
thinking	sexual intercourse	screaming	saving a drowning child
playing solitaire	singing	intoxication	going to cocktail parties

Thus, it is the nature of the human organism that groups and social interaction have a definite role in enhancing the potential drive reduction of the various participants. Many activities other than those illustrated above fall into the type 3 category. One measure of the social interaction in society would be the relative quantities of type 3 activities to other types. A measure of the independence of an individual would be the relative amounts of type 2 activities undertaken. This framework thus offers a way of analyzing and comparing different groups. However, since the nature of the activities themselves and whether or not they are carried out depends upon the group to which an individual belongs, it begs the question of the nature of the group. Therefore, the subsequent query is toward the conditions and aspects of group formation, change, and the effects upon the various members of such groups.

THE FORMATION OF SOCIAL GROUPS

Rather than assuming the existence of a particular group, the following discussion is oriented toward the creation and destruction of groups and subgroups within groups. Here group formation means the act of those forming the group, bringing themselves into contact with one another in a fashion to benefit from this personal interaction. In addition, the concept of a group is more or less an ongoing arrangement among persons. It is a specific agreement to interact for an extended period, rather than being an ephemeral, ad hoc conglomeration of individuals. Usually one would be able to associate goals and objectives with a particular group. The criterion, however, as to whether a group exists or is merely a happenstance collection of people is whether or not the individuals involved made a personal decision to join the group.

The theoretical structure to be developed here is not intended to replace the mass of work in social psychology. Since the questions of this analysis are the aggregate effects or the basic underlying forces in social progress, the conceptual framework can be more general. The structure necessary to analyze particular groups can be simplified by eliminating special details. Thus the theory provides a general basis from which more specific analyses can be derived. For example, March and Simon (1958), Collins and Guetzkow (1964), and Katz and Kahn (1966) all present theoretical structures (or meta-theories or conceptual frameworks) of the social psychology of organization which are compatible with the presentation here. The difference is that the above authors specify a host of environmental parameters consistent with current Western culture and consider the finer details of specific organizations. The emphasis here is on the unifying thread of group interaction and the long-run tendencies. For example, a social psychologist would be interested in precise descriptions of communication flows and how specific knowledge sets change, while the overall ramifications and general tendencies of knowledge change and group interaction are of interest here.

Initially, it will be assumed there is a fixed number of individuals N and that each individual is free to decide whether or not he wants to join any group. Similarly, each group can isolate itself from any individual it does not want to interact with. Any individual can physically or psychologically "drop out" from contact with others. This will be referred to as the free-group-formation assumption.

The process by which these groups maintain or change their size is a portion of the results of this analysis. That is, there are no presumed voting rules imposed, such as unanimity or majority rule; but this aspect of group formation will emerge directly from the inquiry to follow. (Almost all other work on voting and social choice assumes the existence of primitive rules or value judgments as criteria for analysis. No such assumption is employed here)[1].

First, it is clear that any individual considering joining a given group will prefer to join only if he is better off as a member of the group than if he is not. The next question is whether the group decides in some manner to admit the individual. Since this decision will be the result of an aggregative preference process and since drive reduction depends upon the activities of others, one needs to distinguish between the maximizing activity mix and alternative activities

1. Cf. Buchanan and Tullock (1962), Arrow (1963), or Wilson (1969).

which constitute what will be called "threat" sets and "acquiescence" sets.

Define the following terms as:

$S^{i \epsilon G}$ = maximum drive reduction attainable by individual i if he is a member of $G \subseteq N$ and everyone else in G is also doing the best that he can for himself. Only actions of the members of G affect the satisfaction of individual i; that is, $\partial \phi^i / \partial W^j = 0, j \notin G$.

$S^{i \epsilon G, \overline{W}^k}$ = maximum drive reduction attainable by individual i when he is a member of G and individual $k \epsilon G$ is carrying out a set of activities other than the maximizing set of activities for individual k.

Suppose group G' is considering the admission of i such that G' becomes $G = [G', i]$, individual k has a conflict if $S^{k \epsilon G'} > S^{k \epsilon G}$, but $S^{k \epsilon G} > S^{k \notin G}$. That is, k prefers the original group G' to G; the addition of i to G' will lower k's maximum attainable level of drive reduction. However, k also prefers being in the new group rather than withdrawing.

Clearly then, k is opposed to the admission of the new member; k possesses a *valid threat*, with respect to the augmentation of G' into G, if there exists some $[\overline{W}^k]$ such that $S^{j \epsilon G, \overline{W}^k} < S^{j \epsilon G'}$ for all $j \neq k$ and $\phi^k (\overline{W}^k) \geqslant S^{k \epsilon G'}$. That is, k possesses a valid threat if he has some feasible activity mix which will lower the satisfaction of each member of the original group, either directly or indirectly, and those activities will not leave k at a lower level of satisfaction than he could attain if he were a member of the new group G. The activity set $\overline{W}^k$ may imply that k is a member of the new group G, or it may not.

An *idle threat* is defined when there exists for a conflicting (with respect to a group change) individual k a threat set which would lower the drive reduction of every member of the group but would also lower it for k as well; that is, there exists $[\overline{W}^k]$ such that $S^{j \epsilon G, \overline{W}^k} < S^{j \epsilon G'}$ (for all $j \neq k$) and $\phi^k (\overline{W}^k) < S^{k \epsilon G}$. This represents an idle threat because even though k can threaten to lower the satisfaction of everyone in the group, it would also lower his satisfaction to a point where he would be better off to agree to the group change.

It will be assumed that only valid threats are effective in altering the formation of a group. When knowledge is imperfect, an individual could alter others' decisions with what is actually an idle threat; but due to lack of knowledge, others see it as a valid threat. In addition, often without complete certainty of individual abilities, there will be empirical testing of individuals' threat sets for their validity. At this stage full information will be assumed. All individuals know whether or not any other person's threat set is valid or idle. This assumption does serious harm to specific situations, but it corresponds to the long-run and/or aggregate effects of personal interaction.

NEGATIVE THREAT OR "ACQUIESCENCE" SETS

Assume that $N = \{1, 2, 3\}$ and suppose this set is faced with a triangle problem, the maximum attainable satisfactions for all possible groups are as follows (see Table 5.1):

$$S^{1\epsilon1,2} > S^{1\epsilon1,3} > S^{1\epsilon1} > S^{1\epsilon N}$$
$$S^{2\epsilon2,3} > S^{2\epsilon1,2} > S^{2\epsilon2} > S^{2\epsilon N}$$
$$S^{3\epsilon1,3} > S^{3\epsilon2,3} > S^{3\epsilon3} > S^{3\epsilon N}$$

Assume individuals 1 and 2 initially form a group and individual 3 is in isolation; let this be represented by G'.

$$S^{1\epsilon G'} \text{ is 1's maximum}$$
$$S^{2\epsilon G'} \text{ is 2's second best}$$
$$S^{3\epsilon G'} \text{ is 3's third best}$$

Let G represent a regrouping to $\{2,3\}$ and 1 in isolation. The change from situation G' to G would be preferred by both 2 and 3 but not by 1. In fact, for any combination of two from $N = \{1,2,3\}$ two of the individuals will always prefer a change. Thus the equilibrium group will depend upon the acquiescence of the individuals. It may be possible for 1 to prevent the change from G' to G by carrying out a set of activities $[\overline{W}^1]$ such that the following conditions hold:

$$S^{1\epsilon G,\overline{W}^1} > S^{1\epsilon G}$$
$$S^{2\epsilon G,\overline{W}^1} > S^{2\epsilon G}$$

Since $S^{1\epsilon G',W^1} \leqslant S^{1\epsilon G'}$ by definition, this represents a "giving in" on the part of individual 1 to prevent the change and he will remain better off than if the change had occurred. A similar argument holds

Table 5.1. Preference table of preferred group formations based on everyone pursuing a maximizing course

Choice	Individual		
	1	2	3
1st	1, 2	2, 3	1, 3
2nd	1, 3	1, 2	2, 3
3rd	1	2	3
4th	N	N	N

for each of the other two individuals. Which one makes the sacrifice (acquiesces) will depend upon the friction of the changing process, the initial conditions, the extent of each individual's activity sets, and the like.

Clearly, an acquiescence set is included in the concept of a threat set. An acquiescence set is a set of activities undertaken by an individual to affect the activity mix of the others (to stop an individual from going to another group). If the activity w_1^i represents individual i forming a group, individual j can affect i's activity by "giving in," that is, carrying out activity w_a^j, or $w_1^i = w_1^i (w_a^j)$.

This distinction of negative threats or acquiescence sets is useful only in pointing out the wide range of activities which could potentially be included in a threat set.

A WORLD GREATER THAN THREE INDIVIDUALS

Group formation and change when there are more than three individuals will depend on the interaction of the threats and degrees of acquiescence available to the various members. Under the proposition of potential individual isolation, either by the rest of a group or by a single person himself, the threat set is only relevant where the conflicting individual is more valuable to the group than is the contemplated change. The conflicting individual must have some position of power from which to operate, otherwise he could merely be replaced in the composition of the group. Therefore, it necessarily follows that if a conflicting individual k has a valid threat, that is,

$$S^{j\epsilon G, \overline{W}^k} < S^{j\epsilon G'}, \text{ for all } j\epsilon G, j \neq k; \phi^k (\overline{W}^k) \geqslant S^{k\epsilon G}$$

and letting $G'' = [G] - [k]$, then $S^{i\epsilon G''} < S^{i\epsilon G'}$, for all $i\epsilon G''$. In other words, conflicting individual k is indispensable to the group G''.

The above discussion has been essentially limited to minor group change (namely, augmenting the group size by one), and a valid threat has been defined as the conflicting individual being able to affect the entire group. Under the definition of a valid threat, $S^{j\epsilon G, \overline{W}^k}$ represents the drive reduction or satisfaction of the individuals comprising the group G, with k carrying out nonmaximizing activities. No mention of the possibilities of other threat sets was given. The notation $S^{j\epsilon G, \overline{W}^k}$ is the maximum drive reduction attainable due to k's threat set being carried out. It may in turn cause several other individuals to implement threat sets. The following theorem will illustrate this more clearly.

Theorem 5.1
A conflicting individual k can stop the change of a group G' into G if and only if he possesses a valid threat set.

Proof

IF: The if portion of the proof follows directly from the definition of a valid threat and the assumption of free group formation. Under k's valid threat everyone prefers the original group G'.

ONLY IF: This is the much more difficult portion of the proof and follows by induction. Upon change of a group G' into G, the activity set open to any conflicting member can have the following possibilities:

1. k has no social interaction.
2. k has social interaction but no threatening activities in his choice set.
3. k has threats but of an idle nature.
4. k has partially valid threats; he can affect a portion of G adversely.
5. k has a valid threat.

Item 5 has already been discussed under the *if* portion of the theorem. In items 1 and 2 there is nothing k can do about the addition of i to the group G'. In item 3, k could adversely affect some or all members of G, but under the assumption that there is full information, the group change will take place.

This leaves only item 4 to be analyzed. k will have a partial threat if the initial effects of k's actions divides G into two subgroups α and β as follows:

$$\alpha: \quad S^{j\epsilon G, \overline{W}^k} < S^{j\epsilon G'}$$

$$\beta: \quad S^{j\epsilon G, \overline{W}^k} > S^{j\epsilon G'}$$

Subgroup α is now opposed to the change in light of k's threat, while subgroup β is still in favor of the change. If individual i, the new member of G, is contained in subgroup α, then β is empty and k has a valid threat. Subgroup β then must contain i and at least one or more members of the group G'.

Since those in α are opposed to the change in light of k's threats alone, they will implement any valid threat sets which could either increase the numbers in α or in β. After all valid threat sets have been implemented and if G and G' are still the best forms of social interaction, there are three forms for subgroups α and β:

1. $\alpha: \quad S^{j\epsilon G, \overline{W}^k, \overline{W}^1}, \cdots < S^{j\epsilon G'}$ for all j

   β: empty

This means that k's threat set and the subsequent addition of other threats has caused all individuals to be opposed to the change; k has a valid threat and the evolution of G' into G will not occur.

2. β: $S^{j \epsilon G, \overline{W}^k, \overline{W}^1, \cdots} > S^{j \epsilon G'}$ all $j \neq k$

   α: empty

Then k does not have a valid threat, even though he had a partially valid one. His initial threats were offset by others adversely affected; k does not have a valid threat and the change will take place.

3. α: $S^{j \epsilon G, \overline{W}^k, \overline{W}^1, \cdots} < S^{j \epsilon G'}$

   β: $S^{j \epsilon G, \overline{W}^k, \overline{W}^1, \cdots} > S^{j \epsilon G'}$

Here all valid threats have been exhausted; and since G or G' are the two best groups, i will be allowed to join the group. There is nothing more those in α can do to stop those in β from joining the group.

The only other alternative is for completely new groups to form. Let G_1 and G_2 be two possible groups formed from G. If they do form, then $S^{j \epsilon G_1} > S^{j \epsilon G}$. Thus k possesses a valid threat. In this case, G_1 is a result of k's threats.

On the other hand if groups do not form, $S^{j \epsilon G_1} < S^{j \epsilon G'} < S^{j \epsilon G}$, or k does have a valid threat and has stopped the change of G' into G. In the case where new groups G_1 and G_2 form, the evolution would be from G' into G_1 and G_2 rather than G' into G. For example, k may have a valid threat for the change of G' into G but may not possess a valid threat for G' into G_1 and G_2. This completes the *only if* portion and the theorem is proved.

Theorem 5.1 says that regardless of whether arbitrary rules of group change exist, a conflicting individual can only prevent such a change if he (or they) possesses a valid threat. It may be that threat sets of individuals exist only because of such given rules, constitutions, and the like. Whatever the origin of the threat sets, group change will occur only with unanimity of opinion in light of all valid threat sets which exist. For example, the minority agrees to abide by majority opinion because of the threat sets associated with changing the institution of majority rule.

At this point it is worthwhile to emphasize the interpretive content of the above analysis. The maximizing solution for an individual who is a member of any given group includes many of the concepts often described as "interdependence of utility." It includes all activities that an individual can undertake which will prompt particular responses from others in the group. The question of group change is only relevant when the change affects individuals adversely; and by excluding one or more individuals (or by separating them) or by changing the decorum of the group, greater satisfaction is attained by those making the change.

The range of activities which any individual can undertake for purposes of a threat or acquiescence would include such things as side payments of money, temper tantrums, physical violence, restricting and controlling tempted responses, and so on. In short, it includes all forms of possible power plays and submissions. A certain amount of analysis has been carried out in economic literature concerning monetary side payments and logrolling.[2] These are valid within their narrow conceptual framework, but in a broader context where multifarious activities infringe upon individuals, money or vote exchanges would not represent in general the best alternative for an individual. Thus the literature does not give an adequate picture of the dynamics of group change.

There are many cases of group change and formation where no money changes hands or no explicit "deals" are made. This is the more typical case in spite of the belief of some writers that monetary payments solve everything. Almost every example in public goods and externality analysis where a monetary side payment would produce an equilibrium is not solved in that manner in the real world. When a neighbor builds a fence or plants flowers, the existence of money subsidies is not a real-world phenomenon, and this is precisely because there are more efficient activities available to those involved, for example, threatening to tear down the fence or telling others what a wonderful, flower-planting neighbor one has.

INTERPRETATION OF GROUPS

Within this quite general analysis of group interaction are included many different types of organizations and internally cooperating bodies. Families constitute a particular kind of group, and individual members provide one another with various benefits from division of labor to more personal affectations. In a particular culture many of the interpersonal, intrafamily activities derive their legitimacy from the cultural ethic as learned by the family members, but nevertheless this ethic provides the necessary values for family stability. The nature of the creation of these values and social mores is more a problem of the establishment of knowledge sets and is dealt with in other sections.

The concept of the firm is another specialized example of a group. In this case the division of labor afforded by the formation of a firm is represented by the interpersonal activities. Most of these specialized jobs can be classified as purely social activities in that a

---

2. E.g., Buchanan and Tullock (1962).

single individual would never undertake these in isolation. The indirect stimulation for these social activities arises from wages and salaries for the workers and labor services and products for the organizer or for those individuals performing the entrepreneurial function. In classical economic analysis the entrepreneur or the captain of industry has a position of power enabling him to control the formation of this specialized group because he has access to capital not available to the average individual, he has particular skills in marketing the products or services, he has control over knowledge and/or the means for production such as patents or copyrights, or he has other similar sources of power making him master of his employees. As these reasons for control of the group change or wither away due to advancing technology, the power structure within the group necessarily changes. Any group is a mutually benefiting aggregation of its independent decision makers. Anyone becoming a member of the group is doing better for himself than he could by not participating. The ability to control change depends upon the individual and the degree to which he becomes dependent upon the existence of such a group.[3]

As the power structure in a firm changes, the decision-making process changes along similar lines. The "rules" become more and more democratic, not because of the magnanimity of the entrepreneur, but due to the increased technological development and the consequent change in power. At this point, much of this decision-making process is inextricably intertwined with a learning process which itself requires resources. As a consequence, rules of thumb or institutions are created in the short run which are applicable to many situations. A fuller discussion of these phenomena of society is presented below.

In addition to economic agents, the analysis of group interaction is applicable to clubs, fraternities, and so forth. While each such organization merits particular discussion, some general comments also apply. In general the force behind such agglomerations is one of economy of information or economy of effort for interpersonal interaction. Groups often provide status for members, (convey information to other members of the society), or they provide a vehicle for exploiting the benefits of personal interaction. Cities, political parties, and nations also constitute special forms of groups. However, many of the pertinent and interesting aspects of these larger groups are included in the analysis of the interaction of smaller groups.

3. For similar theses developed in a different context, see Veblen (1904) or Galbraith (1967).

GROUP INTERACTIONS—COALITIONS

Even though groups are formed for the purpose of enhancing the drive reduction or satisfying individuals comprising the group, some groups are often purposely formed to interact with others (for example, firms and nations), or subsequent to formation the group finds it necessary or beneficial to interact with other individuals or groups. Many of the advantages of particular groups often stem from interaction with other such organized bodies.

A coalition will be defined as a particular group which interacts with others outside the group, and the objective function for this extragroup interaction is well defined. The group must be sufficiently well organized so that it is able to make a collective decision on how it will act as a body with those not in the group. For a group to be a coalition this group decision must at least order the alternatives. It must be possible to aggregate the individual objective functions of the members to form an objective function for the group which has at least the properties of a transitive, binary preference ordering over alternatives open to the group. A firm whose objective function is solely defined in terms of profits would be a coalition if more profit in dollar terms is preferred to less. This does not mean that groups not becoming coalitions do not make collective decisions or interact with other groups on an ad hoc basis but these decisions need not be consistent or transitive.

Some Conditions for a Coalition

When a group is interacting as a group with other agents in the social framework, the analysis of individual participation in the decision-making process within the group is analogous to the above discussion of group change. If a group deals with others, the consequences to any particular individual are equivalent to the effects of group change. Thus for any conflicting individual to prevent the group from making some extragroup transaction, he must possess a valid threat. It can further be concluded that if any individual goes along with such a change, he is doing the best he can for himself. He might not be as well off after as before, but he is better off than he could be in any other feasible agglomeration of individuals.

For a group to function as a coalition, the desires of the individuals must be sufficiently similar so that for some action space a well-defined objective function for the group results. If a market exists where the various individuals can buy and sell their own activities as well as those of others, money can be included in the drive-reduction function as a surrogate for interpersonal activities, that is,

$$S^i = \phi^i(w^i_1, \ldots, w^i_m, M_i) \tag{5.3}$$

Near the maximum solution of the individual calculus, the drive-reduction equation can be approximated by Equation 5.4.

$$S^i = X^i(w^i_1 \ldots, w^i_m) + \lambda_i M_i \tag{5.4}$$

where λ_i is the marginal value of a money payment which is transferable into real goods and services.

It is now possible to approximate a group objective function in the following way. Define W^* as preferred by the group to W^{**} if and only if $\phi^i(W^*) > \phi^i(W^{**})$ for all i, where ϕ^i is approximated by Equation 5.4.

Theorem 5.2

For $G = [1, 2, \ldots, n]$ there exists $M_1, M_2, \ldots, M_n$ such that

1. $\displaystyle\sum_{i=1}^{n} M_i = 0$

2. $X^i(W^*) + \lambda_i M_i > X^i(W^{**})$ for all $i \epsilon G$ if and only if

3. $\displaystyle\sum_{i=1}^{n} [X^i(W^*)]/\lambda_i > \sum_{i=1}^{n} [X^i(W^{**})]/\lambda_i$

Proof

ONLY IF: From item 1, since $\lambda^i > 0$,

$$[X^i(W^*)]/\lambda_i + M_i > [X^i(W^{**})]/\lambda_i$$

then if

$$\sum_{i=1}^{n} M_i = 0$$

$$\sum_{i=1}^{n} [X^i(W^*)]/\lambda_i > \sum_{i=1}^{n} [X^i(W^{**})]/\lambda_i$$

IF:

$$\sum_{i=1}^{n} [X^i(W^*)]/\lambda_i > \sum_{i=1}^{n} [X^i(W^{**})]/\lambda_i$$

either they agree:

$$X^i(W^*) > X^i(W^{**})$$

for all $i \epsilon G$. Then let

$$M_i = 0$$

or there is a conflict between members:

$$X^i(W*) < X^i(W**), i \epsilon G_1 \subset G$$
$$X^j(W*) > X^j(W**), j \epsilon G_2 \subset G$$

Therefore, $[X^i(W*)]/\lambda_i < [X^i(W**)]/\lambda_i$, since $\lambda > 0$. There exists an M_i' such that

$$[X^i(W*)]/\lambda_i + M_i' = [X^i(W**)]/\lambda_i, i \epsilon G_1 \subset G$$

Add and subtract M_i' from item 3 to obtain

$$\sum_{i \epsilon G_1} \frac{X^i(W*)}{\lambda_i} + \sum_{i \epsilon G_1} M_i' + \sum_{j \epsilon G_2} \frac{X^j(W*)}{\lambda_j} - \sum_{i \epsilon G_1} M_i'$$

$$> \frac{X^i(W**)}{\lambda_i} + \frac{X^j(W**)}{\lambda_j}$$

Since

$$\sum_{i \epsilon G_1} \frac{X^i(W*)}{\lambda_i} + \sum_{i \epsilon G_1} M_i' = \sum_{i \epsilon G_1} \frac{X^i(W**)}{\lambda_i}$$

let

$$\sum_{j \epsilon G_2} M_j' = \sum_{i \epsilon G_1} - M_i'$$

then

$$\sum_{j \epsilon G_2} \frac{X^j(W*)}{\lambda_j} + \sum_{j \epsilon G_2} M_j' > \sum_{j \epsilon G_2} \frac{X^j(W*)}{\lambda_j}$$

There exists a number $\epsilon > 0$, such that

$$\sum \frac{X^j(W*)}{\lambda_j} + \sum(M_j' - \epsilon) > \sum \frac{X^j(W*)}{\lambda_j}$$

Let

$$M_i = M_i' + \epsilon$$
$$\Sigma M_j = \Sigma(M_j' - \epsilon)$$

then

$$\sum_{i \epsilon G_1} \frac{X^i(W*)}{\lambda_i} + \sum_{i \epsilon G_1} M_i > \sum_{i \epsilon G_1} \frac{X^i(W**)}{\lambda_i}$$

and

$$\sum_{j \in G_2} \frac{X^j(W*)}{\lambda_j} + \sum_{j \in G_2} M_j > \frac{X^j(W**)}{\lambda_j}$$

which completes the theorem.

The foregoing theorem asserts that the objective function for the group near the optimum can be approximated by Equation 5.5 for an n-person group.

$$S^G = \phi^G(W) = [X^1(W)] / \lambda_1 + \cdots + [X^n(W)] / \lambda_n \tag{5.5}$$

where λ_i = marginal value of money side payments at the optimum for individual i.

In the absence of money side payments the general conditions for group acceptance of any set of activities are an immediate generalization of the theorem on group change for conflicting individuals. For the group objective function, $\phi^G(W) > \phi^G(W*)$ if and only if $\phi^i(W) > \phi^i(W*, \overline{W}^k)$ for all $i \epsilon G$ and $\overline{W}^k$ are valid threat sets. Feasible monetary side payments "smooth over" the various threats generated by different proposed activity mixes. The existence of money puts dollar values on both threat and acquiescence sets and provides a precise ranking of various proposals. Without money and markets the group objective function is a unanimous opinion in light of the valid threat sets. This is a very particular approach to the problem of aggregating individual preferences which has been rather extensively discussed in economic literature beginning with Arrow (1963). Unlike the approach of Arrow and others, the above is not particularly concerned with whether the objective function for the group appears as dictatorial or imposed. This approach merely attempts to note the conditions which will necessarily follow from an interacting group. In the above analysis, the welfare implications are enmeshed in the question of the possession of various activities which serve as threats or create the power structure of any group. This question, aside from the learning process expounded above, will be dealt with more fully later.

THE CREATION OF INSTITUTIONS AND THEIR ROLE
IN A SOCIAL SYSTEM

An institution will be defined as a system of rules applicable to established practices and generally accepted by the members of a social system. These guidelines of interaction may be either explicitly delineated by laws, charters, constitutions, and so forth, or they may be implicit to a particular culture such as customs, mores, generally accepted ethics, and so forth. The essential point is that an institution specifies consequences of individual or group action which can be expected. Given an existing institution, an individual or a group knows to some extent the reaction its activities will evoke.

Examples of different institutions could reach infinite proportions. However, the following list might stretch the reader's imagination to encompass the broad context within which this analysis applies. In the area of social mores, institutions include the proper dress for various occasions and similar rules of "proper" etiquette, the language which is acceptable in different company, general religious beliefs, and so on. Laws and similar legislated acts have more well-defined prescripts for response to individual actions. Whether these laws are in the area of thievery, murder, tariffs, monopoly, or bigamy, they prescribe procedure and penalties for these activities. Various customs are another general type of institution and include a diverse mixture of rules of thumb for individual action. Customs include holidays; hours of business; language and writing systems and the like; the number of times and appropriate foods for meals; group responses such as applause, casual idioms, and greetings; and so on.

The roles of institutions in a social system can be categorized into the following three types.

To provide information. One function which institutions serve in social interaction and which has been more or less dismissed in the previous discussion of individual and group interaction is that of providing information. When an individual decides to carry out an activity, he does so with varying degrees of belief over the possible outcomes. The existence of an institution serves to limit the range of these results or to specify the precise results when there is what might be termed a perfect institution. An institution specifies a functional relation between the individual's activity and the consequent activity or activities it produces. If $w_j^g = f(w_j^i)$, the institution specifies f. In case of a perfect institution, i would know f with certainty.

Another potentially significant method by which institutions provide information is as a source of drive reduction or satisfaction itself. Institutions specify "correct" activities and responses for personal interaction. If these institutions are lacking, the individuals involved must establish rewards and consequences. If this activity of deciding what is right and wrong, good or bad, and so forth, in the calculus process is itself drive enhancing, the lack of an institution becomes a source of anxiety. The individual who does not have specified institutional arrangements to tell him right from wrong or good from bad may find this a source of great discomfort. Suppose some institution is eliminated by society. Since institutions are in a sense generalized habits, suddenly the individual has a greater demand on his personal resources. He must now do for himself what was being done for him; this could be quite disquieting. His concept of a stable, known environment may be shattered. Suddenly the individual finds it very portentous and distressing not to know all the answers. Consequently, he spends much time and effort trying to decide what is in fact true. If this process has a negative total effect on drive reduction, the individual would have been receiving some drive reduction directly from the existence of the institution.

Many examples can be given demonstrating this value of institutions in a society. Suppose we have a number of people who decide that the traditional Western institutions of sex and sexual relations are passé, and they decide that limiting sex to one's spouse is unnecessary with the current high level of affluence; the necessity of a stable traditional family is no longer needed. The dispensing of one institution necessitates the establishing of a new one if stability remains a goal of the group. Suddenly there are a host of unanswered questions. The traditional institution says that one becomes highly insulted if his spouse commits adultery. What should be the response if these institutions are discarded? Should lovers be discreet or open? Should the new sexual liberty be personal between two participants or is group sex better? How does one include or exclude the children? And so on. In the face of these unanswered questions, the various individuals may experience extreme inner conflict, trying to come up with the best answers, knowing that these answers have rather wide consequences.

In general when any institution is discarded, the participants are likely to undergo a significant change in knowledge, finding that the institution provided a great deal more information and prescription than was originally perceived. If this is true and if this knowledge change is drive enhancing, the value of an institution may be very difficult to ascertain.

To serve as a constraint, either absolute or tolerant. An institution might effectively serve to fix certain individual activities. This will be called an absolute institution. The institutional penalty or response to particular individual activities may be so severe as to essentially fix the level of an activity. For example, an absolute institution might set $w_k^i = 0$, where k is the activity of murdering individual j.

A more permissive institution or a tolerant institution might prescribe some level which the individual cannot exceed, for example, $w_k^i \leqslant w_k$, where k is drunkenness. This says that some lower levels of drunkenness are permitted but more than w_k would bring sufficient social penalties to be inhibitive for individual i.

To make personal interaction more efficient. Perhaps one of the more important economic functions of an institution is in the area of efficiency. Suppose that without an existing institution individual i can carry out activities $\overline{w}_k^i$ and $\overline{w}_n^i$ which will produce the response $\overline{w}_j^g$ by person g, that is, $\overline{w}_j^g = f(\overline{w}_k^i, \overline{w}_n^i)$. Given an institution $\overline{w}_j^g$ could be elicited by person i without the activity $\overline{w}_n^i$, that is, $\overline{w}_j^g = f*(\overline{w}_k^i)$. Where by use of the term efficiency, it is implied that $(\partial \phi^i / \partial \overline{w}_j^g) > 0$. Thus the institution transforms f into $f*$, where $f*$ is more efficient than f. In this case the creation of the institution is a type of technological change as discussed in Chapter 3.

Whatever the type, the value of an institution can be determined by the resources it saves. Suppose an individual would make an identical decision with or without the institution. Without the social decorum the individual must expend certain resources (for example, time and money) which would not be necessary given an existing system. If this were a market, the individual might have to search for another trader, while the existence of a marketplace would have avoided this personal expenditure. Or, if the institution specified the consequences or reactions to an activity, the saving in resources would be the individual's time and energy which he would have to use to carry out the calculus process himself. If this personal calculus resulted in a higher level of drive reduction, this would have to be considered in the evaluation of the institution. The presence of an institution permits each individual to attain a certain level of drive reduction $S*$, and without the given institution some other level S is attainable, where $S < S*$ if the institution has a positive value for the individual.

To establish the social value of the institution, the aggregation problem has to be overcome. One approximation is the additional dollar value of goods and services made possible. This may or may not be an accurate index of drive reduction, depending upon how the various individuals make use of their additional freedom and the marginal effects on drive reduction. If the institution serves to alter the decision of the individual, the evaluation of such an institution in terms other than drive reduction becomes much more complex. In general the only accurate measure is the increased drive reduction attainable.

The establishment of an institution is quite analogous to the analysis of both group change and creation of group policy as presented above. Institutions are created by the interaction of groups acting as coalitions and singular individuals, and thus the analysis of personal interaction applies. If any individual or coalition of individuals is made worse off by an institution (that is, it would not be the optimal social rule for those adversely affected, for example, those with insomnia would attain a higher level of satisfaction if business hours were conventionally set at night), he can stop its creation or alter its form if he possesses sufficient power to do so with the activities at his disposal. Alternatively, he may also have the choice of isolating himself from such institutional rules and their consequences.

The evaluation of institutions has rather wide ramifications for welfare and efficiency concepts. Consider the work-leisure choice facing an individual in the current institutional structure of the United States. This is often put forth as an inefficient institutional "all or none" bargain. The individual can choose to work 40 hours a week or not work at all, and it is argued further, that this is not consistent with the marginal adjustment process, thus it is inefficient. However, such an institution provides an economy of information and therefore is of value to many individuals in the society. Bookkeeping is easier, employers and employees can plan more accurately on how much of their time will be occupied, and so forth. Its existence allows resources which would be utilized in solving the problems handled by the institution to be put to better uses.

Thus, to compare the alleged inefficiencies of such an "all or none" bargain, one must aggregate over the differences between drive reduction attainable with the institution and what is attainable without it. One can analyze the existence of such an institution as a 40-hour workweek in terms of the threat sets and acquiescence sets of the various components of the social structure. When a sufficient number become in favor of institutional change, the change does in fact take place. Such is the case with the evolution of the workweek from 60 hours, to 48 hours, to 44 hours, to 40 hours. The evolution and occasional revolution of various institutions which comprise the social fabric of an agglomeration of individuals will be analyzed in greater detail in Chapter 10.

SUMMARY

In this chapter the analysis has been extended to include a specific statement of personal interaction and the formation of groups. In particular, the abstract, necessary, and sufficient conditions for an individual to control group change were presented. Also the conditions for a coalition, a group with a well-defined objective function, were given. Rules of a social system are analogous to rules for groups except that social institutions are formed by the interaction of groups.

chapter 6

Public Goods and Group Formation

HERETOFORE, emphasis has been upon goods and services which affect only single individuals and in turn may affect others, but indirectly. Food and fiber consumed by individual A benefits individual B indirectly as A becomes more amiable and pleasant, rather than being inimical and disagreeable. However, there are particular goods and services which do not diminish in quantity with additional consumers. These goods, which will be termed public goods, warrant special attention because they are amenable to joint consumption and hence to cooperative or group provision. Consequently, one individual providing a public good will affect the decision calculus of another, who may be able to share this good without cost or by sharing the cost in some manner.

THE TRADITIONAL APPROACH TO PUBLIC GOODS

In the body of economic theory there is specific recognition of the possibility of joint consumption of a particular quantity of public goods. Formally, Samuelson (1954a, 1954b) developed the conditions for the Pareto optimal mix of purely public and purely private goods and services as shown in Model 6.1.

MODEL 6.1—Samuelson conditions for Pareto optimal mix

Define the following terms as:

x_i = a purely private good if the quantity produced is equal to the sum of quantities consumed by all individuals, that is, $x_i = \Sigma_{k=1}^{n} x_i^k$, where there are n individuals. x_j = a purely public good if the quantity produced is equal to the quantity consumed by each individual, that is

$$x_j = x_j^1 = x_j^2 = \ldots = x_j^n$$

$F(x_i, x_i) = 0$ is the transformation function representing the trade-off in the maximum possible outputs of x_i and x_j. $F(x_i, x_j) = 0$ represents the production possibility frontier for a given set of resource supplies and level of technology.

$U_k = U_k \; x_i, x_j$ = the utility index of individual k, $k = 1, \ldots, n$

By straightforward maximization techniques, the Pareto optimal mix of public and private goods (a mix of the two goods such that it is impossible to make someone better off without making another individual worse off) must be one where the sum of the marginal rates of substitution (MRS) for all individuals is equal to the marginal rate of transformation (MRT):

$$\sum_{k=1}^{n} \frac{\partial U_k / \partial x_j}{\partial U_k / \partial x_i} = \sum_{k=1}^{n} MRS_{j:i}^k = \frac{\partial F / \partial x_j}{\partial F / \partial x_i} = MRT_{j:i}$$

Before developing the actual provision in some particular models, it is worthwhile to point out the kinds of goods and services about which the Model 6.1 is concerned. The Samuelson purely public good is one where the marginal cost of adding additional consumers is zero. The amount available for additional consumers is not diminished by the number consuming it. Given the specified utility functions in Model 6.1, there is no personal interaction with respect to decisions on consumption; there are no "externalities" of consumption or production. No individual is benefited by another individual *consuming* a good. He may be benefited by another individual *providing* a quantity of the public good. This depends upon whether exclusion is possible. The term exclusion refers to the possibility of prohibiting or allowing additional consumers. If exclusion is possible in a social system with private property rights, the owner or provider of the public good could decide whether to permit other consumers to enjoy the public good. Alternatively, if exclusion is not possible, given that a particular quantity of the public good is provided under Model 6.1, everyone is forced to consume that amount. Likewise, no one can be refused the public good; it is there, freely and forceably available to all.

What kinds of goods would fall under the Samuelson model? Under the possibility of exclusion, such things as the Grand Canyon, movie theaters, and swimming pools in an uncrowded condition would qualify if there were no externalities of swimming with others, if viewing vistas or movies was not affected by the presence of others, and so forth. When exclusion is not possible, such things as national defense or mosquito control on a small island might qualify. Once land is protected or a cesspool is cleaned, all individuals in the area are benefited. Similarly, the impossibility of exclusion implies that once a country is attacked or more mosquitoes are imported, each individual who is a member is affected.

PROVISION OF THE PUBLIC GOOD WITH VARIOUS MARKET MODELS

In this section various simple market models will be constructed and the resulting output of the public-private good mix will be compared. In particular, the models will assume that firms exist, are independent of the consumers involved, and maximize profits. The purpose of this chapter is to establish the fact that Samuelsonian purely public goods motivate group formation. In order to focus on this aspect, simplifying assumptions will be employed.

First, the role of goods in activities and whether a good is a purely general or purely divisible one will be subsumed into a simple ordinal utility function. Given the properties of a particular good and their efficacy in activity fulfillment, an individual will be able to state a preference for one batch of goods vis-à-vis another. These preferences are described by an ordinal utility indicator. Second, a simple budget constraint will be assumed to be the only relevant constraint. This is primarily for didactic purposes.

The models will assume that the individual does not change his beliefs in the products and their serviceability. Consequently, there is no information provided by firms except the price. In models where a limited kind of learning does take place, a very simplified form of the process described in Chapter 4 will be used for illustrative purposes. Any interpersonal relations among individuals and activities will be basically subsumed in the following models.

MODEL 6.2—Samuelson purely public good with exclusion[1]

If exclusion is possible, exclusion properties are significant only if the supplier is a monopolist. This is a clear case of perfect economies of adding additional consumers. Given these zero marginal costs of expanding the market to additional consumers,

---

1. For other models of the provision of public goods with exclusion properties by a private market see Thompson (1968) and Demsetz (1970).

any competitive market structure would be autophagous. Furthermore, even if the market structure were not a single firm, there would be no way to take advantage of the possibilities of exclusion. Thus a competitive market structure under exclusion would not be able to take advantage of the properties of exclusion.

In the special case where all purely public goods are provided by a profit-maximizing monopolist with zero bargaining costs in a market where all such goods possess an exclusion property and all purely private goods are provided by a perfectly competitive industry, the condition for a Pareto optimum will be fulfilled. To prove this contention, first assume that each public-good-producing monopolist is a perfect price discriminator. Thus we have $\pi = p_j x_j - c(x_j)$, where $p_j = \Sigma_{k=1}^{n} p_j^k$ and p_j^k is equal to the maximum price which can be charged to individual k for the quantity x_j of the public good. Perfect price discrimination means that $x_j p_j^k$ is equal to the area under the demand curve, that is,

$$\max p_j^k x_j = \int_0^{x_j} MRS_{j:i}^k \, dx_j$$

where x_i is any purely private good. Thus profits are

$$\max \pi = \sum_{k=1}^{n} \max p_j^k x_j - c(x_j) = \sum_{k=1}^{n} \int_0^{x_j} MRS_{j:i}^k \, dx_j - c(x_j)$$

A necessary condition for a maximum is that

$$\frac{d\pi}{dx_j} = \frac{d}{dx_j} \left(\sum_{k=1}^{n} \int_0^{x_j} MRS_{j:i}^k \, dx_j \right) - \frac{dc(x_j)}{dx_j} = 0$$

or

$$\sum_{k=1}^{n} MRS_{j:i}^k = dc(x_j)/dx_j$$

If all firms minimize costs,

$$MRT_{j:i} = \frac{dc(x_j)/dx_j}{dc(x_i)/dx_i}$$

Since the x_i market is competitive, $dc(x_i)/dx_i = p_i$ which we may take as the numeraire price, that is, $p_i \equiv 1$. Thus we have the desired result:

$$MRT_{j:i} = dc(x_j)/dx_j = \sum_{k=1}^{n} MRS_{j:i}^{k}$$

Next, if we relax the assumption that the monopolist has complete knowledge of the utility function of each individual, will marginal revenue still equal $\sum_{k=1}^{n} MRS_{j:i}^{k}$? The answer is yes if the monopolist bargains with each consumer individually. Let us prove that proposition by induction.

First, consider the case of a one-consumer, one-producer world with two goods: money m and the public good x_j. The consumer has the usual convex indifference curves, but the producer is solely interested in profits. If the marginal cost (MC) of production is constant, isoprofit lines will be linear, as shown in Figure 6.1. $\pi_o \pi_o'$ is the isoprofit contour where profits are zero. $\pi_1 \pi_1'$ is an isoprofit curve where $\pi > 0$. The line labeled cc' is the contract curve. Point c is equivalent to an all or nothing bargain, which is the perfectly price-discriminating bargain. Point c' is the best the consumer can do, given the costs of production.

Now suppose that a bargain such as represented by point y is reached. The monopolist does not have perfect information as to

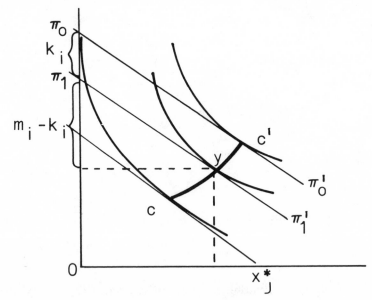

Fig. 6.1. The contract curve for a single producer–single consumer world.

the consumer's preferences and believes that point y is the best he can do. Since the slope of the isoprofit line is MC, the distance m_i is equal to $x_j^* MC + k_i$.

With two consumers the slope of the isoprofit line, as far as the producer is concerned, must sum to MC. Since there are two consumers who will both have the same amount of the public good finally chosen, the summed isoprofit curve with constant marginal costs will equal its original slope. Similarly, for n consumers the isoprofit lines will sum to MC. Total revenue (TR) is thus

$$TR = \sum_{i=1}^{n} x_i MC_i + \sum_{i=1}^{n} k_i = x_i MC + \sum_{i=1}^{n} k_i$$

where k_i is the constant difference between MC and m_i won in the bargaining from each individual. Clearly, it follows that marginal revenue is equal to MC, which is equal to $\Sigma_{i=1}^{n} MRS^i$ due to the bargaining position of the monopolist producer.

When exclusion is possible, in order to obtain any of the public good, the individual must bargain with the monopolist; and the monopolist and each consumer will bargain until they reach a point on the contract curve. Even though the monopolist has no knowledge of the preferences of an individual, if he obtains the best bargain he can from each, the result will be one where his marginal revenue is equal to $\Sigma_{k=1}^{n} MRS^k$. Thus in equilibrium the Pareto optimal conditions will be fulfilled. To argue to the contrary that a monopolist bargaining with individual consumers will not have a marginal revenue equal to ΣMRS is to argue that two individuals will not reach the contract curve in an Edgeworth box trading diagram.

It should be noted that the above requires more trial and error bargaining with each consumer than simply setting a price and observing the quantity sold. But to maximize profits with zero bargaining costs, this problem is not relevant.

MODEL 6.3—Samuelson purely public good with exclusion not possible and perfect competition

In this model it will be assumed that there are two classes of goods as in Model 6.2—purely public and purely private goods. However, the public goods in this model do not possess an exclusive property. Once a given quantity is provided, it must be consumed by all. When exclusion is not possible, there either may be some sort of collective action to provide the public good (or goods) or all public goods may be provided privately with each individual reacting to the quantity of public and private goods which are freely available to him at any point in time.

In this model the latter case will be examined. Since the model involves reactions, it is a comparative static model depicting the change in the quantities of the public and private goods over time and the long-run equilibrium quantities.

For simplicity, two consumers will be assumed initially. For each we have the following ordinal utility indices and budget constraints:

$$U_1 = U_1(x_j, x_i^1), \partial U_1/\partial x_j > 0, \partial U_1/\partial x_i^1 > 0, p_j x_j^1 + p_i x_i^1 = M_1$$

$$U_2 = U_2(x_j, x_i^2), \partial U_2/\partial x_j > 0, \partial U_2/\partial x_i^2 > 0, p_j x_j^2 + p_i x_i^2 = M_2$$

It should be noted that the utility indices of each are a function of the total amount of x_j being *provided*, $x_j^1 + x_j^2$. The budget constraint for the individual is only a function of the amount purchased by him, x_j^1 or x_j^2. Further, the prices of the two goods are assumed constant and equal to the marginal cost of production of each; that is, $p_j/p_i = MRT_{j:i} = $ constant.

Given the above utility indices, each consumer will act independently of the other per se and will decide on how much x_j to buy himself depending on the amount being provided currently, on prices, and on his money income. The optimal quantity which maximizes U is the total amount $x_j = x_j^1 + x_j^2$. To find the equilibrium amount in such a market structure, suppose the two individuals always make simultaneous changes in their purchases of public and private goods and that initially the optimal solution for each consumer includes some of the public good. That is, initially each individual purchases x_j and x_i so that

$$MRS_{j:i}^1 = p_j/p_i \text{ and } MRS_{j:i}^2 = p_j/p_i$$

This means that each consumer will end up having more than the optimal amount of x_j to consume for himself. Clearly each will be better off than planned, and only under rigid conditions would each be in equilibrium. Specifically, since the prices to the individuals are unchanged, the additional amount of the public good would have to leave the marginal rate of substitution unchanged. This requires in turn that

$$(U_{jj}/U_i) - (U_j U_{ij}/U_i^2) = 0, \text{ or } U_{jj} = (U_j/U_i)U_{ij}$$

Thus under the assumption that both goods have positive marginal utility, if the public good gave diminishing marginal utility, the cross-partial U_{ij} would have to be negative. If $U_{jj} = 0$, then $U_{ii} = 0$; and if $U_{jj} > 0$, then $U_{ij} > 0$. If both consumers had identical tastes, the total amount of x_j would be double the perceived optimal amount for each. In general each individual could be expected to reduce his outlays on x_j and the total amount would decrease. This subsequent decrease would cause further adjustment by each until some equilibrium was reached.

If no corner solution is reached in the individual calculus (that is, the optimal additional provision of x_j by an individual is zero because $MRS_{j:i} < p_j/p_i$ with all money spent on x_i and x_j being provided by the other individual), the equilibrium must be one where for each individual $MRS = p_j/p_i$. Hence, it must be an equilibrium position which does not fulfill the condition for Pareto optimality.

However, since an individual is not free to sell the public good which is being provided by the other individual, a corner solution is at least more likely than in the all purely private goods case. In Figure 6.2 this is illustrated more clearly. The heavy line mm' is the budget constraint; mm' represents at all times the purchases of the individual. With no provision of x_j by anyone else, individual 1 would purchase the quantity q. With individual 2 providing x_j^2, the feasible consumption space is now greater,

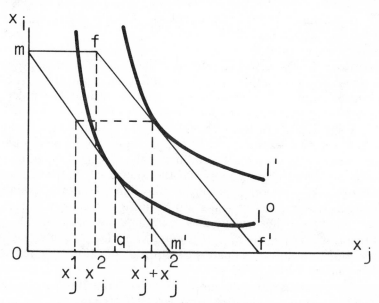

Fig. 6.2. Budget constraint and feasible consumption space for individual 1, with individual 2 providing x_j^2.

namely mff'. Thus individual 1 will be in equilibrium by purchasing the quantity x_j^1 in Figure 6.2, making the total amount
$x_j^1 + x_j^2$, and individual 1 will be in equilibrium on indifference
curve I'. Given the particular indifference map as represented in
Figure 6.2, x_j^1 is less than q. In Figure 6.3 individual 1, in the

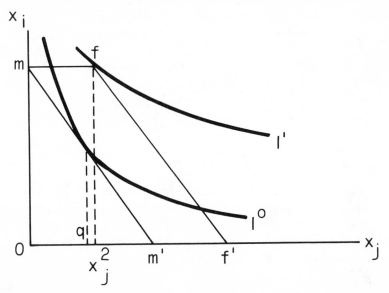

Fig. 6.3. Budget constraint and feasible consumption space which has a
corner solution.

absence of others, would purchase the quantity q of x_j. With
individual 2 purchasing x_j^2 of the public good, individual 1's best
position is at f, a corner solution, and individual 1 is not purchasing any of the public good.

In general there will be a series of adjustments by each individual reacting to the quantity of the public good which is being
provided by the other. This adjustment process is limited by the
total of the purchasing power of the individuals involved, which
may or may not converge to an equilibrium. However, given the
individual's preferences and his purchasing space, he will react to
the quantity being provided as in Figures 6.2 and 6.3. Thus in
general we may write $x_j^1 = f(x_j^2)$ and $x_j^2 = g(x_j^1)$. These reaction
functions are quite analogous to Cournot reaction functions for
duopolists.

The various possible kinds of final outcomes can be seen
more clearly in Figures 6.4 to 6.6. In Figure 6.4 the curve
labeled $\bar{x}_j^1$ represents individual 1's provision of the public good

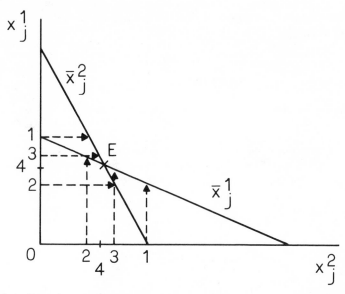

Fig. 6.4. Reaction functions for individuals 1 and 2, with a stable equilibrium at E.

as a function of the amount being provided by individual 2. The curve labeled $\bar{x}_j^2$ is the provision of the public good by individual 2. Under the above model of sequential decision making, both individuals would move from the origin to the points labeled 1 on the respective axes. The process converges to the equilibrium point labeled E.

Mathematically, the model can be formulated in terms of difference equations. If the reaction curves are linear (or taking a Taylor's expansion and neglecting all terms greater than the first derivative), the simultaneous provision of the public good would be

$$x_j^1(t) = \alpha_1 x_j^2(t-1) + \alpha_o, \quad \alpha_1 < 0$$
$$x_j^2(t-1) = \beta_1 x_j^1(t-2) + \beta_o, \quad \beta_1 < 0$$

where α_1 is the slope of $\bar{x}_j^1$ and $1/\beta_1$ is the slope of x_j^2 in Figure 6.4. Solving for $x_j^1(t)$, one finds

$$x_j^1(t) = [\pm(\alpha_1\beta_1)^{1/2}]^t\, x_j^1(0) + E, \quad E = (\alpha_1\beta_o + \alpha_o)/(1 - \alpha_1\beta_1)$$

This further implies that $\alpha_1 > 1/\beta_1$ for a stable equilibrium, or that the slope of individual 1's reaction curve is greater than that of individual 2.

If there is a slight change in timing of purchases so that individual 1 gets slightly ahead of individual 2, the difference equations change somewhat but the conditions for equilibrium remain the same. Under an alternating purchasing scheme,

$$x_j^1(t) = \alpha_1 x_j^2(t-1) + \alpha_o, \qquad \alpha_1 < 0$$
$$x_j^2(t-1) = \beta_1 x_j^1(t-1) + \beta_o, \qquad \beta_1 < 0$$

or

$$x_j^1(t) = (\alpha_1 \beta_1)^t x_j^1(0) + E, \qquad E = (\alpha_1 \beta_o + \alpha_o)/(1 - \alpha_1 \beta_1)$$

which again requires that $\alpha_1 > 1/\beta_1$ for E to be reached.

Although the above would seem to be a likely scenario, the reaction functions could be as depicted in Figure 6.5. If indi-

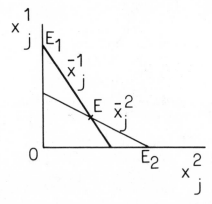

Fig. 6.5. Reaction functions for individuals 1 and 2, with an unstable equilibrium at E and a stable equilibrium at E_1 and E_2.

viduals 1 and 2 simultaneously change their purchases of x_j, the output would alternate from zero to $E_1 + E_2$ as individuals 1 and 2 respectively purchased E_1 for individual 1 and E_2 for individual 2 and zero amounts of x_j. Any slight change in the timing of purchases by individuals 1 or 2 would produce an equilibrium at E_1 or E_2 with the other providing zero of x_j, depending on who provided x_j first. The point E in Figure 6.5 is an equilibrium point but an unstable one.

Other possibilities are illustrated in Figure 6.6. In panel A the reaction functions are coincident, and all points are unstable equilibrium points. A slight deviation from some point on the curves will not produce any tendency to return to that point. Also in panel A under the conditions of Model 6.3, the simultaneous provision of the public good by individuals 1 and 2 would result in an infinite alternating of both providing an amount denoted by 1 on their axes and 0. Any slight change in timing would be an equilibrium.

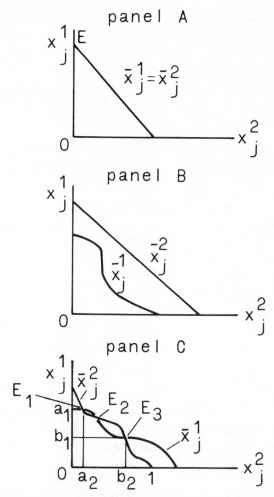

Fig. 6.6. Possible other general shapes of reaction functions for individuals 1 and 2 with a public–private good position.

In panel B the reaction curve for individual 2 lies entirely outside that of individual 1 with the resulting equilibrium at E. That is, in panel B individual 2 will end up being the sole provider of the public good when all decisions are made by the individuals with no contact (bargaining) with others.

In panel C there are three equilibriums: E_1 and E_3, which are stable, and E_2, which is unstable. However, E_1 is only stable in the sense that a slight perturbation from that point will cause a return to E_1. If both simultaneously move from 0 to 1 on their respective axes and continue simultaneously to make decisions, the model will, as time goes to infinity, produce an alternation of a_1 by individual 1 and b_2 by individual 2 to b_1 by individual 1 and a_2 by individual 2.

Whether there is an equilibrium point or not (which depends upon the reaction functions which were derived from the interaction of the individuals' private decisions on the basis of their preferences, feasible purchasing space, and the amount of the public good being provided by other individuals), the conclusion of this model is that the condition for Pareto optimality can *never* be attained. One or the other or both individuals must be equating $MRS_{j:i} = p_j/p_i$, and hence $MRS^1_{j:i} + MRS^2_{j:i} > p_j/p_i$ unless one individual is satiated (which was implicitly assumed away under the assumption that $\partial U/\partial x_j > 0$). Clearly this conclusion is immediately generalized to the case of n consumers.

This particular model lacks realism in the small-group case because it would seem reasonable that if individuals were in close proximity to one another (that is, realized each others actions), some sort of cooperative effort or bargaining would emerge. This possibility is examined further in Models 6.4 and 6.5.

MODEL 6.4—Samuelson purely public good with no exclusion and recognition of actions of others

In this model the individual will be permitted a slight bit of cognitive ability with respect to activities of others but not with respect to others per se. In Model 6.3 every purchase of the public good prior to equilibrium is wrong; that is the expectations of the individuals are never fulfilled as to what the total quantity of the public good will be. Each time a decision is made, each individual assumes that others will not alter their purchases of the public good.

To relax this restrictive assumption, first assume that both individuals in Model 6.3 have identical linear reaction curves:

$$x_j(1) = x_j^1(1) + x_j^2(1)$$

$$x_j^1(1) = \alpha_1 x_j^2(0) + \alpha_o = \alpha_o$$

$$x_j^2(1) = \alpha_1 x_j^1(0) + \alpha_o = \alpha_o$$

$$x_j^1(t) = \alpha_1 x_j^1(t-1) + \alpha_0$$

$$x_j^2(t) = \alpha_1 x_j^1(t-1) + \alpha_o$$

This means that assuming a simultaneous provision of an initial amount of α_o by both individuals, $2\alpha_o$ will actually be available for each to consume. The next decision calculus will result in identical reactions by both individuals. As a result the rate change in the total amount of the public good Δx_j relative to individual 1's purchases Δx_j^1 is equal to 2, that is, $\Delta x_j / \Delta x_j^1 = 2$.

This constant input of empirical information (that the purchase of one unit results in two units of x_j to consume) means that the effective price of the public good is $p_j/2$. If in fact $p_j/2$ does replace p_j in each individual's knowledge set, a decision by both, with this new parameter in this model, will result in an equilibrium which *does* satisfy the conditions for Pareto optimality. That is,

$$MRS_{j:i}^1 = p_j/2\, p_i = MRS_{j:i}^2$$

and

$$MRS_{j:i}^1 + MRS_{j:i}^2 = p_j/p_i = MRT_{j:i}$$

It should be emphasized that each consumer decides upon the optimal mix of public and private goods on the basis of the parameter $p_j/2$ but purchases just half the optimum amount. Similar conclusions are reached if the number of individuals is n.

However, the model is very restrictive. For example, if the reaction functions differ from each other in the case of two individuals as

$$x_j^1(t) = \alpha_1 x_j^2(t-1) + \alpha_o$$
$$x_j^2(t) = \beta_1 x_j^1(t-1) + \beta_o$$

then

$$x_j(1) = \alpha_o + \beta_o$$
$$x_j(2) = \alpha_1 \beta_o + \alpha_o + \beta_1 \alpha_o + \beta_o$$
$$\Delta x_j = \alpha_1 \beta_o + \beta_1 \alpha_o$$

and

$$\Delta x_j^1 = \alpha_1 \beta_o$$

also

$$\Delta x_j^2 = \beta_1 \alpha_o$$

and therefore, from individual 1's point of view,

$$(\Delta x_j / \Delta x_j^1)|_1 = 1 + (\beta_o / \alpha_o)$$
$$(\Delta x_j / \Delta x_j^1)|_2 = 1 + (\beta_1 \alpha_o / \alpha_1 \beta_o)$$
$$(\Delta x_j / \Delta x_j^1)|_3 = 1 + (\beta_o / \alpha_o) \ldots$$
$$(\Delta x_j / \Delta x_j^1)|_{t\,even} = 1 + (\beta_1 \alpha_o / \alpha_1 \beta_o)$$
$$(\Delta x_j / \Delta x_j^2)|_{t\,odd} = 1 + (\beta_o / \alpha_o)$$

and from individual 2's point of view,

$$(\Delta x_j / \Delta x_j^2)|_1 = 1 + (\alpha_o / \beta_o)$$

$$(\Delta x_j / \Delta x_j^2)|_2 = 1 + (\alpha_1 \beta_o / \beta_1 \alpha_o)$$

$$(\Delta x_j / \Delta x_j^2)|_3 = 1 + (\alpha_o / \beta_o), \ldots$$

$$(\Delta x_j / \Delta x_j^2)|_{t\,even} = 1 + (\alpha_1 \beta_o / \beta_1 \alpha_o)$$

$$(\Delta x_j / \Delta x_j^2)|_{t\,odd} = 1 + (\alpha_o / \beta_o)$$

In other words, the rate of change in the total amount with respect to individual 1's purchases of x_j alternates depending upon whether or not the decision time is odd or even. If the slopes of the reaction functions are equal, $\beta_1 = \alpha_1$, the rate of change every period is

$$\Delta x_j / \Delta x_j^1 = 1 + \beta_o / \alpha_o, \qquad \Delta x_j / \Delta x_j^2 = 1 + \alpha_o / \beta_o$$

Consequently, the effective price for each becomes

$$p_j^1 = \frac{p_j}{1 + \beta_o / \alpha_o}, \qquad p_j^2 = \frac{p_j}{1 + \alpha_o / \beta_o}$$

and reacting to these new parameters respectively will produce an equilibrium which fulfills the necessary condition for Pareto optimality, that is,

$$\Sigma MRS_{j:i} = \frac{p_j / (1 + \beta_o / \alpha_o)}{p_i} + \frac{p_j / (1 + \alpha_o / \beta_o)}{p_i} = p_j / p_i$$

In summary, a reaction by the individuals to the rate change in the total quantity of x_j with respect to their own purchases under very restrictive conditions will produce an amount of x_j and x_i which is commensurate with the condition of efficiency, $\Sigma MRS = MRT$, but in general it will not result in an optimal mix of the public and private goods.

MODEL 6.5—Group formation, collective decision making, and collective provision of public goods

Heretofore, the models have not permitted individuals to mutually provide the public good. The possibility of forming a group and collective provision of the public good has not been considered.

The initial question is, Under what conditions will a group form? For a group to form, it is necessary that at least one individual be made better off and every other individual be as well off under the terms of the group than he was by not being a member. Anytime there is a public good, a group or collective provision is as good or better than the consequences of private decisions under the assumption of zero costs of collective decision making. With or without exclusion possible for the public good, a collective or cooperative provision will always be potentially better. These propositions are considered in detail in the following submodels.

MODEL 6.5a—Samuelson purely public good—private good, exclusion possible

For simplicity assume two consumers and two goods as follows:

$$U = U(x_j, x_i^1)$$
$$I = I(x_j, x_i^2)$$

x_j = Samuelson purely public good
x_i = purely private good = $x_i^1 + x_i^2$
m = budget for U
m' = budget for I
p_j, p_i = constant prices of x_j and x_i respectively

From Models 6.2–6.4 it is clear that any private decision calculus with the given parameters m', m, p_j, and p_i will not be Pareto optimal. In Figures 6.7 and 6.8, the private solution for I and U is shown where the exclusion properties have been enforced. In Figure 6.9 the potential for collective provision is shown. The budget constraint in Figure 6.9 is $m + m'$. The

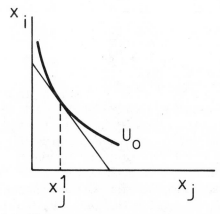

Fig. 6.7. *U*'s best condition with private provision.

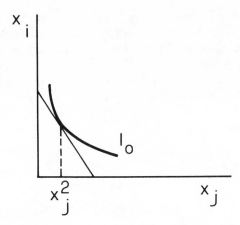

Fig. 6.8. I's best condition with private provision.

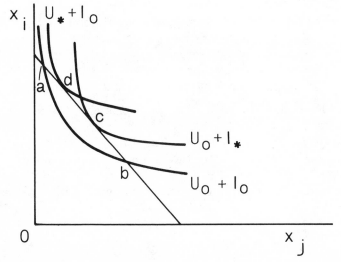

Fig. 6.9. Possible provision under collective arrangement for U and I.

points a or b leave I and U just as well off as they were in the private provision framework. The curve $U_o + I_o$ is the vertical summation of the curves U_o in Figure 6.7 and I_o in Figure 6.8. The slope of this vertical summation is $MRS_{j:i}^I + MRS_{j:i}^U$. The conditions for a Pareto optimum require that $\Sigma MRS_{j:i} = p_j/p_i$. However, an infinity of such curves exist which are tangent to the combined budget constraint. For example, the curve $I_o + U_*$ represents I being just as well off under the collective provision and U extracting all the gains from the combinatorial arrangement. Alternatively, the curve $U_o + I_*$ is the other extreme; I usurps the benefits from combining resources. Between the tangencies of $U_o + I_*$ and $U_* + I_o$ (that is, c and d) an infinity of other "aggregate" indifference curves exist, depending upon how the benefits are shared between the two. The principle of exclusion assures that the collective provision will be between the points c and d. Just where, however, depends upon other interactions between the two (if there are any) or the ethics decided upon by the group. For example, they could agree to share the the gains "equally" or "fairly." This, however, means nothing without information as to how an individual cardinally evaluates the gains of another.

MODEL 6.5b—Samuelson private good, purely public good without exclusion

This model is equivalent to Model 6.5a except the public good does not possess exclusion properties. That is, if some of the good is provided by either I or U, it is available to the other. This change vitiates the results of the foregoing model in that either individual has the option of not cooperating in a collective provision and freely enjoying what the other will provide privately.

Again assume that Figures 6.7 and 6.8 represent the private provision by U and I respectively. Since either have the option of waiting for the other to provide x_j privately, their ex post consumption spaces (that is, after the other has made a private decision) are illustrated in Figures 6.10 and 6.11 for U and I respectively.

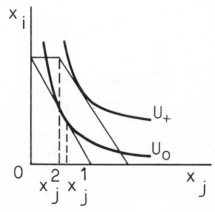

Fig. 6.10. Feasible consumption space for U after I provides x_j^2 privately.

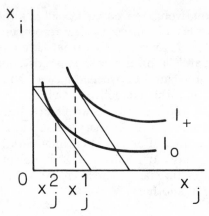

Fig. 6.11. Feasible consumption space for I after U provides x_j^1 privately.

As shown in Model 6.3, the private provision can never be Pareto optimal. That is, whether I waits for U to provide x_j^1 or U waits for I to provide x_j^2, they can always improve their lots by combining. (Again, insignificant costs of collectivization are assumed. However, these costs could be subtracted from the aggregate potential to alter the results appropriately.) The difference is that the outcome of the collective decision must lie

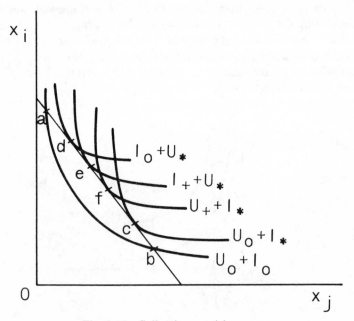

Fig. 6.12. Collective provision space.

between the points e and f rather than the points c and d in Figure 6.12. The point e represents the vertical summation of I_+, the best I can do if he waits for U to provide x_j^1, and U_*, U's maximum leaving I on I_+. The point f similarly is the vertical summation of U_+, and I's maximum given U has a satisfaction of U_+.

Model 6.5b reduces the core of the collective decision. That is, if the collective decision were one as represented by the point c, U can block that outcome. He could refuse to participate, drop out of the collectivity and wait for I to provide x_j^2, and then end up with a satisfaction level of U_+. As in Model 6.5a the final outcome in the core ef in Figure 6.12 depends upon other information of the interaction between I and U. However, the collective decision when no exclusion is possible requires the gains from collective provision to be shared more equally than the case where exclusion is possible.

MODEL 6.5c—Two Samuelsonian purely public goods, no private goods

In this model the special case of two purely public goods and no private goods is considered. This is of interest under the condition that all goods in an economy have public-good characteristics or when considering the way a group will divide its purchases between two public goods (alternatively, this could be thought of as how a firm will regulate the level of two activities which affect all members of the firm). In addition, this model adds a specific example to the theory developed in Chapter 5, specifically to the results of Theorem 5.2.

Assume:

x_k and x_j are two purely public goods

$U = U(x_k, x_j)$

$I = I(x_k, x_j)$

$F(x_k, x_j) \geqslant 0$, $F(x_k, x_j)$ = the transformation function or the constraints of production of x_k and x_j.

Suppose we proceed in the usual fashion to find the conditions for Pareto optimality. Maximize $U(x_k, x_j)$ subject to the constraint of the transformation function and that

$$I(x_k, x_j) - \bar{I} \geqslant 0$$

that is, I's satisfaction is at least $\bar{I}$. The Lagrangian function is

$$\lambda = U(x_k, x_j) + \lambda_1 F(x_k, x_j) + \lambda_2 [I(x_k, x_j) - \bar{I}].$$

The Kuhn-Tucker conditions require

$$\partial\lambda/\partial x_k = \partial U/\partial x_k + \lambda_1(\partial F/\partial x_k) + \lambda_2(\partial I/\partial x_k) \leqslant 0$$
$$\text{if } \partial\lambda/\partial x_k < 0, x_k = 0$$
$$\partial\lambda/\partial x_j = \partial U/\partial x_j + \lambda_1(\partial F/\partial x_j) + \lambda_2(\partial I/\partial x_j) \leqslant 0$$
$$\text{if } \partial\lambda/\partial x_j < 0, x_j = 0$$
$$\partial\lambda/\partial\lambda_1 = F(x_k, x_j) \geqslant 0, \text{ if } \partial\lambda/\partial x_1 > 0, \lambda_1 = 0$$
$$\partial\lambda/\partial\lambda_2 = I(x_k, x_j) - \bar{I} \geqslant 0, \text{ if } \partial\lambda/\partial\lambda_2 > 0, \lambda_2 = 0$$

First of all if it is assumed that

$$\partial U/\partial x_k, \partial U/\partial x_j, \partial I/\partial x_k, \partial I/\partial x_j > 0$$

and since $\lambda_1, \lambda_2 \geqslant 0$, this requires that either the first or second equation hold with equality and in turn that $F(x_k, x_j) = 0$ or $\lambda_1 \neq 0$. Second, λ_1 can be interpreted as the marginal utility to U of an increase in technology. λ_2 is an interpersonal weighting of utility between I and U. Specifically, λ_2 is the marginal rate the optimal value of U decreases if $\bar{I}$ is increased.

Whether $\lambda_2 = 0$ depends upon the indifference maps and the transformation function. The two possibilities $\lambda_2 = 0$ and $\lambda_2 > 0$ are illustrated in Figures 6.13 and 6.14 respectively. In Figure

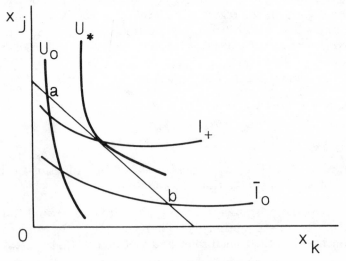

Fig. 6.13. Two purely public goods and two individuals, $\lambda_2 = 0$.

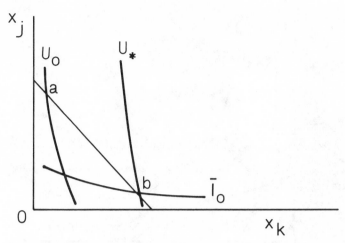

Fig. 6.14. Two purely public goods and two individuals, $\lambda_2 > 0$.

6.13 the curves labeled U_o and $\bar{I}_o$ represent the best that U and I can do in isolation, that is, in a situation where the purchase of the public goods x_k and x_j do not affect anyone else and are not affected by other's purchases of such goods. In Figure 6.13 the maximum U_* is attained only by increasing the utility of I from $\bar{I}_o$ to I_+, so $\lambda_2 = 0$. In Figure 6.14 the maximum U_* leaves I just as well off as he was in private, thus $\lambda_2 > 0$. Since the budget constraint in both diagrams is the combination of the private budgets, the solution of a collective provision must lie between the points a and b in either figure.

As a final conclusion of Model 6.5c, the case of two purely public goods, three individuals I, U, and M, and a majority rule is presented. The result is similar to much work on voting schemes in the literature, namely, the "middle of the road" or "median" opinion will dominate. However, it is presented here in the graphical context above.

In Figure 6.15, the curves U_o, I_o, and M_o represent the best that U, I, and M can do in private, given their budgets and the two purely public goods x_k and x_j. The budget constraint for the three-member group is the combined resources of the three. Under a voting scheme of majority rule, M is able to effect the decision to provide $\bar{x}_k$ and $\bar{x}_j$ collectively and he attains the maximum possible. Given the preferences of I and U, M will always be able to play one against the other so that he attains the best of all possible worlds.

It should be further noted that it is not necessary to have a

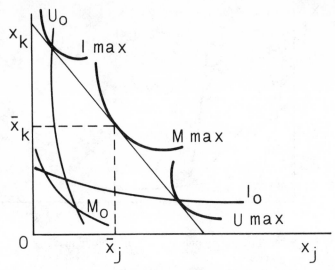

Fig. 6.15. Two purely public goods and three individuals with majority rule.

rule of majority for M to control the group as if he were a dicta-
tor. As long as there are no other significant interacting activities
for the three individuals (that is, no other bases for threat sets),
individual M possesses the threat of cooperation with only *one* of
the others. That is, M and I could exclude U from the group if he
refuses to cooperate, or M and U could exclude I if he refuses to
cooperate. In any event the median preference has the upper
hand in the collective decision process regardless of whether a
constitution exists.

*MODEL 6.6—Private goods with external effects, the giving of
        gifts*

In this model another class of goods is analyzed where goods
are not purely private in their effects upon the satisfaction of individuals. The goods in this model will be assumed to be purely
private in the physical sense. When a commodity is consumed by
one individual, it is physically used up. However, some of the
goods will be assumed to have external effects. The consumption
of one good by an individual affects another because he *consumes* it, not because he *purchases* it. Thus, this model is a
special case of the interpersonal influence of activities carried out
by individuals as analyzed in Chapter 5. The model will be limited
to interacting economic activities and the activity function ab-

sorbed in the satisfaction function. Formally, assume

$$U = U(x_i^1, x_j^1, x_j^2), \partial U/\partial x_i^1, \partial U/\partial x_j^1, \partial U/\partial x_j^2 > 0$$

$$I = I(x_i^2, x_j^1, x_j^2), \partial I/\partial x_i^2, \partial I/\partial x_j^1, \partial I/\partial x_j^2 > 0$$

$$x_i^1 + x_i^2 = x_i, \qquad x_j^1 + x_j^2 = x_j$$

and

$$F(x_i, x_j) = F(x_i^1 + x_i^2, x_j^1 + x_j^2) \geqslant 0$$

The good x_i is a purely private one with no external effects. The amount consumed by U does not affect I and vice-versa. On the other hand, x_j is a purely private good in the physical sense as $x_j^1 + x_j^2 = x_j$. However, the good x_j possesses external effects. The consumption of x_j by individual U, x_j^1 affects I because U consumes x_j and vice-versa for I's consumption of x_j.

The necessary conditions for Pareto optimality can be derived as follows. From the Lagrangian function:

$$\lambda = U(x_i^1, x_j^1, x_j^2) + \lambda_1 F(x_i^1 + x_i^2, x_j^1 + x_j^2) + \lambda_2 [I(x_i^2, x_j^1, x_j^2) - \bar{I}]$$

The Kuhn-Tucker conditions require

$$\partial\lambda/\partial x_i^1 = \partial U/\partial x_i^1 + \lambda_1(\partial F/\partial x_i) \leqslant 0$$

$$\partial\lambda/\partial x_j^1 = \partial U/\partial x_j^1 + \lambda_1(\partial F/\partial x_j) + \lambda_2(\partial I/\partial x_j^1) \leqslant 0$$

$$\partial\lambda/\partial x_j^2 = \partial U/\partial x_j^2 + \lambda_1(\partial F/\partial x_j) + \lambda_2(\partial I/\partial x_j^2) \leqslant 0$$

and

$$\partial\lambda/\partial x_i^2 = \lambda_1(\partial F/\partial x_i) + \lambda_2(\partial I/\partial x_i^2) \leqslant 0$$

and for the most interesting case the strict equality can be assumed in each. Thus eliminating λ_1 and λ_2, the above reduces to

$$\frac{\partial U/\partial x_j^1}{\partial U/\partial x_i^1} + \frac{\partial I/\partial x_j^1}{\partial I/\partial x_i^2} = \frac{F_j}{F_i}$$

and

$$\frac{\partial U/\partial x_j^2}{\partial U/\partial x_i^1} + \frac{\partial I/\partial x_j^2}{\partial I/\partial x_i^2} = \frac{F_j}{F_i}$$

In other words, U's MRS of U's consumption of x_j for U's consumption of x_i plus I's MRS of U's consumption of x_j for I's consumption of x_i must be equal to the marginal rate of transformation. Also, the sum of the effects of I's consumption of x_j on I and U as weighted by their own marginal utility of x_i must equal the marginal rate of transformation F_j/F_i. Graphically, the optimal quantity would be a vertical summation of the *MRS* curves for *U*'s consumption of x_j and a vertical summation of the *MRS* curves of *I*'s consumption of x_j, then a horizontal summation of the two as shown in Figure 6.16.

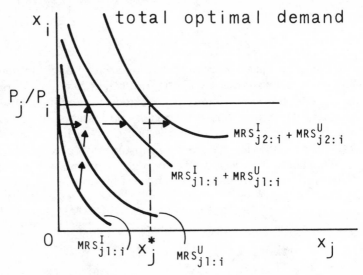

Fig. 6.16. Graphical interpretation of an optimal quantity x_j^* of a good with external effects.

These necessary conditions for maximum efficiency can be contrasted to what will happen if all decisions are made privately. For individual *U*, the problem is to maximize

$$U(x_i^1, x_j^1, x_j^2)$$

subject to

$$p_i x_i + p_j(x_j^1 + x_j^2) = M$$

for which the necessary conditions are that

$$\frac{\partial U/\partial x_j^1}{\partial U/\partial x_i^1} = \frac{\partial U/\partial x_j^2}{\partial U/\partial x_i^1} = \frac{p_j}{p_i}$$

or

$$MRS_{j1:i}^U = MRS_{j2:i}^U = \frac{p_j}{p_i}$$

In other words, when *U* is in equilibrium he will add to *I*'s consumption of x_j so that the marginal rate of substitution of his own consumption of x_j relative to x_i is equal to his MRS for I's consumption of x_j relative to x_i. Consequently, if I was not spending enough on x_j so that $MRS_{j1:i}^U = MRS_{j2:i}^U$, U would give I a gift of x_j. Again this is the equilibrium condition, and some sort of dynamic process of adjustment between I and U could be constructed to analyze the movement to equilibrium. Whatever the dynamic process is, the equilibrium will not be Pareto optimal. The reason is that U and I in their private calculus and the given prices fail to consider the other's direct satisfaction from the consumption of x_j. As a consequence, under the usual assumptions of positive marginal utility the output of the *good* with external effects will be too low. It is possible to make both better off by increasing the output of x_j and reducing the output of x_i.

If the assumption that all marginal utilities are positive is relaxed, there are some changes in the foregoing conclusions. First, if U becomes satiated with I's consumption of x_j, that is, $\partial U/\partial x_j^2 = 0$, to be in equilibrium U must reduce I's consumption of x_j (assuming he is not satiated with his own consumption of x_j). However, if U is not contributing x_j to I and I is in equilibrium, U would have to bribe I to reduce his consumption. Often the costs associated with such activities are above the gains, or the existence of institutional restrictions on individual behavior precludes U from efficiently bargaining to reduce I's consumption. This aspect and similar problems where the external effects are negative, that is, $\partial U/\partial x_j^2 < 0$, have been widely discussed in the literature of public goods.

MODEL 6.7—Samuelson purely public good with external effects

As a final example of the public goods models and group interaction, the case of mixed goods will be considered; that is, where there is a good with both external effects and physical properties of the purely public good. The model is

$$U = U(x_i^1, x_j^1, x_j^2), \qquad I = I(x_i^2, x_j^1, x_j^2)$$
$$x_i = x_i^1 + x_i^2, \qquad x_j^1 = x_j^2 = x_j$$

and

$$F(x_i^1 + x_i^2, x_j) \geqslant 0$$

The Lagrangian for Pareto optimality is

$$\lambda = U(x_i^1, x_j^1, x_j^2) + \lambda_1 F(x_i^1 + x_i^2, x_j) + \lambda_2 [I(x_i^2, x_j^1, x_j^2) - \bar{I}]$$

from which the Kuhn-Tucker conditions require, in the case of strict equality, that

$$\frac{\partial U/\partial x_j^1}{\partial U/\partial x_i^1} + \frac{\partial U/\partial x_j^2}{\partial U/\partial x_i^1} + \frac{\partial I/\partial x_j^1}{\partial I/\partial x_i^2} + \frac{\partial I/\partial x_j^2}{\partial I/\partial x_i^2} = \frac{F_j}{F_i}$$

The conditions for private equilibrium in Model 6.7 will be exactly the same as in Model 6.6. In the dynamic adjustment process there will be two aspects of x_j to adjust to: (1) U may or may not give x_j to I, given I's consumption of x_j, likewise for I to U; (2) as in Models 6.2 and 6.3, both I and U will find their feasible consumption spaces are greater than their budget space if the other is providing some of the public good x_j. In equilibrium a private decision cannot fulfill the Pareto optimality conditions unless the price parameters are altered as in Model 6.4 or the group forms a collectivity as in Model 6.5.

SUMMARY

Only under restrictive and rare circumstances will a nongroup decision (when there are purely public goods, in the physical sense, or when there are goods with external effects) meet the conditions for Pareto optimality. This in turn implies an impetus for group formation and collective provision of such goods. The presence of such goods may give particular individuals unequal power over the decisions of a group because of the given mix of preferences of the members.

chapter 7

The Variable Preference Model and the Multiproduct Firm

THE FIRM is a specialized group with an accompanying structure of institutions which acts as a coalition in dealing with other firms and individuals within the social system. In this chapter, the analysis of individual behavior and the interaction of individuals in a group as presented in Chapters 5 and 6 will be specifically applied to the economic act of production of goods and services. Firms ranging from the single entrepreneur to the large conglomerate corporation are considered.

If the firm is construed as an individual workman engaged in a simple manufacturing process, there is no difference between this and the general model of consumer preferences developed in Chapter 3. If anything, the independent artisan would conform to the model more closely in that he would be faced with fewer institutional restrictions. For example, the amount of time he could devote to any particular activity would only be constrained by the total time in a day, while the individual laborer is often faced with "all or none" bargains such as the 40-hour workweek.

CONSIDERATION OF RESEARCH AND DEVELOPMENT

In the case of production of goods and services, the set of feasible activities can be viewed as including research and development activities. As with any other feasible activity, the individual must decide the time and energy he can optimally devote to such endeavors. Possibly the research activity could be either drive reducing or drive enhancing in and of itself. In addition to this primary return there are secondary aspects as well. The individual must draw upon his inductive powers to ascertain the degree of belief in future rewards

143

from the unpredictable or unknown results of inventive activities. He must also determine the subjective weighting he gives to the various possible outcomes.

Under the Bayesian learning model developed in Chapter 4, any such formulations will depend upon the range of past experience, the degree the individual feels that these experiences are applicable, the results of previous predictions, and so on. In general, the greater the degree of past experience and the greater the ability to perceive the essential underlying forces, the greater are the chances that such predictions will be accurate. Also it would seem that after some minimal amounts the more experience one has, the greater the faith and confidence one places in his prognoses.

The outcome of economically motivated research, development, and innovation depends to a large extent upon the relevant institutions or the social superstructure, that is, the social values which determine the reward or compensation for each activity. As an example, inventions may be protected by patent laws, or the rewards to the developer may be in the form of kudos and accolades via some subjective form of remuneration. In more restrictive cultures, on the other hand, the social superstructure may inhibit change and development. Improvements, no matter how economically advantageous, may be met with scorn and social degradation for various reasons. Thus in any society of interacting social, political, and economic systems the process of change is a product of these forces, mitigating or improving, or altering or reinforcing methods and processes of human activity. Technological change creates pressures on existing institutions forcing reorganization which in turn allows or inhibits further technological change, which may either impel the complex of systems into a rapid upward spiral of improvement or into a vicious circle of intransigence.

The import of these tangential remarks is that the social value of innovation depends upon the particular existing confluence of institutions within the social system. What is optimal in one system may be completely infeasible in another. Thus generality must yield to specificity in the following analyses with a caveat that the applicability will be maintained only so long as technology and the level of affluence dictate the necessity and usefulness of such institutional arrangements under discussion.

In Model 7.1 institutional arrangements are assumed which are conformable to the traditional presumptions of Western economic analysis. Included in the institutions are money and the existence of markets. Model 7.1 assumes a single decision maker who is able to purchase physical commodities at the going price and also able to sell transformed commodities in markets in which he can affect the price by the quantity he sells and by other activities such as advertising.

MODEL 7.1—The individual as a firm

The individual is assumed to have several activities with which he can maximize drive reduction. Since the individual is now limited to being a firm, all the relevant activities are assumed to be economic. The decision is to find a set of activities which maximize

$$S = \phi(w_1, \ldots, w_n)$$
$$w_i = \gamma_i(x_1, \ldots, x_k)$$

where

$$x_1, \ldots, x_j = \text{inputs}$$
$$x_{j+1}, \ldots, x_k = \text{outputs}$$

subject to

1. $M = \Sigma_{i=1}^{k} P_i x_i \geqslant 0$, where $P_1, \ldots, P_j$ are given and

   $$P_i = P_i(x_{j+1}, \ldots, x_k, w_{h+1}, \ldots, w_n), \quad i = j + 1, \ldots, k$$

   where $w_1, \ldots, w_h$ are production activities and $w_{h+1}, \ldots, w_n$ are nonoutput activities.

2. $T = \psi(w_1, \ldots, w_n) \leqslant T_o$

3. $x_1, \ldots, x_j \leqslant 0$
   $x_{j+1}, \ldots, x_k \geqslant 0$
   $w_1, \ldots, w_n \geqslant 0$

4. $P_1, \ldots, P_k \geqslant 0$

Suppose for discussion purposes w_i is a particular research activity. The inputs $x_i, \ldots, x_j$ would be the raw materials, human skills, and so on, used up in any such process. The outputs $x_{j+1}, \ldots, x_k$ can be thought of as capabilities to produce a new product. The price or value of this capability must be given some degree of belief, and these degrees must be given the subjective weighting which the firm feels is appropriate. When the output is knowledge, skills, or capacity for future production, this capability can be thought of as an output which the firm buys from itself in the next period.

All prices are discounted to the present time if they are for future sales. Also assume that even though many of the functions are not known with certainty, each function selected is used in the calculus process as if it were the true relation. The individual's decision process of selecting such a function is dependent upon his past experiences and consequently can be expressed in terms of a Bayesian learning model as developed in Chapter 4.

The price of each output or product of the firm is affected in general not only by nonoutput activities such as advertising but also by the other products the firm produces. For many of the inputs and outputs, the effect of a change in quantity x_h on their price would be equal to zero, that is, $\partial P_i/\partial x_h = 0$, for some $h \in (1, \ldots, k)$, $h \neq i$. Likewise many of the nonoutput activities undertaken by the firm would have no effect on the price. However, the generality of the equations allows for either complementary or competitive outputs, that is, $\partial P_i/\partial x_h \gtrless 0$, and explicitly includes such things as sales promotion and advertising activities.

The degree of correspondence between maximum profits and the optimal solution to Model 7.1 depends upon the relation between the various activities and drive reduction. If one activity w_p is defined as making profits (a proxy for the individual's private life) and all other activities have an equal effect on drive reduction, that is,

$$\partial \phi/\partial w_i = \partial \phi/\partial w_j \text{ all } i, j \neq p$$

the goal max S can be replaced in Model 7.1 by

$$\max M = \Sigma \, P_i x_i \geqslant 0$$

Since $(w_{h+1}, \ldots, w_n)$ are nonoutput activities of the firm, they must have a positive effect on the revenue of the outputs such that $\Sigma_{i=j+1}^{k} (\partial P_i/\partial w_g) x_i \geqslant 0$; for all $g = h + 1, \ldots, n$, evaluated at the optimum.

If M is quasi-concave and the constraint set convex, the Kuhn-Tucker conditions are both necessary and sufficient for a maximum; that is, the Lagrangian equation is

$$\lambda = \sum_{i=1}^{k} P_i x_i + \lambda_1 \psi(w_1, \ldots, w_n) + \lambda_{2_1}[w_1 - \gamma_1(x_1, \ldots, x_k)]$$

$$+ \cdots + \lambda_{2_n}[w_n - \gamma_n(x_1, \ldots, x_k)]$$

or in vector notation;

$$\lambda = Px + \lambda_1 \psi(W) + \lambda_2[W - \gamma(x)]$$

The Kuhn-Tucker conditions for inputs or outputs i not at a zero level are

$$\sum_{j=1}^{k} \left(\frac{\partial P_j}{\partial x_i} x_j + P_i \right) + \lambda_1 \sum_{j=1}^{n} \frac{\partial \psi}{\partial \gamma_j} \frac{\partial \gamma_j}{\partial x_i} + \sum_{j=1}^{n} \lambda_{2j} \frac{\partial \gamma_j}{\partial x_i} = 0$$

Letting

$$R_{x_i} = \sum_{j=1}^{n} \frac{\partial P_j}{\partial x_i} x_j + P_i = \text{marginal effect on revenue by } x_i$$

$$\psi_{x_i} = \sum_{j=1}^{n} \frac{\partial \psi}{\partial \gamma_j} \frac{\partial \gamma_j}{\partial x_j} = \text{marginal effect on time}$$

$$\gamma_{x_i} = \left(\frac{\partial \gamma_1}{\partial x_i}, \ldots, \frac{\partial \gamma_n}{\partial x_i} \right)$$

the conditions become

$$\gamma_{x_i}/\gamma_{x_h} = (R_{x_i} - \lambda_1 \psi_{x_i})/(R_{x_h} - \lambda_1 \psi_{x_h}) \qquad (7.1)$$

or

$$R_{x_i}/R_{x_h} = (\lambda_1 \psi_{x_i} - \lambda_2 \gamma_{x_i})/(\lambda_1 \psi_{x_h} - \lambda_2 \gamma_{x_h}) \qquad (7.2)$$

or

$$\psi_{x_i}/\psi_{x_h} = (R_{x_i} + \lambda_2 \gamma_{x_i})/(R_{x_h} + \lambda_2 \gamma_{x_h}) \qquad (7.3)$$

In other words Equation 7.1 says that the marginal rate of technical substitution, that is $\gamma_{x_i}/\gamma_{x_h}$, is equal to the ratio of the marginal revenue effects weighted by the marginal effect on time multiplied by the shadow price of the time constraint λ_1. Equation 7.2 says that the marginal revenue ratio is equal to the ratio of the implicit value of time and the implicit value of technology constraints. Equations 7.2 and 7.3 are merely rearrangements of Equation 7.1.

If the individual firm manager does not act solely to maximize profits, the optimum conditions stated above will be biased in favor of higher levels of those activities which are satisfying (or least dissatisfying) in and of themselves. If the making of wine, activity w_i, has a greater effect on drive reduction than the making of grape juice, activity w_j, other things being equal, $\partial \phi/\partial w_i > \partial \phi/\partial w_j$; the individual will not maximize profits—he will carry out the wine-making activity at too high a level. Under Model 7.1 the interpretation of inputs could be expanded to include labor only if it is a very simple type.

That is, the use of such labor is completely unrestrained and the labor enters the production process without affecting the decision-making process in any manner. In other words, the model assumes that the labor is equivalent to cold, hard steel as far as the entrepreneur is concerned. Realistically, for this condition to be satisfied, the skill level of the labor must be of a very simple nature. This question of the firm as a group will be further explored, but before this a simplification of Model 7.1 will aid in pointing out the relevant forces operating for the single decision maker.

MODEL 7.2—Inclusion of nonoutput activities, advertising, and research[1]

   Assume:

1. All units are measured over the period of T_o.
2. Two inputs are used:
   x_k : capital (physical) and
   x_l : labor (simple).
3. Two outputs are marketed:
   x_c : current consumer commodity and
   x_f : future commodity.
4. Three activities are known or possible:
   w_c : production of x_c,
   w_f : production of x_f (research), and
   w_a : advertising.
5. There is a limited managerial time, T_o.
6. Input prices are given as P_k, P_l, and P_a.
7. The firm is an imperfect competitor in the output market.
8. In each output market x_c and x_f the relations between quantity sold, advertising, and the price are interdependent. That is, once P_c and w_a are set, x_c is determined; or in general, when any two variables are set, the third is simultaneously established.
   Therefore, any two variables can be considered independent in each market.
9. The output markets are independent, that is,

$$\partial x_c / \partial P_f \equiv 0$$

10. The goal of this simple multiproduct firm is to maximize profits over the period T_o.

---

1. Model 7.2 basically follows Holdren (1968).

11. Patents and technology developed, x_f, are worth an amount equivalent to the discounted price, P_f, per unit to the firm, and this is dependent upon the advertising, w_a, of the firm.
12. Inventory change must be zero at the end of the period.

Since

$$x_f = x_f(P_f, x_a)$$
$$x_c = x_c(P_c, x_a)$$
$$\text{cost} = C(x_c, x_f, x_a)$$
$$T = \text{managerial time} = \psi(x_c, x_f, x_a) \leqslant T_o$$

and the objective is to maximize profits, the Lagrangian equation is

$$\lambda = P_c x_c (P_c, x_a) + P_f x_f(P_f, x_a)$$
$$- C(x_c, x_f, x_a) + \lambda_1 [T_o - \psi(x_c, x_f, x_a)]$$

Let the independent variables be P_c, P_f, and x_a, then at the optimum

$$\frac{\partial \lambda}{\partial P_c} = x_c + P_c \frac{\partial x_c}{\partial P_c} - \frac{\partial C}{\partial x_c} \frac{\partial x_c}{\partial P_c} - \lambda_1 \frac{\partial \psi}{\partial x_c} \frac{\partial x_c}{\partial P_c} \leqslant 0$$

$$\text{if } \frac{\partial \lambda}{\partial P_c} < 0, P_c = 0$$

$$\frac{\partial \lambda}{\partial P_f} = x_f + P_f \frac{\partial x_f}{\partial P_f} - \frac{\partial C}{\partial x_f} \frac{\partial x_f}{\partial P_f} - \lambda_1 \frac{\partial \psi}{\partial x_f} \frac{\partial x_f}{\partial P_f} \leqslant 0$$

$$\text{if } \frac{\partial \lambda}{\partial P_f} < 0, P_f = 0$$

$$\frac{\partial \lambda}{\partial x_a} = P_c \frac{\partial x_c}{\partial x_a} + P_f \frac{\partial x_f}{\partial x_a} - \frac{\partial C}{\partial x_a} - \lambda_1 \frac{\partial \psi}{\partial x_a} \leqslant 0$$

$$\text{if } \frac{\partial \lambda}{\partial x_a} < 0, \quad x_a = 0$$

$$\frac{\partial \lambda}{\partial \lambda_1} = T_o - \psi(x_c, x_f, x_a) \geqslant 0; \text{ if } \frac{\partial \lambda}{\partial \lambda_1} > 0, \lambda_1 = 0$$

Case 1

Assume $\lambda_1 = 0$, or that the time constraint is not binding and that $\partial \lambda / \partial P_c = \partial \lambda / \partial P_f = \partial \lambda / \partial x_a = 0$, that is, output prices and the amount of advertising purchased are not equal to zero. Define the marginal revenue of the price change ($MR_{\Delta P}$) and the marginal expense of a price change ($ME_{\Delta P}$) as follows:

$$MR_{\Delta P_c} = x_c + P_c(\partial x_c/\partial P_c)$$
$$MR_{\Delta P_f} = x_f + P_f(\partial x_f/\partial P_f)$$
$$ME_{\Delta P_c} = \partial C/P_c = (\partial C/\partial x_c)(\partial x_c/\partial P_c)$$
$$ME_{\Delta P_f} = \partial C/\partial P_f = (\partial C/\partial x_f)(\partial x_f/\partial P_c) \tag{7.4}$$

Analogously for advertising, the marginal revenue and marginal expense are defined as:

$$MR_{\Delta a} = P_c(\partial x_c/\partial x_a) + P_f(\partial x_f/\partial x_a)$$
$$ME_{\Delta a} = \partial C/\partial x_a = P_a + (\partial C/\partial x_c)(\partial x_c/\partial x_a) + (\partial C/\partial x_f)(\partial x_f/\partial x_a)$$
$$\tag{7.5}$$

Thus the firm will equate

$$MR_{\Delta P} = ME_{\Delta P} \tag{7.6}$$
$$MR_{\Delta a} = ME_{\Delta a} \tag{7.7}$$

Another way of viewing the same conditions is to define $M\pi_x$ as equal to marginal profits of producing commodity x

$$M\pi_x = P_x - (\partial C/\partial x)$$

then Equation 7.7 can be written as

$$MS_{x_c} M\pi_{x_c} + MS_{x_f} M\pi_{x_f} = P_a \tag{7.8}$$

where $MS_{x_c} = \partial x_c/\partial x_a =$ marginal sales effect of advertising on product x_c. Then if advertising has no effect upon the x_f market but only on the current market, Equation 7.8 becomes

$$MS_{x_c} M\pi_{x_c} = P_a \tag{7.9}$$

That is, the firm would advertise until the price of advertising is equal to the marginal sales effect of advertising multiplied by the marginal profits of producing commodity x.

Case 2

If the time constraint is binding on managerial time, $\lambda_1 > 0$. This is essentially no different from Case I except that the marginal expense of a price or advertising change must include not only the monetary costs, that is, $(\partial C/\partial x)(\partial x/\partial x_a)$, but the marginal time cost multiplied by λ_1, which is the shadow price imputed to managerial time. The equality of Equations 7.6–7.9 still holds at the optimum but only under this expanded interpretation of marginal expense.

Once the experience vector of a unit of advertising is determined[2] and given initial consumer conditions, the marginal sales effect can be established. For illustrative purposes suppose that the amount of x_c sold is a linear function of the degree of belief as expressed by the expected probability that x_c fulfills a desired activity for consumers, that is,

$$x_c = \sigma[E_x(\lambda_{x_c})] + \beta \qquad (7.10)$$

σ and β are constants, λ_{x_c} is the probability of x_c being "true," and E_x is the expectation operator.

If each unit of advertising carried out by the firm provides r units of success and s units of failure toward establishing this consumer belief, by slight algebraic manipulation one can solve for the optimal amount of advertising the firm should purchase.

Aside from the potential empirical applicability of Model 7.2 or its simplification, the model has quite a capacity for including many of the "problems" on which the current theory of the firm is silent. Although Model 7.2 is quite simplistic (that is, it can be extended to include such things as learning on the part of the firm itself; a more general objective function in addition to profits; and a further delineation of various relevant constraints such as imperfect capital markets, corporate control, and the like), it nevertheless adds a great deal of intuitive insight to the workings of a multiproduct firm and further helps explain firm activities.

MANY-PERSON FIRM

The subsequent step in this theoretical model-building process is to consider the firm as a group rather than a single person manipulating inanimate factors of production. Whenever the single entrepreneur finds it advantageous to form a group, the above analysis is modified so that the objective function represents a coalition rather than the single individual. When this entrepreneur and individuals with more than the simplest of skills (hence individuals who are able to attain a position of power) coalesce, the objective function changes accordingly.

When does a group decision-making process replace the single decision maker? Basically, it occurs when the advantages of forming a group cannot be represented by a monetary side payment. In the analysis of a group preference function in Chapter 5, it is assumed that the individual preference functions were separable. For those

2. See Chapter 4.

activities where the cross-partial derivative is not equal to zero, the presumption of an existing market for those activities permitted a side payment which negated this cross-partial derivative effect. Therefore, whenever such a market does not exist (or it is not the most efficient form of interpersonal activity exchange) and these activities have a tradeoff with those activities which are available in a market, the decision of the group is determined by group interaction rather than by the single decision maker. Wages and salaries then become only one facet of intragroup exchange.

To add further intuitive understanding, consider a simple example of a shopkeeper and a cabinetmaker. Since both individuals can have more by forming a group, they decide to do so. By ascribing the initiative to the shopkeeper, he may also be designated as the entrepreneur. The contract between the two specifies, implicitly or explicitly, a set of activities to be exchanged, for example, the type of cabinets to be built by the artisan, where he will build them, who will obtain the wood and other raw materials, the wage paid to the builder, and so on. In other words, they establish an institutional arrangement or a contract which is reached in light of some perceived environmental conditions. Given an agreed upon set of rules governing their relationship and the way they will react toward those outside their group, no further decisions need to be made. The rules and prescriptions for behavior are established and need not be altered unless those forming this group change their opinion of the environmental conditions. A situation may arise which was not specified in the formation of the group. The individuals' concepts of the extensive effects of group action may have been in error or incomplete. Thus, unless there is a change in the knowledge sets, there is no need for decisions. However, the typical situation is one where a great deal of learning takes place.

Suppose the entrepreneur decides to expand the group by adding another builder when he sees that output could be increased so that his profits are increased. In other words, there is a change in the perceived environmental conditions; there is a change in the knowledge sets of the individuals involved. Whether the original artisan will take part in this decision depends upon his particular drive-reduction function and also upon his interaction with the other proposed members of the new group of three. Thus the entrepreneur will be the single decision maker if the laborers have no available threat sets other than their demand for wage payments and other activities of the entrepreneur which affect their satisfaction are uniquely and readily expressible in monetary terms.

INFLUENCES OF INDIVIDUALS ON THE FIRM'S ACTIVITIES

A single individual will maintain his position as the decision maker only as long as he has sufficient power (activities or threats to limit the bargaining of laborers). The traditional economic model of the firm implicitly implies a single decision maker and that labor can be hired at the going market price. If there are no costs associated with replacing one worker with another (training costs and the like) the entrepreneur possesses a threat set of replacing the worker if and when he demands more than the going market wage rate. Clearly as production processes become more complicated, these transition costs rise. Also, it becomes more efficient for the entrepreneur to delegate decision-making powers to others. One reason for this is a physical limitation on his time and energies for making decisions.

Another example of a decision process which is perhaps more relevant to the phenomena of changing technology follows. Suppose the cabinetmaker proposes a change in design. Even in the case where the marketer is the nominal entrepreneur of this two-person group, unless he is sufficiently skilled in the art (or science) of cabinet building, he will not be able to render an opinion because of lack of knowledge. If he does veto the proposal, he is still not able to offer meaningful alternatives. The advantages of a division of physical labor are equally applicable to the labor of decision making. With more and more complex technologies, a division of the decision making not only becomes more efficient but becomes the only feasible method of group decision making.

The objective function of a coalition is an adopted institution concomitant with the other decorums established when the group is formed. It will be one of profit maximization only so long as the drives of the various members can be most efficiently satisfied by monetary payments, given the makeup of the group. The objective function is a bargained institution which specifies how the group should deal with those outside the group. Of course, the specification of the institution could vary from a general plan which allows one member to act for the group in outside activities to a complete specification of an agent's activities with those outside the group. In any event, as with all institutions when knowledge sets change and/or other parameters in the environment of the group change, the institution may be subject to pressure and consequent revision.

Traditional economic theories of the firm, in maintaining the assumption of profit maximization, implicitly assume that a variety of other conditions are fulfilled. If one were dealing with a large conglomerate corporation in the United States and the question was what would be done with research and development funds, the actual decision process would involve more than the single individual. In any complex manufacturing process a single individual can hardly be expected to have an adequate knowledge of all facets of the enterprise. Thus the decision of where and when to innovate depends upon the alternatives. And how are the alternatives generated? Even though many may come from outside the technocracy, many sections will have the power to review and eliminate certain proposals due to their implicit (if not explicit) power position which is directly a function of their specialized knowledge. The decision process generally involves many individuals in the firm and cannot easily be aligned with a single goal. In the case where monetary side payments cannot efficiently compensate for interpersonal transactions, the profit maximization hypothesis is neither an accurate nor an adequate description of the firm's activities.

In the following discussion the objective function of the firm will be assumed to be basically the same as in Model 7.2; however, it will be assumed to be a product of group interaction. It also will be shown that the changing objective function for the coalition is mathematically equivalent to that of the single individual under limited types of knowledge change, even though the actual knowledge set change (or other parametric change) occurs initially in the various members comprising the group.

In Chapter 5 the conditions which must hold in order for an institution to be adopted by the group were presented. These conditions can be interpreted in terms of the firm in the following way.

$S^i = \phi^i(W^i, W^F)$ = drive-reduction function attainable
$\qquad$ by individual i

W^i = vector of i's personal activities

W^F = vector activities carried out by the firm

W^F would include both the firm's dealings with those within its organization and the dealings of the organization with those outside. For example, included in the vector W^F would be wage payments to i; working conditions; maximizing profits for the firm, given outside revenues and outside costs; or the firm's subsidizing of orphans and widows.

If $W^F = (w_1^F, \ldots, w_f^F)$, the effect of individual i on the activities of the firm can be represented as

$$w_i^F = w_i^F(w_1^i, \ldots, w_n^i, \omega_1^i, \ldots, \omega_m^i)$$

and, in turn, the maximizing conditions for all individuals determine the level of each of the firm's activities. The firm's activities depend upon the individuals' available sets of activities and their interaction with others in the group. Suppose I represents activities which maximize profits and II represents the same activities except that orphans are sold output at cost. Suppose further that everyone in the firm aside from individual i wants II as the rule of the firm's activities. That is, $\overset{*}{S}{}^{j\epsilon II} > \overset{*}{S}{}^{j\epsilon I}$, but $\overset{*}{S}{}^{i\epsilon I} > \overset{*}{S}{}^{i\epsilon II}$.

Suppose $\overset{*}{S}{}^{j\epsilon I, \overline{W}^i} > \overset{*}{S}{}^{j\epsilon II} > \overset{*}{S}{}^{j\epsilon \Omega/I,II}$ for all j who are members of the firm, $j \neq i$. $\overline{W}^i$ is a set of nonmaximizing but threatening activities of i, and $\Omega/I, II$ is the set of all possible sets other than those described by I or II. Then i will have recourse to a threat set. It will be a valid threat if $\phi^i(\overline{W}^i) \geqslant \overset{*}{S}{}^{i\epsilon II}$ and an idle threat if $\phi^i(\overline{W}^i) < \overset{*}{S}{}^{i\epsilon II}$. And of course if it is only an idle threat, knowledge of this fact would result in the firm's adopting the subsidizing policy II; while a valid threat would result in the firm maximizing profits if no other members of the firm had a valid threat over i.

THE EFFECTS OF KNOWLEDGE CHANGE

Suppose there is a change in the knowledge sets of one (or more) of the members of the firm. What effect will this have on the objective function, other rules of the firm, and its members?

First, in order for the change in knowledge to be relevant to the institutions of the firm it is necessary that $\overset{*}{S}{}^{i\epsilon F'} > \overset{*}{S}{}^{i\epsilon F}$, for some i, where F' is a new set of institutions envisioned by individual i as a result of the knowledge change and F is the original set of institutions.

Second, the change must be such that it is possible for individual i to induce it either directly or indirectly. The process, the argumentation, the trouble, and so forth that individual i must go through to change policy cannot outweigh the advantages of the change. This is analogous to the analysis in Chapter 3 of the effect of learning and the level of drive reduction. If person i has to carry out activities, such as arguing or teaching, which lower his drive reduction in order to convince others in the group, i would compare total streams of drive reduction. If $\int S^{i\epsilon P} \, dt > \int \overset{*}{S}{}^{i\epsilon F} \, dt$, where P represents the process i must go through to change policy from F to F', then i will bring about the change. If $\int S^{i\epsilon P} \, dt \leqslant \int \overset{*}{S}{}^{i\epsilon F} \, dt$, even though i would be better off under the new institutional arrangements and could bring about this change, the necessary trouble and red tape completely eliminate those advantages. This is calculated with respect to some knowledge set; that is, the individual must estimate the costs and benefits. It is not expected that the individual would be correct in all cases. Sometimes he will bring about change with less effort and sometimes he will find it much more costly. These represent further changes in his knowledge set and lead to a continual recalculation of the costs and benefits involved in continuing or abandoning his efforts.

LATENT DESIRED INSTITUTIONAL CHANGE

With less than perfect knowledge by those comprising the firm it is possible to build up latent desired institutional change. Suppose that for some subset $G' \subset G$ a change in institutions is preferred, $\overset{*}{S}^{i \in F'} > \overset{*}{S}^{i \in F}$, $i \in G' \subset G$, but also each member of G' feels the effort offsets the benefits, $\int S^{i \in P} dt \leqslant \int S^{i \in F} dt$. Thus we have a situation analogous to the problem in public goods theory. All G' would benefit from the change, but no single individual acting alone is willing to bring it about. If $\int \int S^{i \in P'} dt \, dG' > \int \int S^{i \in F} dt \, dG'$, where P' is the procedure that the subgroup would have to go through in order to bring about change, greater information would produce a cooperative effort among those comprising G' to instigate the change. By the nature of the model this could only occur under conditions of less than perfect knowledge. Otherwise, the cooperative aspects of bringing about the change would be included in the set P or for each individual, $\int S^{i \in P} dt > \int S^{i \in F} dt$. Many situations, where institutional change has been brought about, are conformable to the former concept of latent change. The last straw that broke the camel's back is a cliché which emphasizes that once some individual takes the initiative, and demonstrates favor to change (hence changing the knowledge sets of others as to their presumption of the difficulty of change), this results in a snowball or bandwagon effect. This fact that changing information is a contributing aspect to the bandwagon effect has been well documented by social psychologists.[3]

THE SIZE OF THE GROUP COMPRISING THE FIRM

Since a firm is a particular group drawn together by the benefits or joint production, the existing environment will significantly affect the size of the firm.[4] For simplicity, initially assume that the benefits of interpersonal interaction are solely those of money income. In other words, drive reduction from working with others is zero.

3. See Katz and Kahn (1966) and Collins and Guetzkow (1964).
4. For an early discussion of this see Coose (1937).

Each individual will be willing to join the firm as long as his income is greater in that firm than it would be in any other. To avoid problems with the length of time the individual wants to work per time period, assume the workweek is fixed institutionally and the individual must work a fixed period per week no matter which firm he joins. Under these assumptions the individual will decide to join a particular group solely on the basis of the tendered wage rate. On the other hand, the firm will be willing to bring the individual into the group if the additional cost is less than the additional revenue. The cost of an additional member is his wages and materials (since benefits and the like have been assumed unimportant). If the group has a single decision maker, this entrepreneur will hire from plentiful labor just up to the point where the marginal expense is equal to the marginal revenue product of that laborer, as traditional economic analysis contends. This reduces to the marginal revenue product of labor being equal to the wage rate in the special case where labor is homogeneous and the threat set of the firm is much greater than that of the individual.

Now the question is, Why do not all individuals engaged in the production of a commodity form a single firm? What determines the limits of cohesion of individuals into a single firm under the above assumption of income maximization?

The binding together of individuals as a group for production and distribution must increase their income and must be more efficient than changing the size of the group. Traditionally, the explanation of firm efficiency has been one of a specialization of labor. With individuals concentrating on simple tasks, the output is greater. With any production process there are economies of scale associated with each phase of the operation. For example, the procurement of a place of operation, a plant site, is a fixed cost and does not affect the marginal cost of production (at least for quite wide ranges of output). The editing of a book is required once whether one or 100,000 copies are printed. One assembly line foreman may be required to coordinate two workers, whereas he could just as easily manage fifty. Additional bookkeeping for doubling of output may merely require the use of different figures with no alteration of time and effort expended. One salesman can take an order for fifty units as easily as five. For research and development to be worthwhile, there must be some assurance of continued existence of the firm. Gathering information as to the quantity which can be sold may be identical in cost whether the quantity is large or small. Similarly, the information flow from the firm to potential purchasers may exhibit significant economies of scale.

Economies of scale are associated with financing a firm, use of other resources besides human labor, and economies of stability from a diversified operation when there are costs of startup and shutdown. The point being that as a firm expands production it expands in particular directions with respect to skills and knowledge needed for additional members.

Since each individual must bring a surfeit to the firm in order to be accepted, the division of this extra value will depend upon the distribution of threat sets among the members of the firm. Traditional economic analysis assumes the entrepreneur has an overwhelming threat set over common labor. Consequently, the size of each firm is determined by economies of scale. If economies of scale are at low levels of output relative to the market, more and more firms will form as total production increases and perfect competition results. If economies of scale are achieved only at high levels relative to total market production, the result is monopoly.

To gain further insight into the distribution and determination of wages and salaries, consider the following example. Suppose there is a monopolist, that is, a group of individuals forming a firm which is the sole producer of a commodity x_j. Furthermore, assume that x_j is the sole commodity used in activity w_i for all consumers and that activity w_i carries a relatively high drive-reduction value. Any single individual or subgroup of individuals within the firm will be able to increase their share of the market revenue minus material costs if they possess a sufficient threat set. And in this case one significant aspect of their threat set is the formation of another firm. If a subgroup could do better by forming another firm than they are doing in the original firm, they would have a valid threat. In the case of full information as to which threats were valid and which were idle, the resulting firm size would be solely dependent upon the economies-of-scale production. That is, if economies of scale were continually increasing, a monopoly would remain with various individuals sharing the profits, depending upon their threat sets. And as noted above, sources of power for threat sets would include access to capital in an imperfect capital market, specialized knowledge, specialized abilities, and so forth.

As conditions change over time, various individuals' threat sets change as well. If a change in technology favors a larger scale of production and thus increases the management's threat set due to an imperfect capital market, it may become efficient for the laborers to bind together in a labor union and bargain collectively.[5] As

5. This is essentially Galbraith's thesis of countervailing power, Galbraith (1956).

technology expands and requires very specialized skills and knowledge, individual threat sets replace the advantages once found in a labor union.

In general the size of the firm will not be optimal from a purely profit point of view as the assumptions employed above are violated. If any individual dislikes working with others, he will produce outside the group at a lower implicit wage than the group would offer. A monopoly may give rise to a waning duopoly because one subgroup believes it has a valid threat while another believes the threat is only an idle one. Various groups have different internal policies or institutions which impinge upon individual behavior. Without considering the special characteristics of each group and its production activities, little more can be said.

The institutions of the firm represent what is analogous to the knowledge set of the individual. An alteration of these institutions or policies represents a change in knowledge on the part of the firm. Thus the firm can be viewed as having an objective function, implicitly or explicitly stated, which is part of an adopted policy or set of institutions. The firm then maximizes this objective function subject to the various technological and extrafirm institutional constraints which impinge upon its behavior. The comparative static analysis of policy change on the part of the firm follows precisely along the lines of individual knowledge change as developed in Chapter 3. The difference is the process of how these institutional arrangements are altered over time, the difference between how an individual's knowledge set changes and how group interaction produces a change in the objectives and constraints facing the firm. (More specific analysis of particular firms and individuals comprising these firms represents a vast and interesting area for future research. The detail of conditions necessary to effect change under particular groups and sizes should furnish a plethora of useful information, insight, and policy criteria for particular situations. Given the general characteristics of the various members of a firm, much greater detail of institutional change within a firm could be derived.)

SUMMARY

The firm as an economic unit can be viewed as a single individual with an objective function which is part of the institutional arrangements of those comprising the group. The knowledge set of this unit can be viewed as the complete set of institutions governing group interaction. When the knowledge sets of the individuals in the firm change, the knowledge set of the firm will change when the "enlightened" ones are able to produce an institutional change.

Product Innovation and Imitation

ANY COALITION of individuals exists within an environment which affects the knowledge sets of the individuals and their decision-making processes; hence it affects the objective function adopted by a firm. This chapter concentrates on the aspects of exchange within a given institutional framework typical of current Western society. Specifically, the firm is construed as functioning in a marketing environment where the decision variables of any individual or group do not affect these institutional arrangements.

THE EFFECTS OF INSTITUTIONAL STRUCTURE ON REWARDS

In an economically motivated culture such as the twentieth-century United States, the existing system of protection and rewards favors centralized agglomerate units with respect to research, development, and product innovation. Simultaneously, it enforces the development of complex technologies, that is, those which are not easily imitated. To the extent that this is favorable to further development, it is desirable under the traditional hedonistic assumptions of value. Information, knowledge, and skills are considered by the conventional wisdom of Western culture to be public goods, and their common acquisition is encouraged and reinforced by the social structure. An increase in one's knowledge is considered to be his own property with no debts incurred to the originator, and in general no taboos exist against implementing and developing skills and knowledge which are not purely one's own product.

While the legal system protects property rights of physical objects, neither this nor the social mores protects ownership of non-physical factors. Thus it becomes necessary to construct artificial ways of maintaining ownership if rents (the payoff for ownership) are to be derived. And of course the greater the rents, other things being equal, the greater the feasibility of acquiring ownership. In the case of research and invention, ownership acquisition per se is equivalent to the development of unknown skills or knowledge. (Whether activities which do not maintain ownership and produce rent are initiated is of lesser importance, since economic units which do carry out high rent activities will be the ones which are successful and survive.)

Paradoxically, the reward system in academic research is quite the opposite. Revolutionary ideas whose ownership is easily transmitted to others, (that is, those which are simple and easily understood), receive the greatest amounts of social currency. However, one can view the rent-generating activities of the academician as being those which develop a recognition of ability, that is, convince others of his ownership of capacities to invent, develop, and teach (the ownership of which is institutionally assured to be maintained). The problem is to convince others that indeed such a capability does exist. The entire reward system of grades, continual testing, journal articles, seminar appearances, and so forth, are immutable evidence of this existing reward system. No such grading scheme exists for General Motors. The reward system is essentially profit oriented or a by-product of the profit concept. One remembers the Henry Fords and Andrew Carnegies who were able to maintain a high rent position. But who developed credit cards? Neither Henry Ford nor Andrew Carnegie actually *invented* anything significant. They each exploited existing, useful technology to the fullest. They were excellent *innovators*. They had the keen ability of establishing and maintaining a nearly impregnable high rent position. Even the criterion as to what has been significant to the human race in terms of physical goods and services is often based upon its rent maintenance capacity.

The threads of Schumpeter's argument [Schumpeter (1950)] of the optimality of the ephemeral monopoly come into question at this point. But optimality and monopoly are inconsistent; the monopoly rent position implies maintenance and growth of a particular corporation. Thus any free-market system allowed by the legal and social complex to develop and advance will be autophagous. The rewards for complex technological change will become more certain, and similarly, the confidence of the large, agglomerate firm concerning the probability distribution over the various types of research activity will increase.

The research and development undertaken by a firm which has been nurtured in the market mechanism will be almost exclusively devoted to high rent items. Clearly, as pointed out above, the degree of rent which becomes the return for innovation and invention depends upon two factors: the profitability from demand considerations and the degree that exclusive rights can be maintained. The quantity of a good which a firm can sell depends upon the price and the other facets of the offer which the firm makes (guarantees, credit conditions, sales environment, amount of advertising, and so forth). It also depends upon the competition in the market.

MARKETING A NEW PRODUCT

For any one product x_f the mechanics of efficient marketing, design, advertising, and the like, are to maximize the profit from that product, all other things constant. Maximize

$$\int_0^\infty p_f \cdot x_f \, (p_f, w_{h+1}, \ldots, w_n) - C(x_f) \, dt \qquad (8.1)$$

where

$$x_f = \text{quantity sold}$$
$$p_f = \text{price of } x_f$$
$$C(x_f) = \text{cost of selling } x_f$$

$w_{h+1}, \ldots, w_n$ are the offer variations associated with x_f. However, this need not have any a priori correspondence with the total quantity sold on the market. In Figure 8.1 a hypothetical situation is

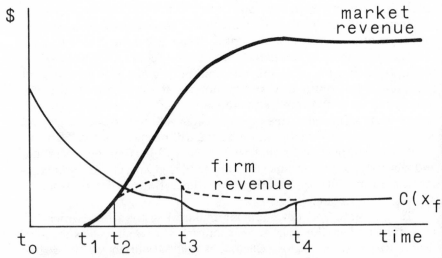

Fig. 8.1. Hypothetical path of market and firm revenues.

presented showing the change in the relative market share of revenue obtained by an innovating firm. At time t_o the firm experiences costs of innovation (invention, market start-up, and so forth). At t_1 marketing begins, and until t_2 the firm is a monopolist in the market; at this time others begin to imitate this product. At t_3 the reduction in the firm's costs and accompanying reduction in the market revenue share could be a result of external economies of additional firms entering this field. At t_4 the entrance of additional firms with some associated diseconomies of industry size have reduced the market to a competitive one where the profits have been eliminated. For a firm the method of efficient innovation would be to vary its price and nonprice offers (in consideration of the effects these will have on other firms entering the market, the total quantity it can sell, its share, and so forth) to maximize the area under the dashed line minus the area under the cost curve, $C(x_f)$. The decision process concerning which products to continue producing and in which areas to innovate is discussed in detail in Model 8.2.

The import of all this is simply that complex technologies, other things being equal, are less easily imitated by other firms. Thus if a simple technology and a complex technology produce the same market revenue as in Figure 8.1, but the complex technology keeps out many competitors, the firm would be better off with the complex technology. (The implications for social welfare are not as clear as they seem; this is taken up later.)

From the foregoing propaedeutics of marketing, several interesting and pertinent questions arise. From the firm's point of view what is the best procedure for introducing, marketing, advertising, and servicing a new product? In fact, what is the best method to predict and estimate the critical parameters necessary for optimal (profit-maximizing) product innovation? From a more general point of view, what is a socially optimal method of product innovation? Which methods create a vast waste due to overexpansion of an industry? What market structures will result from a rapidly expanding technological economy? What market structures will be conducive to further technological change and product innovation? The subsequent analysis will examine these questions in a theoretical manner and as completely as possible.

MODELS OF OPTIMAL SALES CURVE CREATION

Consider the problem faced by a large firm in deciding whether or not to introduce a new product and just how to do so. Traditional economic theory has basically ignored the details of this ques-

tion.[1]   However, these decisions have a very significant impact on the
firm's profits, the stability of an industry and the total economy, and
the efficient use of resources.

In Figure 8.1 at least three functions clearly need to be estimated
for determining a profit-maximizing method of product innovation:
(1) the market revenue function, (2) the imitation rate on the part of
other firms and hence the firm's revenue function, and (3) the cost
function over time. Each have several facets to consider. The market
revenue function will depend upon the price and nonprice offers of
both the innovating firm and of others who also enter this product
line. It will depend upon the feasible sets of the consumers, their
initial knowledge sets, and the effects of the firm's offers on these
feasible and knowledge sets. As time passes, such things as the
durability of the product and future innovation add additional com-
plications to the estimation process.

The innovating firm's revenue function will depend upon the rate
at which it is imitated by other firms. This will entail the feasible
and knowledge sets of other firms and the effect of the innovation,
the price offer, and the nonprice offer on these sets. Likewise, the
cost function will vary in general with the rate of imitation by other
firms and the consequences on factor costs and economies of industry
size.[2]   Also, further technological advance and increased efficient
production techniques which arise from repetition of the production
and marketing process may significantly affect the costs and profits
of the firm. Finally, ex post parametric estimation and its ex ante
use in decision-making processes are no mean tasks. Vital to the applicability of information about past product innovation to future innovation is the analysis of the underlying motivating forces of demand and knowledge change.

Since the Euler-Lagrange conditions for Equation 8.1 to be
maximized are well known, the problem reduces to one of including
the relevant variables in Equation 8.1 and relating ex post parametric
estimation to ex ante decision making. While a precise specification
would vary with the particular commodity, firm, consumer group,
and so forth, the following model is illustrative of this maximizing
technique.

MODEL 8.1—Durable good innovation

Assume that firm f_o is considering the innovation of good x_1^*
which is technologically superior to good x_1. Currently, good x_1

1. Recent models which go somewhat beyond traditional theory include
Scherer (1967) and Baldwin and Childs (1969).
2. Fuller discussion of this particular topic can be found in Griliches (1957)
and Arrow (1962, 1969) along with some empirical observations.

is used by consumers in activity $w_1 = \gamma_1(x_1)$. The technological superiority of x_1^* is that it releases more units of service per unit of time than does x_1. For simplicity assume that both goods have equivalent durability; that is, both x_1 and x_1^* will last for the same number of years T_o.

The first question is, What are the characteristics of the market revenue function? From the analysis of the individual calculus process, Figure 8.2 represents a typical feasible set of a consumer. All other activities are aggregated as activity w_a requiring an aggregate commodity bundle x_a with an associated price p_a. Assume that the functional time-activity relation is linear, and for each consumer the maximum occurs where both constraints are binding (point α in Fig. 8.2). The description of point α is given in Equations 8.2 and 8.3,

$$t_1 x_1 + t_a x_a = T_o \qquad (8.2)$$

$$p_1 x_1 = p_a x_a \qquad (8.3)$$

The relation of time use and x_1^* is shown in Figure 8.2 as $T^* = T_o$ and in Equation 8.4.

$$t_1^* x_1^* + t_a x_a \leqslant T_o \qquad (8.4)$$

If it is assumed that the isodrive reduction curve between w_1 and w_a is linear, the maximum price the innovating firm could charge for x_1^* and have the consumer (as represented in Figures 8.2 and 8.3) purchase x_1^* over x_1 is shown by M' in Figure 8.3. This assumption is not as restrictive as it may sound; in fact it is the most general. The maximum price the innovating firm could charge is less than if the indifference curves had the traditional convex-to-the-origin shape, since the feasible set under the new technology dominates the former set. Thus by setting the price at p_1^*, each consumer will be at least as well off regardless of the

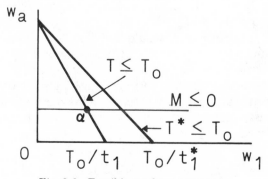

Fig. 8.2. Feasible set for a consumer.

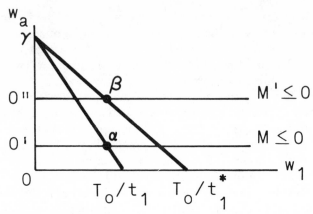

Fig. 8.3. Change in a feasible set for a consumer from $0' \alpha \gamma$ to $0'' \beta \gamma$ if x_1^* is priced at p_1^* max.

actual shape of his indifference curves. This assumption is described in Equations 8.4 and 8.5. The maximum new price would then be determined by point β in Figure 8.3.

$$p_1^* x_1 = p_a x_a \qquad (8.5)$$

Solving Equations 8.2–8.5, Equation 8.6 shows that the maximum change in price $\Delta p_1 \equiv (p_1^{*\,\mathrm{max}} - p_1)$ is simply related to the technical time-saving advantage of x_1^*, namely, $\Delta t_1 \equiv (t_1 - t_1^*)$.

$$\Delta p_1 = (p_a/t_a)\, \Delta t_1 \qquad (8.6)$$

The durable, indivisible nature of this good (as shown by $M \leqslant 0$ and $M' \leqslant 0$, the budget constraints, being parallel to the w_1 axis) means that as long as $\Delta p_1 \leqslant (p_a/t_a)\, \Delta t_1$ and the consumer becomes informed of x_1^*, he will purchase one unit of x_1^*. If $\Delta p_1 > (p_a/t_a)\, \Delta t_1$ then he will purchase one unit of x_1. (Note that the analysis holds equally well for those consumers who already have purchased x_1. In this case the original budget constraint $M \leqslant 0$ would be coincident with the w_1 axis, and point α would be equal to T_0/t_1. Also since x_1 is by assumption a durable good, Equation 8.3 would become $p_a x_a = 0$.) However, each consumer has in general a different income and a different aggregate activity mix w_a. This implies that t_a and p_a would vary among consumers. Thus by establishing m classes of initial consumer conditions $(p_a/t_a)_i$, where M_i is the number of consumers in each class, the quantity x_1^* that this firm could sell after all were informed would be

$$x_1^* = \sum_{i=1}^{m_0} M_i, \text{ where } \Delta p_1 = (p_a/t_a)_{m_0}\, \Delta t_1$$

and

$$(p_a/t_a)_1 < (p_a/t_a)_2 < \cdots < (p_a/t_a)_{m_o} \qquad (8.7)$$

Thus Equation 8.7 gives quantity sold of x_1^* as a function of the price p_1^*. Alternatively, in continuous terms, let $C = p_a/t_a$ and $f(C)$ be equal to the distribution of consumers. Then

$$x_1^* = \int_0^{C^*} f(C)\,dC$$

where $\Delta t_1 C^* = \Delta p_1$. For example, if $f(C)$ is approximately a normal distribution, x_1^* would be the cumulative normal function.

The subsequent question is, What is the cost of informing the consumers of the availability of x_1^* and its advantages over x_1? This amounts to adding $w_1 = \gamma_1(x_1^*)$ and $\psi*(x_1^*, \ldots, x_m) \leqslant T_o$ to each individual's knowledge set so that, depending upon his income and preferences, he can choose either $0'\alpha\gamma$ or $0''\beta\gamma$ (Fig. 8.3) as the relevant feasible set. This would entail estimating the effect of advertising on the subjective believability of each consumer toward establishing that $w_1 = \gamma_1(x_1^*)$ and

$$\psi*(x_1^*, \ldots, x_m) \leqslant T_o$$

were true. Among other things this would depend upon the initial beliefs of the consumers and the degree of believability they placed in the advertising.

For example, the number of individuals reached by various information systems in the different classes could be related to the cost of this information. In other words, $M_i = g(X_c)$, $i = 1, \ldots, m$; X_c is the vector of various advertising commodities available to the firm. Again, in continuous terms, if $f*(C)$ is the original distribution of uninformed consumers,

$$f(C) = g[f*(C), X_c]$$

where $f(C)$ is now the distribution of the informed consumers.

Having established the market revenue function as dependent upon price p_1^* and advertising, the market share function can now be given further consideration. This will be approached from the point of view of the potentially imitating firm. Presumably, then, the innovating firm would attempt to empathize and put itself in the place of potentially imitating firms.

Among the many facets determining whether a firm will imitate are the learning experiences of the imitating firm about the new product and its associated technology and the feasibility or profitability of imitation relative to the imitator's other alternatives.

Learning on the part of the other firms about the existence of the product and its potential activity-servicing qualities would seemingly be as rapid or more so than learning on the part of consumers. This would take place when the innovating firm informed others of the new product's availability. A rare and unlikely possible violation of this learning would entail a special subgroup of consumers who could be cryptically informed and were not potential producers or information transmitters themselves. On the other hand, other firms could learn about the existence of a product and its market potential through industrial grapevines, trade journals, organized espionage, and the like.

Concomitant with gathering information about the existence of a technologically new product, the potential imitating firms would also gain information about the costs of imitating. Their imitation could be essentially the same product technologically or could be a further improvement. It will be assumed in the models to follow that the innovating firm does not believe that the imitating firm will be able to improve on their improvement. The innovating firm feels that it has the best feasible improvement. This assumption is not likely to be completely general, but the basic concern is the large innovating firm who would have access to the same or greater economies of scale as any of the possible imitating firms.

If a firm decides to imitate, it must have a sufficient subjective belief in basically the same information as the innovating firm. The apparent cost of imitation would depend upon the complexity of the product, the current state of the firm's knowledge in the area of the product's related technology, and so forth. For example, the potential imitator must decide whether the technology for producing the product is apparent from the product. If not, how much further investigating is necessary to understand the new technology? Given that the copying firm feels it understands the technology, is it easily adaptable to its current physical and human resources? In other words, what are the costs of retooling the physical plant, the technocracy, the sales force, and the managers for the new product? Is this new product complementary to current areas of the imitating firm's endeavors and hence indicative that the costs of imitation would be less? For example, the new product might add to the completeness of a product line or be easily included in the current marketing processes.

A third question which is perhaps quite relevant to an imitating firm is that of new areas of technological expansion. Is this new and perhaps foreign area of technology a profitable one for expansion? It may be that by imitating a product in a new area of technology, the firm may gain experience that promises to be profitable in the future. Thus even though imitation results in a loss, it may represent the most efficient form of educating the members of a firm in a new area of technology. The loss from imitating may be much less expensive than the cost of training personnel by sending them to formal classes or the cost of expanding the group making up the firm to include those who were trained in this area. For example, General Electric Corporation has continually operated its information systems business at a loss. By their own statement, "Although experiencing current operating losses, the Company is establishing *a base* for profitable, worldwide participation in this key growth industry."[3]

Given that a firm has established a particular set of beliefs as to the product and its associated technology, the question of feasibility of imitation can be tackled. This will depend upon the profitability of imitating the product improvement in the context of other available alternatives open to the imitating firm. That is, determining the profitability determines only a parameter of the firm's objective function, and whether it will be carried out in the maximizing solution depends upon the other variables.

Model 8.2 is a specific analysis of the above aspects of firm imitation under simplified assumptions. The purpose of Model 8.2 is to demonstrate how firms will imitate and how an innovating firm would use such a model for estimating its market share function.

MODEL 8.2—Product imitation

Assume:

1. There is a given class of potential imitators consisting of p firms $f_1, \ldots, f_p$ which could affect the decision of the innovating firm f_o.
2. Each potential imitator f_i cannot improve technologically upon the new product other than differentiation in brand name, color, packaging, or the like. Each product imitation

3. 1968 Annual Report, General Electric Corporation, p. 16.

does not service the activity set more efficiently than does the product of the innovating firm.

3. $x_t^* P_t^*$ is the market revenue at time t, and this is solely determined by the price and nonprice offers of the innovating firm f_o. In other words, f_o is a price and advertising leader in the sense of influencing the market revenue function. Any advertising (or other nonprice offers) on the part of imitating firms serves only to alter the market shares of each firm, but does not influence the total market demand.

4. Each firm in the market can, by advertising enough, capture his share of the market, where

$$x_t^* P_t^* / N_t = \text{each firm's share of market revenue at time } t$$

$$N_t = \text{number of firms in the market at time } t$$

Furthermore, the functional relation between the imitating firms' advertising and their share of the market is such that if a firm enters the market at all, he will advertise up to the point that he obtains $x_t^* P_t^* / N_t$. The level of "competitive advertising" for market shares is dependent upon the level of market revenue $x_t^* P_t^*$ and hence determined by f_o's pricing and "informative advertising" policies. (A generalization of this assumption which is unnecessarily complicated for this model would be to let $\alpha_t^i (x_t^* P_t^*)$ be f_i's share of market revenue at time t, where $\alpha_t^i = h(x_c^o, \ldots, x_c^j)$; $x_c^j = $ competitive advertising by firm $j\epsilon(0, \ldots, r) = $ index sequence of those firms in the market.)

5. The index i assigned to an imitating firm f_i is such that for the level of output $\bar{x}_t^*$ the costs for f_i are less than or equal to f_{i+1}, that is,

$$C_o(\bar{x}_t^*) = \text{costs for innovating firm } f_o$$

$$C_1(\bar{x}_t^*) = \text{costs for closest imitator } f_1$$

$$C_p(\bar{x}_t^*) = \text{costs for farthest imitator } f_p$$

$$C_o(\bar{x}_t^*) \leqslant C_1(\bar{x}_t^*) \leqslant \cdots \leqslant C_p(\bar{x}_t^*), t > 0$$

a. At time $t = 0$ the costs to f_o include the cost of technological development and informative advertising to sell x_o^*. The costs after $t = 0$ would not entail additional development costs for f_o.

b. $C_o(x_t^*)$ is a nonincreasing function over time, $dC_o/dt \leqslant 0$.

c. $C_i(\bar{x}_t^*) = C_{i-1}(\bar{x}_{t-k_i}^*)$, $i = 1, \ldots, p$, where $0 \leqslant k_i < t$, and k_i is the time lag for firm i. This says that each firm can match the costs of the innovating firm after a sufficient time lag.

The impact of assumptions 4-5c is that "competitive advertising" is equal for each firm $f_o, \ldots, f_p$ if f_i is active in the market.

The potential profit for each firm at time t is given in assumption 6.

6. $\pi_t^i = \int_t^\infty e^{-\rho t} \left[(x_t^* P_t^* / N_t) - C_i(x_t^* / N_t) \right] dt$, where ρ = instantaneous rate of discount.

7. Each firm f_i has a best alternative profit level for the costs of producing $\bar{x}^* / N_t$, namely, $\bar{\pi}^i$. Each firm decides whether or not to enter the x^* market solely on the basis of π^i. Thus assumption 6 can be solved recursively by trial and error, where

$$\text{if } \pi_t^1 < \bar{\pi}^1, \qquad \text{then } N_t^1 = 1$$
$$\text{if } \pi_t^1 \geqslant \bar{\pi}^1, \qquad \text{then } N_t^1 = 2$$
$$\text{if } \pi_t^2 < \bar{\pi}^2, \qquad \text{then } N_t^2 = N_t^1$$
$$\text{if } \pi_t^2 \geqslant \bar{\pi}^2, \qquad \text{then } N_t^2 = N_t^1 + 1$$

$$\vdots$$

$$\text{if } \pi_t^{p^1} < \bar{\pi}^p, \qquad \text{then } N_t = N_t^{p-1}$$
$$\text{if } \pi_t^p \geqslant \bar{\pi}^p, \qquad \text{then } N_t = N_t^{p-1} + 1$$

As a numerical example, suppose there is only one time period so that

$$\pi^i = (x^* P^* / N) - C_i$$

and

$$x^* P^* = 100$$
$$C_1 = 10/N$$
$$C_2 = 15/N$$

Therefore, $\pi^1 = 90/N$, $\pi^2 = 85/N$. Suppose that $\bar{\pi}^1 = 50$, $\bar{\pi}^2 = 40$. Since π^1 will be 45 if f_1 enters and since $\pi^1 < \bar{\pi}^1$, f_1 will not enter. $\pi^2 = 42.5$, which is greater than $\bar{\pi}^2$ and f_2 therefore will enter. Consequently, $N = 2$.

Model 8.2 assumes that the imitating firms have some belief in what the market revenue will be for a product now and in the future. That is, in order to calculate π_t^i, $i \neq 0$, f_i must estimate $x_t^* P_t^*$ which was postulated as being controlled by the innovating firm. Empirical evidence in many markets where overexpansion occurs indicates that many imitating firms are overoptimistic as to either the future market revenue or their share of market revenue. On the other hand, in markets of complex technology empirical evidence suggests there is underexpansion which is due to either pessimism or technical inability to compete in these areas.[4] Consequently, the specific assumptions of firm learning and the spread of technology will determine the market structure and the profitability.

Prior to presenting some submodels of Model 8.2 which incorporate specific assumptions of firm learning, a few comments are in order. First, π_t^i in assumption 6 represents excess profits. The cost function would include all explicit and implicit costs to the firm such as market rate of return on capital and all development costs incurred by the firm.

At this point, a slight problem arises as to the rate of return on capital. A distinction is needed between ex ante or estimated excess profits and ex post or actual profits. For a potential market entrant the symbol π_t^i will denote assumed excess profits before entry at time t for firm i. The cost function would include the cost of procuring and maintaining both physical capital and technical members of the firm consistent with the firm's assumed market revenue share from the present to the future. After any firm has purchased specific physical capital for market entry, the relevant cost of capital for π_t^i is a bit different. The value of a piece of equipment, for example, is generally determined by its discounted future returns, where the discount rate is the market rate of interest. However, ex ante, both future returns and the market rate of interest are subjective quantities. Therefore, in the following analysis it will be assumed that physical capital is valued at cost of production, where competition operates to eliminate excess profits in the capital-producing industries. Different types of physical capital have different degrees of substitutability. A metal lathe may be as adaptable to producing automobiles as agricultural equipment, while a die formed to mold Hula-Hoops may be completely useless for anything else other than scrap. Therefore, physical capital once created will have some best alternative use or return at any point after its formation.[5] For completely adaptable capital this would be given in general by cost less depreciation. For completely unadaptable capital this would be close to zero, slightly positive for scrap value or even slightly negative for disposal costs.

In general then, the rate that determines the cost of capital to be included in the cost function would be the market rate of interest, with the value of capital defined as cost less any physical depreciation. Again physical depreciation is defined relative to the best alter-

4. Mansfield (1968a, 1968b, 1969) reports that the median expected rate of return on research and development expenditures is about 30 percent.
    5. See Bailey (1959).

native use. At any time after the specific physical capital has been created, its value is its best market price and the cost is this market value times the market rate of interest. In order to clarify this more precisely, the following examples are given. Consider a machine which is completely unadaptable and has disposal value of zero (scrap price minus disposal costs equal zero). The value of this machine is zero and its cost in assumption 6 is zero; it is a sunk cost. Alternatively, consider a metal lathe, used in the production of a novelty toy, which is completely adaptable to many other manufacturing processes. Suppose this machine physically depreciates at a uniform rate for five years. If its initial cost in a competitive market were $10,000, after one year of use it would have a market value of approximately $8,000. Since the market price would represent an aggregation of past and expected rates of inflation, if these were all zero the market value would be exactly $8,000. The cost in assumption 6 would be the market rate of interest times $8,000 plus depreciation for one more year of use.[6]

Models 8.3 and 8.4 develop the market structure for an innovated product. Specifically, they investigate the rate at which the market will expand, defined to mean the number of different firms in the market. The criterion of how well the market behaves for descriptive purposes will be as follows. Assume the rate of return on capital is the same in each market. In a partial equilibrium context, then, define optimal excess profits $(\pi_t^i)_o$, which is given by assumption 6 when x^*P^* is the actual market revenue and the cost function is defined as if the physical capital were perfectly adaptable and its cost is determined by the market rate of interest plus depreciation. If $(\pi_t^i)_o$ is positive for any i, the market is underexpanded at time t. If $(\pi_t^i)_o$ is negative for any i, the market is overexpanded at time t.

The above definition of market behavior argues that π_t^i should be sufficiently positive to induce firms to enter the market just fast enough so that if capital were perfectly liquid it could command no higher or lesser rate of return. Basically, this amounts to no more than arguing for market equilibrium both ex post and ex ante. No one firm benefits because the market fails to adjust, and no firm loses because the market overadjusts. If perfect information were available, the market would adjust so that $(\pi_t^i)_o = 0$ for all i and t.

MODEL 8.3—Naive imitators

In addition to the assumptions of Model 8.2, assume that each imitator at time t_o assumes that future market revenue is

6. The above cursory remarks of capital and investment theory can be contrasted to a plethora of literature. For example, see Haavelmo (1960), Dewey (1965), and Jorgenson and Stephenson (1967a, 1967b).

equal to the current level of market revenue, that is, each imitator assumes $x_t^* P_t^* = x_{t_o}^* P_{t_o}^*$.

Then if

$$d(x_t^* P_t^*)/dt > 0, \text{ underexpansion results} \qquad (8.8)$$

$$d(x^* P^*)/dt < 0, \text{ overexpansion results} \qquad (8.9)$$

In Equation 8.8 if ex ante π_t^i is positive then $(\pi_t^i)_o$ will be positive, as not enough firms will be entering the market. In Equation 8.9 if for some firms ex ante π_t^i is positive so that they enter the market, for some $t > t_o$, $(\pi_t^i)_o$ becomes negative. The duration of time that $(\pi_t^i)_o$ is negative will depend upon the adaptability of capital, that is, the difference between the long run and the short run. Thus with completely unadaptable capital a firm could enter the market, and even as $(\pi_t^i)_o$ became negative, π_t^i would remain positive for a time since such costs are irrelevant to π_t^i. Consequently, the market would have overexpanded at t_o due to the false assumptions of the imitating firm.

MODEL 8.4—Simple imitators

In addition to the assumptions of Model 8.2, assume that each potential firm is a linear extrapolator, that is, each firm at time t_o assumes

$$x_t^* P_t^* = t [d(x_t^* P_t^*)/dt]_{t=t_o} + C, C = \text{constant}$$

Each imitator assumes that future market revenue will follow a linear trend through time, where the slope of this trend is the current rate of change.

Then if for all $t \geqslant t_o$

$$d(x_t^* P_t^*)/dt > 0 \text{ and } d^2 (x_t^* P_t^*)/dt^2 < 0, \text{ overexpansion results}$$
$$(8.10)$$

$$d(x_t^* P_t^*)/dt \geqslant 0 \text{ and } d^2 (x_t^* P_t^*)/dt^2 > 0, \text{ underexpansion results}$$
$$(8.11)$$

$$d(x_t^* P_t^*)/dt < 0 \text{ and } d^2 (x_t^* P_t^*)/dt^2 < 0, \text{ underexpansion results}$$
$$(8.12)$$

$$d(x_t^* P_t^*)/dt \leqslant 0 \text{ and } d^2 (x_t^* P_t^*)/dt^2 > 0, \text{ overexpansion results}$$
$$(8.13)$$

In Equation 8.10 the firms are overoptimistic, as exemplified in Figure 8.4 where actual revenue follows a logarithmic path and firms calculate ex ante $\pi_{t_o}^i$ along a linear path. If this is sufficient to induce a number of firms to enter the market (that is, if imitators are not equally overoptimistic in each possible market), $(\pi_t^i)_o$ will become negative. Again as in Model 8.3, if capital is completely adaptable, $(\pi_t^i)_o = \pi_t^i$, and the firm will quickly leave the market with negligible private or social loss.

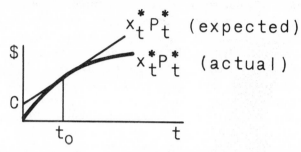

Fig. 8.4. Actual market revenue and linear estimated market revenue.

In Equation 8.11 this situation is just the opposite. Linear extrapolation underestimates the growth in market revenue, and consequently not enough firms enter the market.

Equations 8.12 and 8.13 are quite analogous to Equations 8.11 and 8.10 respectively, except that the market is declining and it is a question of how quickly firms drop out of the market. Still, if firms do not cease operating rapidly enough, the declining market will be overexpanded. If they drop out too fast, the market will be underexpanded. However, consideration of committed capital, nostalgia and intransigence, and other nonprofit objectives of firms would suggest the prevalence of an overexpanded declining market vis-à-vis an underexpanded one.

The results of Models 8.2–8.4 can be generalized in the following fashion. Errors in estimating could occur in any parameter or variable of the model; costs could be underestimated as well as market revenues. Therefore, if all firms underestimate profit levels in potential markets and do so nonuniformly, underexpansion will result. On the other side, if firms overestimate profit levels nonuniformly and capital is not completely adaptable, overexpansion is the consequence.

QUALIFICATIONS AND CONCLUSIONS
OF MODELS 8.2, 8.3, AND 8.4

The results above depend quite crucially upon the postulates and assumptions of the model. First, it is implicitly assumed that the innovating firm disseminates informative advertising that is valid. Consumers are free to decide whether or not to purchase the good x^*; and in evaluating the performance of the market under these conditions, the implication is that consumer decisions would not be improved if the informative advertising were different. In other words, the fact that commodity $x*$ is a bona fide technological improvement is postulated.

Second, it is implicitly assumed that competitive advertising is not a waste of social resources. The role and cost of competitive advertising to reduce excess profits in the market to the zero level raise serious questions. Specifically, the social loss of competitive advertising should be compared with the social loss of an underexpanded market. Wasting resources to bring the costs of production up and to eliminate excess profits is throwing out the baby with the wash water. However, in cases where both overexpansion and purely competitive advertising result there is a clear waste of resources.

Third, the assumption that the innovating firm f_o has complete control over both the market price and the volume of informative advertising reduces the generality of the models. Complete price leadership would imply that the innovating firm could match any price competition on the part of imitators to such an extent that they would be eliminated from the market. Consequently, the threat set with respect to price competition of the innovating firm must be perceived by the imitators as overwhelming, and their only variable is competitive advertising.

It is also interesting to note that under the assumptions of advertising and price leadership the amount of information flowing to the consumer is less than under pure monopoly but is more than under perfect competition, where it would be zero. Obviously, this is due to the public good characteristics (or nonownership properties) of information flows.

This can be shown by the Euler-Lagrange conditions for assumption 6 to be a maximum, that is, maximize

$$\pi_{t_o}^i = \int_{t_o}^\infty e^{-\rho t} \left[\frac{x*(x_c, P_t^*)\, P_t^*}{N(x_c, P^*)_t} - C_o(x_c, P^*) \right] dt$$

where x_c and P^* are the variables.

First-order conditions require

$$\frac{\partial F}{\partial x_c} = \frac{d}{dt} \left[\frac{\partial F}{\partial (dx_c/dt)} \right]$$

where F is the quantity under the integral sign. Since

$$\frac{\partial F}{\partial (dx_c/dt)} = 0$$

then

$$\frac{\partial C_c}{\partial x_c} = \frac{P_t^*(\partial x_t^*/\partial x_c)}{N_t} - \frac{x_t^* P_t^*(\partial N/\partial x_c)}{N_t^2}$$

The innovating firm will equate the marginal cost of informative advertising to $1/N$th of the marginal market revenue *less* the effect this has on bringing in other firms. Even if the number of firms in the market were fixed so that $\partial N/\partial x_c = 0$, the informative advertising would be $1/N$th of the level necessary to equal its marginal cost.

In order to maximize $\pi_{t_o}^o$ with respect to its price variable P_t^*, the innovating firm must empathize and assume how the imitators will react. The results of the naive Model 8.3 require

$$\frac{\partial C}{\partial P_t^*} = \frac{P_t^*(\partial x^*/\partial P_t^*)}{N_t} + \frac{x_t^*}{N_t} - \frac{P_t^* x_t^*(\partial N_t/\partial P_t^*)}{(N_t)^2} \qquad (8.14)$$

which states that the marginal cost of price change is equal to marginal revenue for f_o, less an allowance for bringing in additional firms.

Under the assumptions of Model 8.4 the conditions are quite complicated mathematically but are essentially equivalent to those of 8.3; namely, marginal cost is equated to marginal revenue less the effects of pricing on firm entry.[7]

Anyone interested enough to work it out should end up with the following necessary condition by assuming $N_t = N(x_c, P^*, \dot{P}^*)$, where $\dot{P}^* = dP^*/dt$ and $N_{x_c} = \partial N/\partial x_c$, and so forth:

$$C_{P*} = \frac{x}{N} + \frac{x_{P*} P^*}{N} - \frac{xP^* N_{P*}}{N^2} - P^* \frac{xP^* N_{P*}}{N^2} + \frac{P^* N_{P*} \dot{x}}{N^2} + \frac{x\dot{P}^* N_{P*}}{N^2} + \frac{xP^*}{N^2}$$

$$\times (N_{\dot{P}*_{x_c}} \dot{x}_c + N_{\dot{P}*\dot{P}*} \dot{P}^* + N_{\dot{P}*\ddot{P}*} \ddot{P}^*)$$

$$- \frac{2\,xP^* N_{\dot{P}*}}{N^3} (N_{x_c} \dot{x}_c + N_{P*} \dot{P}^* + N_{\dot{P}*} \ddot{P}^*) \qquad (8.15)$$

In general the welfare implications of the relative amounts of information flow are inscrutable without detailed information of the drive-reduction function. As analyzed in Chapter 3 there is no a priori correspondence between the activity mix selected before and

7. Very recently an analogous approach has been taken for deriving the conditions for monopoly to exist in a dynamic state, see Jen and Southwick (1969). Their approach limits the analysis to price competition and a declining cost function over time. Other general references in the area of traditional market competition are Chamberlin (1948), Bain (1956, 1959), Modigliani (1958), and Fellner (1965).

that selected after knowledge change, hence no correspondence between amounts purchased. However, by revealed preference those
who purchase the technologically improved product are better off
(or at the margin at least as well off), and there are two ways of passing along this benefit: (1) by reducing the price of x^* and (2) by informing more consumers. But without consumers being aware of
their potential satisfaction after a knowledge change or knowledge of
the cost of information, the revealed preferences have no relation to
changes in satisfaction.

Under Models 8.2, 8.3, and 8.4 the implications are clear for improved market structure. Adaptable capital is preferred to unadaptable capital. If a market becomes overexpanded, whether due to mis-
calculation by firms or to a change in consumer preferences,
adaptable capital not only avoids individual capital losses but also
saves social resources. Standardized machine parts, legal systems of
weights and measures, and uniform construction techniques are all
examples of social institutions which have developed to make capital
more adaptable. In part this is due to the private desire to avoid
personal losses, but the mere fact that capital needs to be adaptable
(that is, information is never perfect) would indicate a divergence in
social and private costs.

The second and more significant aspect of the models is the importance of information on social welfare. Information as to how
market revenue will respond to advertising and the degree of the
spread of technological knowledge are vital to ensure dynamically
optimal market structure. Information as to how firms learn and
how individuals learn of the benefits of technological change could
significantly improve the operation and competitive nature of the
market. When change occurs, planning and coordination are not only
vital but crucial to the existence of complex technological production methods and techniques. Statements which express the idea
that all information can be transmitted by means of a single price are
ludicrous.[8]

The next step in the analysis is to generalize Models 8.2, 8.3, and
8.4 in several directions. Essentially, the assumption that one firm
controls both price and informative advertising will be eliminated.
Model 8.5 assumes that the competing firms are selling commodities
with different durabilities. Before proceeding with Model 8.5, a
digression on consumer demand for durable goods is necessary.

8. Cf., for example, Koopmans (1957), Galbraith (1967) and Hurwicz
(1969) for discussion of the information transmission by prices and the other
references cited therein.

SOME ASPECTS OF COMMON DURABLE DEMAND

For a durable good in a market of zero costs of trading, the consumer is buying units of services over time.[9] Given a psychological rate of discount ρ, the purchase of one unit of the durable good is equivalent to the purchase of Q_N units of services, where

$$Q_N = \int_{o}^{N} e^{-\rho t}\, dt = (1/\rho)(1 - e^{-\rho N}) \qquad (8.16)$$

That is, Q_N is the present value of service units contained in a durable good, with a durability of N years yielding one unit of service per year.

If we let p be the rental rate of one unit of the durable good, the quantity rented per unit of time y is determined by the demand function $f(p)$, that is,

$$y = f(p) \qquad (8.17)$$

The present value or market price P_N of an N-year durable good is equal to $Q_N p$, that is,

$$P_N = \int_{0}^{N} e^{-\rho t} p\, dt = Q_N p \qquad (8.18)$$

assuming the rental rate constant over the N-year period. Therefore, we have

$$p = P_N / Q_N \qquad (8.19)$$

and

$$y = f(P_N / Q_N) \qquad (8.20)$$

Suppose that the durability of the good (N) were to change. Under what conditions would the quantity sold remain the same and the price be increased? To solve this, differentiate y with respect to N and set it equal to zero:

$$dy/dN = f\left[\frac{dP_N/dN}{Q_N} - \frac{P_N(dQ_N/dN)}{Q_N^2} \right] = 0 \qquad (8.21)$$

9. Cf. Levhari and Srinivasan (1969) and Swan (1970) for their treatment of durable-good marketing.

Since $dQ_N/dN = e^{-\rho N}$, we have

$$\frac{dP_N/dN}{Q_N} - \frac{P_N e^{-\rho N}}{Q_N^2} = 0 \qquad (8.22)$$

$$dP_N/dN = \frac{P_N e^{-\rho N}}{Q_N^2} > 0 \qquad (8.23)$$

Thus an increase in durability will increase market price as long as the rental rate p is positive.

As a basis for competition, different firms could offer commodities of differing durabilities. The question is, Can the demand curve $f(P_N/Q)$ be segregated by offering goods of varying durability? Q^i for each i will depend upon the perceived service flow x^i and the individual's psychological rate of discount ρ_i. Therefore, if a perfect capital market exists as in Fisher's analysis[10] and if there is no uncertainty, everyone will adjust consumption until his psychological rate of discount is equal to the market rate of discount.

Consequently, if everyone also views x as being the same, $Q^i = Q^j$ for all consumers. It follows that if goods of differing durability and prices are offered, each consumer will select the best buy. If the range of durability is continuous each will equate

$$dP_N/dN = (P_N/Q)\,(dQ/dN)$$

It is therefore not possible to separate the demand schedule under these conditions, and thus this will not provide a basis for product differentiation.

One method of separating the demand for durables would be to limit the range of durable goods available. In Figure 8.5 the demand

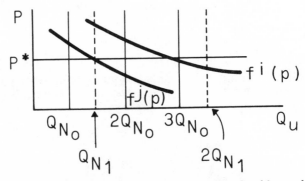

Fig. 8.5. Consumers' demands for indivisible durable goods.

10. See Fisher (1930); also see Hirshleifer (1958) and Bailey (1959) for updated treatments of Fisher's analysis.

curves for individuals i and j are represented as if goods of any durability were available. If only two goods providing service x are available, each consumer must purchase Q in discrete multiples of Q_{N_o} or Q_{N_1}, where $N_1 > N_o$. At the rental price of p^*, consumer j will purchase one unit of the good with life N_1, while i will purchase three units of N_o-year durable good. If p^* is increased slightly, it is impossible to say what each consumer will do. Clearly, each consumer will be off his demand curve, and which durability at what quantity he will procure will depend upon his specific drive-reduction function.[11]

The result will be that in general in the market two distinct demand curves will exist for the goods with different durabilities. It would then be possible for a monopolist or for competitive firms to differentiate on the basis of durability. This would be more likely if there were large economies of scale in producing one kind of durable good.

Another method of generating distinct demand curves for goods of different durability would be to alter the information flow as to the actual number of service units contained in each good and as to the actual life of each durable good. Different individuals will have different initial assumptions as to the life or service flow of a good. By advertising, firms can alter these beliefs as analyzed in Chapter 4. Since $Q^i = x^i(1 - e^{\rho_i N_i})/\rho_i$, as the firm is able to alter consumer i's opinion of x^i and N_i, the quantity Q^i will change. Firms will develop consumer loyalties on the basis that each individual purchasing a particular brand will believe that he is getting the "best buy." From the conditions stated in Equations 8.14 and 8.15, the feasibility of either actually increasing the durability and service flow or using information methods so that consumers believe a firm's good has more depends upon the price elasticity of demand η. Specifically, differentiation is only possible if $\eta > 1$, which is a familiar condition for a monopolist who is maximizing profits. Brand names, specific firm advertising expenditures, and so forth, are only feasible if the price elasticity of quantity demand is greater than one.

In the following model, these aspects of consumer demand will be given general consideration.

MODEL 8.5—Differential marketing game

Assume there are two firms in the economy capable of producing durable goods which will yield a service flow x. This

---

11. This is a familiar problem in integer programming. See, for example, Hadley (1964).

service flow is a constant rate over time regardless of the durability. Assume further that all consumers know this, and their belief in the service flow is unalterable by any form of a nonprice or price offer variation. However, for each consumer i the years of durability that he believes are contained in a firm's product depend upon the built-in durability $\bar{N}$ and the amount of information x_c he receives, that is,

$$N_i = g(\bar{N}, x_c) \qquad (8.24)$$

The following variables relate to firm f^o and firm f':

y = quantity sold by f^o

y' = quantity sold by f'

N = durability of f^o's product

N' = durability of f''s product

$x = x' \equiv 1$ = advertising expenditure by f^o and f'

P_N = price of N-year durable good

From Model 8.2:

$$\pi_{t_o}^o = \int_{t_o}^{\infty} e^{-\rho t} \, [y_t P_{N_t} - C(x_c, \bar{N}, P_{N_t})] \, dt \qquad (8.25)$$

is the present value of profits for firm f^o, where

$$y = \sum_{i=1}^{n} \frac{f_t^i(P_{N_t}/Q_N)}{Q_N^i} \text{ such that } P_N/Q_N^i < P_N'/Q_N^i{}' \text{ for all } i \qquad (8.26)$$

Equation 8.26, the sum of consumer demands for y, implies that y and y' are perfectly divisible. In other words, each consumer purchases y from firm f^o if he believes he is getting the best buy, that being the lowest implicit rental rate for the service flow. Q_N^i is the present value of services in one unit of y, that is,

$$Q_N^i = (1 - e^{-\rho_i N_i})/\rho_i \qquad (8.27)$$

Assume $\rho_i = \rho_j$ for all i and j. Combining Equations 8.24–8.27, y_t can be written as

$$y_t = f(P_N, P_N', \bar{N}, \bar{N}', x_c, x_c') \qquad (8.28)$$

or the quantity sold at time t depends upon the control variables of both firms, f^o and f'.

Assume that the sum of excess profits is distributed such that the goal of f' is to minimize π_t^o, while f^o wants to maximize π_t^o.

For any given level of market revenue it always behooves f' to reduce f^o's excess profits as much as possible. The cases excluded by this assumption (that is, where if f' maximizes π' does not imply that f' minimizes π^o) can be analyzed partially under an assumption of monopoly. In other words, cases where it is better to live and let live can often be analyzed as collusion, albeit implicit.

For simplification it will be assumed that either firm can instantaneously adjust any of its control variables, namely, x_c, $\overline{N}$, P_N for f^o and x'_c, $\overline{N}'$, P_N' for f'. From the assumptions of Model 8.4, differential game theory can now be applied.[12]

In general let

$X \equiv (x_1, \ldots, x_n) \equiv$ state variables describing the condition of the market

$X^o \equiv (x_1^o, \ldots, x_n^o) \equiv$ initial conditions

$\phi \equiv (\phi_1, \ldots, \phi_\lambda) \equiv$ control variables for f'

$\psi \equiv (\psi_1, \ldots, \psi_k) \equiv$ control variables for f^o

Each control variable is subject to some constraint depending upon the state of the market.

$$[a_i(X) \leqslant \phi_i \leqslant b_i(X)]$$

and

$$[c_i(X) \leqslant \psi_i \leqslant d_i(X)] \tag{8.29}$$

Assume that the change in the state variables $(dx_j/dt = x_j)$ can be represented by

$$\dot{x}_j = f_j(x_1, \ldots, x_n, \phi_1, \ldots, \phi_\lambda, \psi_1, \ldots, \psi_k), \quad j = 1, \ldots, n$$

or

$$\dot{X} = f(X, \phi, \psi) \tag{8.30}$$

Since the payoff can be represented as $\pi_f^o \equiv \int G(X, \phi, \psi)\, dt$, then by defining an additional state variable,

$$\dot{x}_{n+1} = G(X, \phi, \psi) \tag{8.31}$$

---

12. The following is adapted directly from Isaacs (1965). Differential game theory, the approach of Pontryagin, et al. (1962) (as well as several other analyses of paths of state variables subject to control), and the classical calculus of variations are similar in subject matter but vary in generality and emphasis. Differential game theory has the advantage of incorporating the classical theory of games developed by von Neumann and Morgenstern (1947).

then

$$x_{n+1} - x_{n+1}^o = \int G(X, \phi, \psi)\, dt \qquad (8.32)$$

The value of the game between f^o and f' is defined as

$$\min_{\phi} \max_{\psi} \pi_{t_o} = V(X^o)$$

from which it follows directly that

$$G(X, \phi, \psi) - \Sigma\, V_j f_j(X, \phi, \psi) = 0 \qquad (8.33)$$

where $V_j = \partial V/\partial x_j$. Further, if $\overline{\psi}$ and $\overline{\phi}$ are the optimal strategies for f' and f^o, differentiating Equation 8.33 with respect to x_k, $k = 1, \ldots, n$ results in the system of equations:

$$G_k(X, \overline{\phi}, \overline{\psi}) - \sum_j V_{jk} f_j(X, \overline{\phi}, \overline{\psi}) - \sum_j V_j f_{jk}(X, \overline{\phi}, \overline{\psi}) = 0$$

Since $V_{jk} = V_{kj}$, then

$$\sum_j V_{jk} f_j(X, \overline{\phi}, \overline{\psi}) = \sum_j V_{kj} f_j(X, \overline{\phi}, \overline{\psi})$$

and substituting $\dot{x}_j = f_j(X, \overline{\phi}, \overline{\psi})$, we have

$$\sum_j V_{jk} f_j(X, \overline{\phi}, \overline{\psi}) = \sum_j V_{kj} \dot{x}_j = V_k \qquad (8.34)$$

From Equation 8.34 then

$$\dot{V}_k = \left[G_k(X, \overline{\phi}, \overline{\psi}) - \sum_j V_j f_{jk}(X, \overline{\phi}, \overline{\psi}) \right] \qquad (8.35)$$

The systems of Equations 8.28 and 8.35 describe the path of the game or the outcome of this two-firm competition for excess profits if both firms play optimally. By allowing instantaneous strategy adjustment within some constraints (Equation 8.29), the optimal strategy for either firm is to begin under the assumption that the other firm will play optimally. The instant that a firm, f^o say, has information that his opponent in this marketing game is not playing optimally, f^o can adjust his strategies and come out with more than the value of the game.

The difference between Model 8.2 and Model 8.3 is in the responsiveness of the competing firms. Essentially Model 8.2 is analogous to the classical calculus of variations where the path of the innovating firm's profits was solely determined by its actions. In Model 8.2 the strategies of the imitating firms were functionally related to the actions of the innovating firm. In Model 8.5, the path of f^o's excess profits is actively affected by the actions of both f^o and f'. This is illustrated in Figure 8.6. Path A results if both players play optimally. Path B results if f' does not play optimally, and path C results if f^o does not play optimally and f' takes advantage of f^o's mistakes.

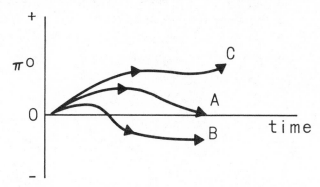

Fig. 8.6. Illustration of optimal and nonoptimal paths of profit over time.

Model 8.5 can be expanded to any number of firms. If one thinks of the sum of excess profits in an economy as being equal to zero and each firm is trying to maximize its own excess profits, the aggregate of other firms can be described as an opposing player whose goal is to minimize that firm's profits.

In terms of the evaluation of the performance of the market from a social standpoint as analyzed in Model 8.2, a market structure can be defined as socially optimal in terms of Model 8.5 if the value of the game is equal to zero and, further, if all participants do in fact play optimally. This requires that the control variables available to the various firms be sufficiently broad to permit this. It also requires a certain degree of information on the part of all participants so that they do play optimally. When the opposing player is an aggregate of firms in general, this would require coordination of independent strategies which may or may not be optimally transmitted by a price system alone. To enhance the social optimality of a given market structure, it may be desirable to require disclosure of advertising methods and volumes, for example. These types of information necessary for socially optimal market performance are often intractable from market prices alone.

SUMMARY

This chapter has presented selected theoretical models of particular markets and market structures, where the flow of information is crucial to the firm attempting to maximize profits. The flow and quality of information is also important to the concept of social welfare. In particular, this chapter has emphasized product innovation and imitation by other firms. It is in this area that information flows are particularly acute. In Models 8.1–8.5 the flow of information determined whether the marketing process would be quite wasteful of resources. The models are not comprehensive of the spectrum of types of markets, but they are indicative.

chapter 9

The Degree of Competition in the Market

FROM THE MODELS developed in the foregoing chapters, it is now possible to categorize some of the facets of commodity exchange. In particular, this chapter is devoted to an assessment of the degree of competitiveness in particular commodity markets. As in the previous chapter it will be assumed that the social system has established institutions for teaching similar to those current in Western societies. This is important to a theory of social process for two related reasons. First, the degree of competition in relative markets will determine the profitability for those engaged in these markets and hence their relative accumulation of wealth over time. Second, the control of market structures by a societal unit (that is, antitrust laws, public regulation, the nationalization of particular industries) represents a threat set on the part of society against those firms. For a more rational decision on market control, it is useful to consider the degree of competition among both suppliers and demanders in light of the foregoing theoretical development.

PRODUCT CHARACTERISTICS INFLUENCING MARKET STRUCTURE

For any given product there are several aspects of the product itself and of the interacting groups and individuals involved in the process of exchange which influence market structure. First, there are a number of different activities potentially serviced by the product. Second, there is a diversity of use by consumers. Further, there is the variable life or durability of each characteristic contained in the product. A good may have the physical properties of a purely public good or it may be a good with external effects.[1] These as-

1. Cf. the development in Chapter 6.

pects will determine the feasibility on the demand side of cooperative provision vis-à-vis private provision of the good. The technology at any point in time will affect the feasibility and cost of combining or separating a product's services into one or many commodities. In light of these considerations each product will have various substitutes and complements.

From the supply side of the market there will be some number of firms competing with like or similar products in each of the above areas, and these firms will have in general a multiproduct line influencing their supplies. Finally, the degree of abstrusity or obviousness of each of these factors will be influential in determining the nature of the marketing process.

FACETS OF MARKET DEMAND

In Chapter 3, x_j was defined as a purely general good if

$$x_j^* = \max_{i \in n_o} x_j^i \qquad (9.1)$$

where n_o is the number of activities using x_j, x_j^i is the amount of commodity j necessary to fulfill activity w_i, and x_j^* is the amount of x_j exchanged in the market.

On the other hand, x_j is a purely divisible good if

$$x_j^* = \sum_{i=1}^{n} x_j^i \qquad (9.2)$$

If $n = 1$, Equation 9.1 and 9.2 are equivalent, and commodity x_j services only one activity, even though it is potentially either purely general or purely divisible. Further, if this holds for all goods j, for all consumers, and for all activity levels, then by assuming full information, the above reduces to the usual demand analysis. That is, for each consumer, if $S = \phi(w_1, \ldots, w_n, \omega_1, \ldots, \omega_m)$ and $w_i = w_i(x_j)$ for $i = 1, \ldots, n, j = 1, \ldots, k$; then one may write

$$S = \phi^*(x_1, \ldots, x_n, \omega_1, \ldots, \omega_m)$$

If the time constraint is not binding, then the noneconomic activities can be ignored, and thus $S = U(x_1, \ldots, x_n)$ is maximized subject to $\Sigma p_i x_i \leqslant 0$.

If $i > 1$, a commodity can service more than one activity. If x_j is a purely general good, the amount purchased will be determined by one activity. If $\max_{i \in n_o} x_j^i$ is unique, all other activities w_i, such that

$i \epsilon n_o$, could be increased or decreased and the amount of x_j exchanged would be the same.

Consider an automobile, for example; a typical one will service several activities. A variety of transportation needs can be fulfilled. In an institutional framework such as current society, it also conveys certain information to other individuals. That is, since the prices in a market are generally known and an individual is subject to a budget constraint, the automobile denotes individual wealth. Consequently, it conveys status.

An automobile also provides a degree of comfort depending upon the construction, weight, and upholstery. Similarly, it could service an entertainment activity such as driving for pleasure or sport, listening to the radio, or dating. The list could be extended indefinitely, depending upon the particular automobile and individual. An automobile may be aesthetically pleasing as a model of craftsmanship and mechanical genius. (It could be just the opposite, of course —aesthetically displeasing and an abominable combination of mechanical ineptitude.)

Suppose for a consumer the automobile is a purely general good and his demand is determined by the transportation activity alone. For another consumer suppose the demand is determined solely by the status-fulfilling properties of an automobile. For the first individual, close substitutes might be airline and train tickets, rental automobiles, or the subway. For the second, however, close substitutes might be a new home, a mink coat for his wife, a private school for his children, or a donation to the local library. The point is that if there is only a single automobile producer in the economy, he may be a monopolist in the eyes of the first individual and a perfect or monopolistic competitor in the eyes of the second.

More generally then, consider the situation where x_j is a purely general good and $\max_{i \epsilon n_o} x_j^i$ is unique for each decision unit. The aggregate demand for x_j will be composed of demands for the various activity-servicing characteristics of x_j. That is, if x_{ji}^k is the consumption of good x_j by activity k by the ith decision unit, the demand for the general good x_j by the ith decision unit is $x_{ji}^{k*} = \max_k x_{ji}^k$. Total demand x_j^* will be the sum total from all decision units,

$$x_j^* = \sum_{k^*} \sum_i x_{ji}^{k*}$$

The decision units could be singular individuals, families, or other organizations depending upon dimensions of x_j such as public good characteristics or externalities.

Alternatively and more relevant for a discussion of market structure, decision units can be arranged according to the purpose for which activity x_j is used. Let

$$x_j^{k*} = \sum_i x_{ji}^{k*}$$

then x_j^{k*} is the demand for x_j directly dependent upon activity $k*$, and hence

$$x_j^* = \sum_{k*} x_j^{k*} = \sum_{k*} \sum_i x_{ji}^{k*}$$

The set of individual units which comprise the demand for x_j due to the $k*$ activity (that is, those whose demand is x_j^{k*}) will be called a consumer group. Different consumer groups will in general be affected differently by a price change in x_j. Those who use x_j in an activity to which it is essential will, other things being equal, be willing to pay a higher price than those who use x_j in an activity for which x_j is not necessary. And this in turn determines in part the willingness and ability of particular consumer groups to coalesce and influence the social institutions which govern markets.

A commodity x_j will be defined as a vital commodity for activity w_i if $w_i = w_i(x_1, \ldots, x_k)$ and, if x_j is less than some constant, then $w_i = 0$. Alternatively, x_j is a nonvital commodity if $x_j = 0$ does not imply $w_i = 0$. A vital commodity must be present in a minimal amount ($x_j \geqslant$ constant) for the activity to be carried out at all. Since any definition of a commodity is an arbitrary aggregation, how vital any particular commodity is will depend on that definition. For example, if w_i is the activity of eating, the commodity sirloin steak would be nonvital for most people, while the commodity food would be a vital commodity for eating.

All this implies that substitution of one commodity for another in response to a price change would be composed of two effects: intraactivity substitution and interactivity substitution. In general one would expect nonvital commodities to have close substitutes (particularly at their minimal levels), while vital commodities would not. In addition nonvital commodities would have a relatively inelastic demand. This is because a vital commodity at its minimal level does not permit intraactivity substitution, and interactivity substitution would not only be spread over all other activities but over all other commodities utilized in the various activities as well. Clearly, however, these generalities need not hold in special cases.

This difference in use of x_j provides an impetus for product variation. If x_j is a purely general good and uniquely determined by one activity, the price is relevant to the $k*$ characteristic of the commodity. For any decision unit in the $k*$ consumer group let $w_{k*}^i = w_{k*}^i (x_1, \ldots, x_p)$; w_{k*}^i is the activity w_{k*} of the ith consumer. Holding constant all x_g, $g = 1, \ldots, p$, where $g \neq j$, then

$$x_{ji}^{k*} = w_{k*}^{i}{}^{-1} (w_{k*}^i)$$

Thus the demand by the $k*$ consumer group can be expressed as

$$x_j^{k*} = \sum_i x_{ji}^{k*} = \sum_{k*} \sum_i x_{ji}^{k*} = \sum_{k*} \sum_i w_{k*}^{i}{}^{-1} (w_{k*}^i)$$

x_j is now defined in physical units as a measurable commodity exchanged containing activity-servicing characteristics. Thus if a firm could vary the characteristics of the product x_j and offer product variations (a physical commodity which contains all the characteristics of x_j but indifferent quantities), the number of different "models" of x_j a firm would find most profitable would depend upon the economies of producing different quantities of each "model"; the elasticity of demand by each consumer group; and the economies and cross relations with other commodities, information flows, and other technical relations within the firm.

If, on the other hand, x_j is a purely divisible good, a change in the price of x_j will change the price of each activity which x_j services for an individual. In this case aggregate demand will not be partitionable in general into consumer groups, since each decision unit will use the commodity in several activities. However, it is still possible for product variations to exist both within a firm and among firms, depending upon the economies of scale and characteristic combinations. For example, with constant returns to scale and a given price for x_j, the firm would vary the characteristic combination for each product variant until the marginal revenue from doing so equaled marginal cost. Consequently, if the characteristics of x_j could be changed with zero marginal cost within some limits, the firm would vary the characteristic combination on each model $i = 1, \ldots, n_o$, until the implicit cost was lowest.

For example, suppose there is a linear relation between w_i and x_j, that is, $a_i = w_i/x_j$. a_i is the level of activity w_i which is feasible with product x_j or a variant of x_j. Further assume that x_j services n_o different activities, and there is some minimal level at which the firm can set each a_i. Given zero marginal cost of characteristic change, this technolgoical combination is subject to the following restriction:

$$\sum_{i=1}^{n_o} a_i = \text{constant}, \qquad a_i \geqslant a_{i_o}$$

Since

$$Pw_i = P_j x_j / w_i = P_j / a_i$$

for model i, the firm would set

$$a_i = 1 - \sum_{j \neq i}^{n_o} a_{jo}$$

and $a_j = a_{jo}$ for $j \neq i$, and this would hold for all models $i = 1, \ldots, n_o$.

To illustrate this point, assume that shoes are purely divisible and can service either work or leisure activities. By definition of a purely divisible good, once these shoes are used for one activity they cannot be used for another. This does not preclude them from being a durable good, however. Therefore, shoes used in a work activity w_1 become unacceptable for leisure w_2. Suppose that the restrictions are $a_1 + a_2 = 1$, $a_1 \geqslant a_{2_o} = .2$, and $a_2 \geqslant a_{2_o} = .3$. Then for the work shoe $a_1 = .7$ and $a_2 = .3$ and for the leisure shoe $a_1 = .2$ and $a_2 = .8$.

FACETS OF THE MARKET SUPPLY

From the analysis of Chapters 7 and 8 the size of a firm, and hence the number of firms in any commodity market, is dependent upon the following technological aspects at any point in time.

1. Economies of division of labor which include:
   a. economies of scale with respect to current production
   b. economies of scale with respect to future production
   c. economies of research and development
   d. economies of finance
2. Economies of information both to the firm and from the firm to the market.
3. Economies of stability through planning and diversity.

In addition, the institutions which exist in a social system may alter the number and size of firms. For example, whether some group is able to pass and enforce antitrust or certain tax legislation and such things as property, patent, and copyright laws will clearly affect the number of firms in a market. It is also shown in Chapter 7 that the number of firms which would result in any social system is

in some respects optimal. If all members of a firm are solely interested in maximizing income and information is sufficiently general,
the number of firms in equilibrium will be efficiently optimal with
respect to the existing threat sets and given institutions (for example,
patents or property rights). If all members are not solely intent on income maximization, the number and size of firms will be optimal in
the sense that no better combination of individuals exists for those
engaged in the production activity. This must be considered relative
to given threat sets and their interaction with institutions and the
knowledge sets of the various individuals.

Thus laws such as antitrust legislation are part of the remainder
of society's threat set which can and will be invoked if necessary.
Formal laws are a specific social institution altering the freedom of
individuals.   Such laws are a specific threat with specified consequences upon violation and conviction. Clearly, these threats are
valid if they can be enforced, otherwise they are merely idle ones.

The "best" market structure is not clear. In fact, this question is
completely confounded with the question of the best or proper distribution of property ownership and property rights. Just property
rights are a value judgment which cannot be divorced from the particular history of a social system, *unless* society in its entirety can
adopt higher ordered value judgments, such as social viability or technological growth, which dictate a necessary distribution of rights to
property. Chapter 10 is an abstract elaboration on these and related
points.

Until these axioms of social progress are forthcoming, the role of
an economist (or any scientist for that matter) in a social system is
limited to improving the state of knowledge so that individuals can
make more rational decisions with respect to formal laws, informal
rules of conduct, social sanction, and the like, which a social system
adopts.

Traditional economic welfare analysis demonstrates that under a
given and quite institutional framework monopolies do not produce
as much output as would a system of many producers who were
price takers rather than price setters.[2]   These rules of social welfare
adopted by traditional economic theory are very heavily entrenched
in an institutional framework, and to alter that framework makes
some individuals worse off than they were before. A change in the
institutional structure which generates few firms to one where many
firms exist requires a change in the parameters which individuals
accept. Those who maximize with respect to one set of institutional

2. Further detail can be found in many sources, for example, Samuelson
(1947), Ch. 8, and Koopmans (1957).

constraints will be harmed if additional constraints limit some of their previous activities, and everyone must learn new "rules of the game." Thus to favor antitrust legislation, for example, an individual does not identify with monopolies.

Another way of viewing the foregoing argument is that commodities are not the sole factor in determining the drive reduction of individuals in a social system. Various other activities also determine that individual's satisfaction. Therefore, to make a statement that everyone will be better off must include these other facets of life that individuals manipulate.

The only feasible way everyone's situation can simultaneously be enhanced is by improving knowledge; that is, to show how an individual or group can attain a given basic goal in a more efficient manner. Among other things this requires consensus on what are basic goals and what merely are derived goals of individuals. For example, racial discrimination may be a derived goal of a desire for security, whereas its consequences are in general quite the contrary in the long run. This in turn requires questioning of the factors which initially determine the knowledge sets of individuals.

SUMMARY

This chapter has done only lip service to the question of market structures and their effects on society. There is a great deal more to be said about each point raised here and others which have been bypassed. However, since the particular aspects of market structures, such as oligopoly versus monopolistic competition, require a treatise of their own and since the broad characteristics suffice for the purposes here, we now turn to social institutions in general.

chapter 10

The Interaction of Groups and Individuals in the Social Process

A SOCIAL SYSTEM is comprised of individuals, acting as individuals or contributing to and participating in group actions. A group is a set of individuals isolated so that they may take advantage of the benefits of personal interaction. Groups which interact as a group with those outside are coalitions. Therefore, the interaction between coalitions and individuals create and determine the nature of the social system. Their interaction produces institutions functioning to enhance this interaction. In precisely the same way that individuals acquiesce to a group environment, various groups and individuals exchange and develop methods of communication on more aggregate levels.

Firms and individuals form a market, and an aggregation of similar markets constitutes an industry. Industries constitute an economy. Local political parties act as a group for special interests in higher level aggregations. Cities, counties, states, and nations are higher levels of this agglomeration process. And so the process goes for any type of organizational structure.

Through the interaction of these organizations and singular individuals the social fabric is woven: a myriad of institutions carrying out their various functions. One question of prime concern is the relevancy and stability of these social superstructures which so greatly affect the individual decision-making processes and consequently play a central role in the course of social systems.[1]

---

1. Rigorous theoretical literature in this area is particularly sparse. See, e.g., Kornhauser (1959), Smelser (1963), Etzioni and Etzioni (1964), Etzioni (1968), and Breton and Breton (1969) for other approaches to a theory of social change.

TYPES OF INSTITUTIONS

Some insight into this and other related questions can be derived from the analysis of the underlying forces operating in the social system and from consideration of the functions these structures serve. As delineated in Chapter 7, institutions (1) provide information; (2) serve as constraints, either absolute or tolerant; and (3) make personal interaction more efficient by being a manifestation of one type of technological change. Consequently, the viability of any institution will depend upon its usefulness relative to its necessity for social interaction.

Consider, for example, an institution of type 1 which provides information. If this information is deemed no longer necessary, the institution will come under pressure to be eliminated or changed. That is, if an old institution specified f in $w_j^g = f(w_j^i)$, and if w_j^g was no longer a relevant activity to individual i, the institution becomes unnecessary for i. Since the usual advantages of institutions are that they serve large numbers of people, as these institutions become irrelevant for some they may remain valuable to others. If these institutions require resources for maintenance, a conflict could develop, with some favoring its elimination and others favoring its retention. Thus a bargaining process will result. The elimination or change of an institution will be blocked only if the groups adversely affected possess the requisite threat sets as analyzed in previous chapters. In a social framework the groups include singular persons and coalitions acting as single units.

As an example, consider the evolutionary changes in the institution of proper dress and its informative properties. As well stated by Veblen (1899), the existence of constraining attire is clear evidence that one is not engaging in heavy manual labor. As the wealth of the society increases, a greater percentage of its members can participate in leisure activities. There is an associated demise in the informational properties of certain styles of dress. Consequently, there is both pressure and resistance to change what is "proper dress." Those who do not perceive of the change in the informational qualities of an institution or who would be harmed by its change resist it. Others who perceive waste in something, which for them has become irrelevant, press for change. In this particular vein there are many examples ranging from white dresses connoting virginity in the antebellum South, to coat and white tie affairs, to styles of swimming apparel, to almost every "convention" of dress over time.

Another example of such institutions is in the area of speech. Clearly, conventions for writing and speaking are efficient compared to no rules for punctuation or intonation. Further than that, the level of speech, in terms of the kinds of words and phrases used, has been and is indicative of the level of friendship or the degree of knowledge about each other in a group. In other words, the social institution as a tacit and efficient transmitter of information has resulted in words having private or internalized meanings in addition to their public or definitional meaning. "Noun" is a word with little private meaning, while "mother" induces a host of private associations. Eminently illustrative of the institutional processes relegating language to implicit as well as explicit forms of communication is the word "fuck." A simple word, yet its use has traditionally indicated a host of relationships among individuals aside from its literal meaning of sexual intercourse. The whole objective of the free speech movement has been to point out that institutions which make the word "fuck" indicative of so many personal attributes and characteristics do not provide a very adequate method of judging the character of an individual. And while this institution may be efficient, it is grossly limited in the volume and relevancy of information which it can convey.

One further aspect more likely to be found in institutions (as opposed to simpler, personal interaction mechanisms) is that since the institution must provide information, it often does so by eliminating other types of information sources. Institutions are often constructed with built-in defense mechanisms initially designed to efficiently produce the desired social effect. However, this aspect is another facet of the existing threat sets available to the members of the social group.

To elucidate this point, think of a hypothetical primitive tribe which initially creates a religious creed and authorizes a medicine man to ward off evil spirits for all. In this way each individual will not have to do it himself, and thus the other members of the group can devote more time to raising cattle. Concomitantly, suppose the medicine man is authorized by this institution to kill those members of the tribe who become infected with the dreaded evil spirits. Clearly, this institutional arrangement vests a substantial threat set in the person of the medicine man. If some individual feels that evil spirits do not exist (are not relevant information) and favors change, he can be eliminated directly because of the institutional provision of threat sets to particular individuals. The point being that institutions themselves are often a source of threat sets.[2]

Another reason for institutional change could emanate from a

2. This explanation of the intransigence of primitive cultures has overwhelming empirical consistency. For example, see Fortes (1965), Murdock (1959), and Southall (1961).

change in technology. Specifically, assume that from individual i's and individual g's drive-reduction function both would be better off if an institution specifying f were transformed to f^*, that is

$w_j^g = f(w_k^j)$, under the old institution

$w_j^g = f^*(w_k^j)$, under a new institution

The process of the institutional change would depend upon those affected and their response to a potential change in the institution. The formal analysis is equivalent to that of a group selection of a public good in Chapter 6. That is, the institution specifies interacting activity effects and responses; as such, both are better off. By its very nature the good is a public good; it affects everyone equally. Consequently, the process will depend upon the threat sets and other institutions in existence at the time.

In the case of type 2 or constraining institutions, the constraint aspect can become no longer necessary or can need alteration in the social decorum for reasons similar to those above. The society could agree to constrain particular activities under one knowledge set that it would find no longer necessary to constrain under an altered knowledge set. Also, at one level of wealth the social system may find it vital to its very existence to constrain many activities. However, with capital accumulation and technological advance, expanded consumption and activity sets become feasible. Consequently, the members of the social system may find it beneficial to "buy back" the constraints which have been partially responsible for the increased affluence.

THE RELEVANCY OF INSTITUTIONS

The underlying thread in the foregoing discussion is that the relevancy of institutions significantly depends upon the level of wealth and technology of the social system in question. This conjecture is certainly not a new one, as this relation is central to the classic works of Marx (1865), Weber (1904), Durkheim (1947), and Veblen (1899). The difference among these theories of social process and the one discussed here is the specification of this relation. In each case, it is naive to dismiss these theories as simple economic determinism. For Marx the economic role of the individual was the key motivating force to conflicting social stratification. Thus, Marxian theory is too narrowly constrained to one activity and tied too closely to the economic conditions of nineteenth-century Europe. Further, it does not contain an analysis of the dynamic process of change, only of increasing institutional conflict. Weber, on the other hand, concentrated on the effect of the institutional arrangement he termed the Protestant ethic on the development of capitalism. Weber's analysis is a monistic specification of the more general analysis presented here. Durkheim emphasized the division of labor and consequent internalization of similar value systems as creating the social structure. Durkheim (as well as Marx) was weak in the dynamical process of change and the consequences of increasingly complex technologies. In other words, in terms of the theory presented here, Durkheim failed to take into account the underlying individual forces at work in the social structure. The essence of this work is perhaps most closely aligned with the work of Thorstein Veblen. In *The Theory of the Leisure Class* and in most of his other works, Veblen cynically attacked the current institutional framework which guided individual activity. Veblen excoriated the social process for its intransigence and fallacies of composition but eschewed any program of change. Here the emphasis is different: first on the dynamical process itself, be it good or bad, and second, on developing a theoretical structure which would be relevant to improving the social process itself.

Institutions are created to increase the activities available for the participants. If this increased feasibility is self-perpetuating and it results in greater amounts of wealth, the institution will in all probability need revision and change. The causality between technological change and increased wealth and the relevant institutional framework is a moot question. Further, it is immaterial. The two are interdependent and complementary. Tolerant institutions which encourage technological change are self-destructing. They produce the increased wealth which leads to their demise. On the other hand, institutions which inhibit and control the wealth and affluency of the social system and maintain the same feasible activity sets for the participants, will remain useful and persist as a permanent, intransigent social structure.

Through this process Western civilization has given rise to a particular set of institutions which in turn has produced particular consequences. For example, private ownership is a result of this complicated process of bargaining and personal interaction. In its initial stages, private ownership is an obvious extension of the biological entity of the human organism. That is, the human organism has control over a number of activities which it can manipulate and thereby produce a series of coordinated muscular actions which amount to a symmetric collection. These collections of activities create effects which are sensuous and stimulating, and which produce and affect drives. The importance of this biological phenomenon is that the individual finds he is able to attain drive reduction by collecting objects and keeping them. Keeping them requires that he prevent others from taking them. However, protecting acquired objects carries an opportunity cost of not being able to spend the time collecting additional units. Consequently, it becomes much more efficient to establish a social order (or an institution) which gives the individual "ownership" of items he has collected. This institution can be enforced collectively where only a "policeman" is necessary to do the guarding of all personal property, the remainder of the group being free to collect further. On the other hand, in cultures where nature has been more prolific in the rudimentary stages of social development, the institution of private ownership has not received such a ubiquitous stimulation. For example, the concept of private ownership of land is unknown in some African and South Sea Island cultures.

With this extension of the human organism to private ownership, as technology and wealth accumulate and the social system becomes more complex, the knowledge sets of individuals and groups carry a "bias" that favors particular institutional change along lines to which they were accustomed. That is, if a new institution which is similar to other, well-known social decorums is adopted by members of a social system, the costs associated with adapting to this institution are less than they would be for an alien institutional form.

Similarly, it is much more efficient if a crude society delegates the creation of mores and codes of conduct to a central authority. High priests can be established to rationalize for the members of the interacting group, thereby relieving the majority from this task—indeed, one which simply could not feasibly be carried out by each member of a society with low levels of wealth. Hence institutions are often another form of division of labor, but one which partly determines the future course of the social system.

Thus the evolution of any social system is dependent upon the process of institution formation. Their purpose is to increase efficiency and to allow members of the system to accumulate higher and higher levels of wealth. But in providing information and prescribing ways and codes for interaction, institutions necessarily create constraints for the individuals and the groups of society. In order to function, institutions must limit the variability of behavior which will occur in any particular situation.

As the level of wealth and technology advances, many of these institutions come under increasing pressure. They have served their purpose and at levels of greater riches they begin to inhibit further progress. At this point the consequences are either an evolution into a form consistent with the progressing system; a defiance until revolution crumbles the outmoded institution; or a cessation of the accumulation of wealth, with the institution withstanding and silencing the pressure for reform.

SOME EXAMPLES OF INSTITUTIONS

While the number of different institutions which could be placed in each category is immense, the following provides an illustration of each type. An example of a more or less orderly evolving institution is that of money or of mediums of exchange. The historic account of the various items which have been used as money shows a rather consistent evolutionary trend. From simple barter of grain for cattle for cloth, common consent (various groups adopted an institution) established simple and scarce commodities as mediums of exchange. Cattle, horses, slaves, salt, tobacco, corn, wine, knives, pots, special rocks, or shells—all have served as an institution of an acceptable medium of exchange. With the increase in availability of precious metals (gold, silver, copper), the commodities were easily replaced with these metals, which were more durable, more easily divisible, and scarcer. Hence, with more durable money and with essentially no vested interests, the institution evolved easily.

Since organized coinage, standards of weight, and so forth offered a great increase in efficiency, sovereigns and formal institutions (governments) took over the issuing of money. Later, the metals were used only as a backing or a reserve until today money is essentially fiat, with most commercial exchange taking place through a simple accounting system of checks. Although monetary history is quite long and detailed, the major path of this institution has been a continual and orderly evolution.

Any political revolution could be placed in the second category as an example where institutions were not malleable to the changing base of man's interaction with man. A singular sovereign may be efficient at low levels of affluence, but increased wealth leads individuals to demand more freedoms and the institution becomes outdated. When those with the vested position of the singular leader fail to recognize the changing basis of their power, increasing conflict develops and culminates in a bloody revolution. In this case, the rules of the social system become so incapable of change, yet incapable of controlling the base upon which they were created, that the only possible consequence is the Marxian forecast of the inevitable revolution. Indeed, this kind of result is the only one considered in the Marxian dialectic. While this may have appeared as an empirical fact to Marx, Lenin, Sorel, and others, the facts of the latter nine-teenth and twentieth century (and also from a purely theoretical standpoint) would indicate that this is only one alternative for the social superstructure. On the other hand, the likelihood of such con-sequences being necessary for particular kinds of social structures should not be ignored.

The third consequence of a social structure is that it completely dominates the mode of life to such an extent that change is squelched. In the so-called "backward" societies of the twentieth century, the institutions have managed to dominate and eliminate the pressures of advancement. The traditional society, where vicious circles maintain the status quo, initially adopted institutions to benefit the members. But these institutions have consequently established such sources of power in a system of limited knowledge sets as to almost ensure their perpetual existence.

It is apparent then that a crucial factor within a social system is the stimulus for innovation. Innovation fathers increased productiv-ity which in turn generates increased wealth (wealth being used in the general sense of indicating a greater wherewithall on the part of in-dividuals), an increased feasible choice space, and thus a pressure and a direction for institutional change. For this reason a more detailed analysis of the stimulus for innovation is presented in the next section.

TECHNOLOGICAL CHANGE AND INNOVATION

Since institutional change and technology go hand in hand with social process, the analysis of the impetus for technological change and innovation is crucial to an understanding and control of the course of social systems. Chapters 3 and 4 define technological change as a subset of individual knowledge change. Specifically, a knowledge change is a technological change if (1) the changed knowl-edge set is associated with commodities, (2) the change occurs at the frontier of knowledge, and (3) it replaces or extends the use of previ-ous knowledge by a significant amount. Clearly, the exact point is arbitrary and identification of technological change in process is extremely difficult.

For any individual deciding upon a mix of activities, institutions (which would include adopted group policies such as those of a firm or a university) play a significant role. First, they partially determine drives. That is, institutions provide stimuli for individuals. These stimuli could be in the form of monetary remuneration, other forms of personal emoluments, or continued admonishments against particular activities. (For example, institutional stimuli against carrying out a particular activity could result in the individual carrying out a learning activity to gain more information.) Concomitantly, institutions also partially establish the drive reduction of the activity mix by establishing accepted rewards or portions of these rewards.

The model as developed in Chapter 3 explicitly recognizes the role of institutions as a constraint upon individual activities. Examined in detail as an example are the requirements of a budget constraint and a time constraint. However, in principle, any constraint could have been included. By serving as constraints, institutions legitimize the transmission of knowledge. That is, they validate the interpersonal transfer of experiences, allowing the dispersion of knowledge to be more efficient than if an individual were required to experience each facet of his knowledge set.

The other codeterminant of the feasible activity set is technology. Included in this concept of technology would be the set of natural resources available to individuals. Materials are only resources insofar as the technology is able to utilize them. Consequently, any physical object is only a resource relative to a given state of technology.

Therefore, for the singular individual each constraint, if relevant, carries a shadow price of the additional drive reduction attainable if it were to be lessened. Any activity designed to alleviate a constraint initially carries a unit value equivalent to the shadow price. For a given knowledge set an individual will include a learning activity in his activity mix if learning activities are known and the drive reduction of learning activities is sufficiently high relative to the drive reduction of available activities. "Knowing" particular learning activities exist means that the individual includes a functional relation in his calculus process. In other words, from the analysis of Chapter 4 the individual has a sufficient subjective belief in an activity and its outcome that it meets the acceptability criterion. This brings up an interesting digression on the capital intensive bias in technological advance. Various authors have argued that relative prices of capital and labor have been instrumental in the development of laborsaving technologies. However, Fellner (1962) convincingly argued that factor prices have no effect since the objective is to minimize total costs. From the above presentation the capital intensive bias is a consequence of the knowledge set. That is, learning activities (methods of experimentation) for physical capital are known. On the other hand, activities which experiment with human beings are institutionally forbidden or unknown. Therefore, experimentation and analysis are "capital intensive," and this results in knowledge change associated with physical capital and a capital-biased technological change. Future advances may result in methods of data collection from humans, which do not violate the institutions of the society and reduce this technological bias.[3]

As a consequence of a learning activity, knowledge will change if the experience generated is positive for change and outside forces do not offset the results of the learning activity. Not only must the new experience vector induce new relationships in the individual's knowledge set, but it must not be negated by incidental experiences and planned teaching activities of other individuals in the society.

If this process does result in a change in knowledge which satisfies the first two criteria of technological change (namely associated with commodities and on the frontier of such knowledge), then this change will be completed upon the fulfillment of the third criterion of transmission and acceptance of this new knowledge by others. The requisites of transmission can be classified as: (1) transmission activities must be known, (2) drive reduction of such transmission activities must be high relative to other activities in the relevant activity mixes, and (3) others agree with the conclusions that new relationships should replace or expand their own knowledge sets. Requisites 1 and 2 are similar in nature to the requirements for a learning activity to be carried out; requisite 3, however, depends upon several other factors. Whether others agree that knowledge has changed depends in part upon the degree of institutional legitimacy associated with transmission activities, the degree in which others value the knowledge change in terms of drive reduction, and whether those adversely affected by this potential change in knowledge possess and implement valid threat sets.

The efficiency of transmission of new knowledge is crucially tied to the institutional structure. If accepted ethic calls for severe penalties for the transmission of false information, for example, the established methods will carry a greater subjective believability to the recipients. Technical journals and the issuing of academic degrees are typical examples of a multitude of social arrangements to facilitate the transmission of information in the current social system.

Clearly, the intended recipients of information have to be receptive to listening. If the drive reduction associated with the offered information is relatively low, the individuals will not take the time nor the energy to understand what is being sent. Individuals can

---

3. For further discussion see Kennedy (1964), Mansfield (1968a, 1968b), and Arrow (1969). Currently, for example, there is also an experiment in negative taxation which promises to greatly enhance the data for social scientists and is described in Watts (1969).

screen out what does not interest them, and the knowledge will not be imparted to them.

Since knowledge and technology play a significant role in the establishment of the power structure of the social system, it is quite likely that any change in knowledge or technology will threaten to destroy these sources of authority and power. Consequently, those who feel in danger of losing drive reduction directly due to a change in knowledge will have an incentive to oppose the transmission of this knowledge. These individuals would be in conflict with a potential change and would prevent the change if they were better off by doing so.[4]

A MATHEMATICAL SUMMARY

The above discussion of the relations between technology, institutions, and the change in both can be symbolically summarized as follows. Specifically, it has been argued that the nature of institutions must correspond to the level of technology and the power structure within the social system (Equation 10.1).

$$I = g(T, P) \qquad (10.1)$$

where

       I = measure of the degree of social institutions
       T = measure of the level of technology
      P = measure of the power of institutions

Equation 10.1 is a social equilibrium relation. That is, as technology grows and the overall wealth of society increases, individuals will demand a reduction in the extent of institutional controls. Institutions or generally accepted rules of society are basically arbitrary in their effects and consequently will generate pressure for their own demise as wealth expands. This can only be offset by an increase in the power structure if institutions are to remain unchanged in their restrictiveness. Institutions are measured by the degree of restrictiveness as shown in Figure 10.1 by a real half-line, where 0 would repre-

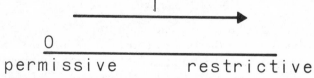

Fig. 10.1. A measure of the degree of institutional social constraints.

4. Cf. Chapter 5.

sent a completely permissive social system in terms of the impinge-
ments effective upon individuals. The hypothesis is, in the relevant
region of the g function (Equation 10.1) for modern history, that
$\partial g/\partial T < 0$, that is, that increased technology causes a diminution in
the restrictiveness of social institutions.

Equations 10.2 and 10.3 summarize the dependency of technological change dT/dt and hence the level of technology on reward
levels R, institutional power structure P, the state of knowledge K,
and institutional validation V.

$$dT/dt = f(R, P, K, V) \qquad (10.2)$$

and thus,

$$\int (dT/dt)dt = T = F(R, P, K, V) + C \qquad (10.3)$$

Equation 10.4 states that a partial effect of an increase of any independent variable in Equation 10.2 (except for P) on the functional
relationship is positive in the relevant range, while an increase in
threat sets has a negative effect.

$$\partial f/\partial R > 0,\ \partial f/\partial P < 0,\ \partial f/\partial K > 0,\ \partial f/\partial V > 0 \qquad (10.4)$$

and also, then

$$\partial F/\partial R > 0,\ \partial F/\partial P < 0,\ \partial F/\partial K > 0,\ \partial F/\partial V > 0$$

The method of measuring each of these variables is both subjectively
and objectively complex. Reward is a proxy for an aggregation of the
drive reduction derived from learning activities resulting in technological change. Institutional power structure P is a proxy for the
power positions or threat sets relevant to technology, while institutional validation corresponds to the effectiveness of transmission
systems.

It is primarily within these two variables that conflict over institutional change is generated. These two facets are the primary determinants of the restrictiveness of institutions. That is, $I = I(P, V)$,
where $\partial I/\partial P > 0$ and $\partial I/\partial V > 0$. However, institutional validation is
not independent of the power structure; that is,

$$V = V(P), \text{ and } \partial V/\partial P > 0$$

Therefore, the power structure and institutional validation move in
the same direction. In the face of expanding technology there is a
need for increased validation—a need for institutions to operate more
efficiently as the opportunity cost becomes greater. But there is also
an income or wealth effect which calls for a reduction in the perva-
siveness of social rules and regulations. And as may be expected,

groups and individuals differ as to which direction institutional change should take.

If both the institutional power structure and institutional validation are increasing (both dP/dt and $dV/dt > 0$), this implies that the society will become increasingly dichotomized with each of the various sectors increasing its power structure. While the model does not predict any further consequences, it does suggest that a social structure based on ever-increasing threat sets would be quite volatile and susceptible to the slightest destabilizing change. This is because the model assumes full information about the threat sets of various social entities, which consequently dismisses the interpersonal "testing" of these threatening activities. However, an ever-increasing power structure implies that the threat sets become harsher and stronger in their potential effects. Consequently, any empirical testing of these expanded threats could result in total, violent, irrational destruction of the system. This might be termed the extreme-right solution to increased expansion of technology.

On the other hand, if both are negative (dP/dt and $dV/dt < 0$), this implies that the society will become increasingly homogeneous, with power structures withering away to nothing and the validation of personal interaction via institutional means also deteriorating. This would then necessitate validation to be on a more personal basis, and this coupled with an eroding power structure would necessitate greater homogeneity. That is, entities comprising the social system would become more homogeneous in the sense that the elimination of threat sets implies that specific knowledge and specific ownership rights are eliminated. Also, for communication to occur, greater personal validation as opposed to institutional validation requires similar characteristics on the part of those interacting. This homogeneity in realms of knowledge does not, however, further imply a society of identical automatons with equal preferences or other characteristics. It does require that the individuals should be basically integrated and broadly educated so that they are not only aware of the social system but are flexible in their own right.

The fact that validation through an institutional matrix is replaced does not imply an absence of institutions or an anarchic system. Rather, it requires that validation not be a consequence of the institutional matrix alone. Institutions still would be quite useful and efficient but would be much more ephemeral than they have been throughout the history of social systems. The structures would necessarily have to adapt and change readily. The mechanism which changes institutions would be more responsive to the changing environment. In other words, since social decorums are an agreement by the participating individuals, institutions would exist only through prior interpersonal validation. This result might be termed the extreme-left solution.

Thus the prospect for ever-increasing technology and a continual upward spiral of prosperity requires either the extreme-right solution or the extreme-left solution. Further, the right-wing solution suggests a highly unstable one, where the slightest bit of false knowledge or misinformation could result in a test of threat sets and a cataclysmic catastrophe.

chapter 11

A Short View of Welfare and Policy: Definition and Applications

A PREREQUISITE to a discussion of social policy which enhances individual welfare is a consideration of the meaning of welfare. From the assumptions of the motivation behind individual behavior, the definition of any one person's welfare follows logically as the quantitative amount of drive reduction. Furthermore, since the individual is able to calculate the drive reduction attainable in different situations and over time, the drive reduction to the individual has a meaningful cardinal difference ratio scale. However, this drive reduction is unique only up to an arbitrary origin and unit of measurement. Even though a difference scale does exist, aggregation among individuals is impossible without identifying (implicitly) with one individual or a group of such individuals. This is due to the arbitrariness of the origin and scale.

Thus, there is no difference between welfare criteria which are based on the drive reduction concept and criteria based on standard ordinal utility, but the scope of the concept is much broader. It would be consistent to argue, for example, that greater equality in income distribution would result in greater amounts of drive reduction for a particular individual or group. Due to personal interaction and the development of threat sets, a "white" group may be better off to increase the economic well-being of a neighboring "black" group so that the "black" group would be less violent, more amicable, and more productive. The consequence would be greater drive reduction for each and every member of the "white" group than attainable by any other method of resource distribution within that group. It is equally consistent to argue that it is better to increase the inequality of income if one believes that by so doing he will be better off. For example, for someone who does not benefit from direct "noneconomic" personal intercourse, bettering others at his expense would be ludicrous.

Social welfare criteria thus depend entirely upon the empirical facts of personal interaction. The degree of general agreement on any derived criteria and policy depend upon the drive-reducing mechanism of the particular individuals and their knowledge sets. The degree of agreement on any normative aspect of the environment depends, first, upon the degree that body chemical and neurological processes are or can be equivalent and, second, upon the similarity of experiences among individuals and the knowledge sets which are thereby created.

The crux of the issue is knowledge and rational behavior toward goal achievement. Although impossible to aggregate different individuals without implicit individual or group identification, it is possible to adopt rules of thumb (adopt social policy or change social institutions) which are applicable to a period of time (depending upon the level of wealth and technology) and which serve to increase the drive reduction of everyone.

In Chapter 5 the formation and change of groups and group policy (adopted institutions by groups) were discussed. The results showed that a group will change (its makeup, its rules of interaction) if those who are benefited from such a change have sufficient strength to bring it about. All change depends upon the interaction of threat sets. One group will exploit and subjugate another individual or group if, in light of all personal interaction, this is the best way to achieve drive reduction. However, human interaction is such that as wealth accumulates and technology advances, ethics and morals and other social decorums evolve to a more magnanimous state. At low levels of wealth and with limited knowledge sets, the solution for maximum drive reduction by one group may very well be enslavement of another. At high levels of wealth and with expanded information about the quality and nature of what stimulates other human organisms, coupled with the advantages of reducing the possibility of enslavement, the social institution changes and such practices are outlawed. Although man is pictured as a very greedy, totally self-centered individual, the best way to attain this self-satisfaction oftentimes is through interaction with others. The drive for self-preservation results in standards which apply to all individuals.

Consider the criterion of Pareto optimality. This, in short, says that a particular configuration of economic activity is optimal if it is possible to make someone better off only by hurting someone else.

This interpretation is usually restricted to physical goods and coupled with the postulate that everyone prefers more goods to less; the result is the "new" welfare economics. Thus this criterion presumes a positive value in human enhancement through interaction. It is an example of a rule of thumb which recognizes this facet of existence. However, the models to which this criterion is applied contradict its basic premise. From the preceding analysis it was shown that a monopoly would develop if it were advantageous. Yet the new welfare economics demonstrates that society could have more if a monopolized industry were made to equate marginal cost to price. This apparent contradiction arises because the models which produce this conclusion accept one set of institutions, (namely, Pareto optimality, given knowledge sets and given resource ownership rights) and propose to eliminate others (namely, the right to form a monopoly). Consequently, what appears to be a "scientific" criterion void of invidious interpersonal comparisons is actually burdened with such assumptions. This is not particularly bad but when such value judgments do exist, the postulate of rational improvement of the state of mankind requires that these be made explicit.

THE CASE OF THE PUBLIC GOOD

Another example in economic theory which is treated in some detail in Chapter 6 is the concept of the public good. This is developed to demonstrate that there are cases where collective economic action is beneficial to all concerned. Specifically, a purely public good is one where the amount available for consumption (providing satisfaction) does not diminish by consumption.

The argument is that it would be possible to make some people better off without hurting the remainder by collectivization of such public goods. This is only consistent with the models of individual behavior if personal interaction is both present and positive. First, personal interaction must exist in order for those who control the potential public good to have reason to "share" it. Second, this sharing of the public good must be beneficial to those who control it originally. If by "sharing" the public good those benefited are in turn willing to share their public goods, both present and future, and to thereby increase the drive reduction of the original controllers, personal interaction would be positive. On the other hand, if "sharing" the public good caused those benefited to acquire new and more powerful knowledge sets which could be transformed into threat sets to the detriment of the original controllers, the personal interaction would be negative.

Thus, the criterion of Pareto optimality in economic models fails to be sufficiently encompassing of institutions and learning on the part of individuals to have genuinely demonstrated that everyone would be better off. Of course the crux of the problem is at the base of scientific analysis itself. Since all abstraction and simplification selects the "relevant" and ignores the "irrelevant," the models are biased to begin with. The assumptions or axioms often appear to be limited to those which generate the desired preconceptions. As a consequence, criteria of welfare are in general little more than an argument to enhance the income of a particular group. Criteria ostensibly designed as impersonal and for the general benefit in practice will harm some members of the social system. If everyone could be better off, why are they not already to that position? The limited case where such criteria are valid for everyone is where knowledge changes and everyone is better off by this. The double criterion should be emphasized. All knowledge change need not be beneficial to all. In light of vested interests of given knowledge sets, it is doubtful that any knowledge change could benefit everyone.

In the next section several examples will be developed which are intended to change the knowledge sets of the readers, to change the intuitive or apparent concept of what transpires in certain phases of human interaction. Particular models will be advantageous to particular groups. For example, a model demonstrating the waste of resources in competitive advertising might provide a rationale for a "consumer" group to place restrictions on a "production" group, while a model of optimal advertising may enable a "production" group to exploit a "consumer" group.

OPTIMAL EDUCATIONAL EXPENDITURES

Since the amount of drive reduction attainable depends upon the knowledge set of the individual, it might be possible to alter this, giving him a greater attainable level of drive reduction with the same or less resources. Similarly, from a given level of satisfaction, additional resources can be used either to fulfill activities by the old knowledge sets or to change the knowledge sets. The method which produces the greater level of drive reduction would be more efficient. This assumes that one could determine a priori the learning which occurs from a given set of resources. While this is not an easy task, equivalent measures occur every day with respect to the education systems in the world and other forms of persuasive activity such as advertising and other sales promotion. Presumably, in these cases the benefits are greater than the costs. The question remains as to what extent these benefits diverge from the costs involved. For example, in referring to advertising by business firms, Doyle (1968b, pp. 594–95) states, "Though the firm is conscious that its advertising outlay is a potent and often essential weapon for maintaining or increasing its sales, it is often impossible for it to decide, even approximately, how much it should spend to maximize its long-run profits. Bemused or unaware of the problem, many firms employ a rule of thumb procedure for deciding the appropriate size, while much of the research into the problem has avoided the central goals of profitability and concentrated on limited objectives." For an efficient use of social resources, it is necessary that those expended in improving information be increased to the point where the marginal social cost is just equal to the marginal social benefit. Objectively, one can easily measure the cost of resources which go into education under a given price system; the problem is ascertaining the benefits objectively. By using the model developed in Chapters 3 and 4, some insight can be gained as to how this could be accomplished. It should be reiterated that the learning concept as used in this chapter deals solely with the ascertainment of the conditions of the world about the individual. This benefit to the individual has been virtually ignored, aside from a passing comment, "The value of education . . . is far more than financial. . . . Education is a vital segment of the full life . . ."[1] by those attempting to measure the value of education. These measurements approach the value of education entirely from the view of investment in capital or from the view of ascertaining skills. The model presented here offers a way to measure the contribution of education to the "full life."

In Chapter 4 it was shown that beginning either from a position of ignorance (no $\gamma_i(X_s)$ function was used in the calculus process) or from a position where the individual changed his opinion, the number of experiences necessary to change the knowledge set could be determined. Therefore, disregarding the usual public characteristics of resources spent in changing knowledge sets, the value of education could be calculated for the single individual as simply the difference in the resources necessary to alter the knowledge set to achieve a higher level of drive reduction and those necessary to achieve the same level through known commodity-activity combinations. Model 11.1 exploits this possibility further.

1. Weisbrod (1966), p. 10; Becker (1964); Blaug (1968); Schultz (1960). Also see Becker (1964) for his argument about the rate of psychic return from education.

MODEL 11.1—The value of education for one individual

Assume there are three activities w_1, w_2, w_3, where w_2 is labor and $\partial\phi/\partial w_2 < 0$, while $\partial\phi/\partial w_1$ and $\partial\phi/\partial w_3 > 0$ but $\gamma_3(x_3)$ is unknown. That is, the expected value of any $\gamma_{3i}(x_3)$ is less than P_o, the decision criterion. This is pictured graphically in Figure 11.1.

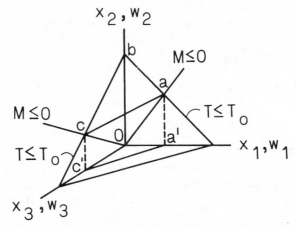

Fig. 11.1. Three activities and three products.

With only w_1 and w_2 known, the equilibrium solution is at a in Figure 11.2 or a' in Figure 11.3. If w_3 were known, the solution would be at d in Figure 11.3. Suppose there is an increase in productivity such that the individual's satisfaction could be increased to S^1 by increasing his wage rate as in Figure 11.4 or, alternatively, by informing him of activity w_3.

The cost of attaining S^1 by using more x_1 directly is $(x_1^{**} - x_1^*)$ units of x_1. Now assume that α units of x_1 could be used in an educational activity such that $w_3 = \gamma_3(X_3)$ would be

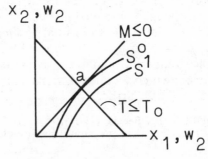

Fig. 11.2. Maximum solution with only w_1 and w_2 known.

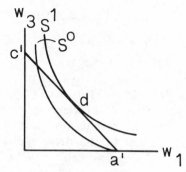

Fig. 11.3. Maximum solution with w_1, w_2, and w_3 known.

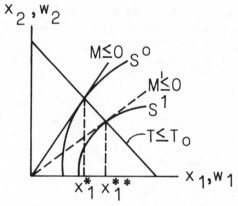

Fig. 11.4. Shift in relative prices necessary to attain S^1 by activity w^1 alone.

included in the calculus process. For example, if x_1 yielded r successes and t failures toward establishing the credibility of $\gamma_3(x_3)$ and if m is the total number of successes and n is the total number of failures,

$$m \geqslant \frac{P_o(n + 2) - 1}{1 - P_o}$$

is a necessary condition for the individual to include $\gamma_3(X_3)$ in his calculus process; and, assuming that r and t are constant for each unit of x_1 used, then α units of x_1 will be necessary for $\gamma_3(X_3)$ to be believed, where

$$\alpha \geqslant \frac{2P_o - 1}{r(1 - P_o) - P_o t} > 0$$

For example, if $P_o = .75, r = 4, t = 1$, then

$$\alpha \geqslant (1.5 - 1)/(4 - 3 - .75) = .5/.25 = 2$$

or two units of x_1 would be necessary.

For the educational activity to take place, some of the other activities in which the individual is currently engaged must be reduced. To maintain focus on the value of the educational experience, assume that the drive reduction lost by reducing the current activity mix is equal to the drive reduction gained by the information process. Mathematically, if w^* is the current mix of activities, assume that $\Sigma \partial \phi / \partial w_i^* = -\partial \phi / \partial w_e$, where $\partial \phi / \partial w_i^*$ is the marginal value of the ith activity and w_e is a learning activity.

Further, assume only one future time period exists and the price of x_3 is equal to the price of x_1. The value of education for the current period is the saving in x_1 resources, $(x_1^{**} - x_1^*) - \alpha$; or, if $x_1^{**} - x_1^* = \beta$, the value of education under the given price system is equal to $P_1^o(\beta - \alpha)$. The value for several future time periods would be

$$\text{Value of education} = \sum_{t=0}^{\infty} P_1^t - \alpha$$

where future prices P^t are properly discounted.

In general, the objective valuation of education could be formulated as follows. Assume:

$$S^1 = \phi(w_1^*, \ldots, w_n^*, \omega_1^*, \ldots, \omega_m^*) \qquad (11.1)$$

and

$$S^1 = \phi(w_1^{**}, \ldots, w_n^{**}, w_{n+1}^{**}, \omega_1^*, \ldots, \omega_m^*) \qquad (11.2)$$

are possible. S^1 is a particular level of drive reduction, and the activities in Equations 11.1 and 11.2 would, in general, use different commodities:

$$w_1^* = \gamma_1(X_{s_1}^*)$$
$$\vdots$$
$$w_n^* = \gamma_n(X_{s_n}^*)$$
$$w_1^{**} = \gamma_1(X_{s_1}^{**}) \qquad (11.3)$$
$$\vdots$$
$$w_{n+1}^{**} = \gamma_{n+1}(X_{s_{n+1}}^{**})$$

Assume Equation 11.2 comes about only as a result of education. The value of resources used under a given price system by Equations 11.1 and 11.2 respectively would be

$$\sum_{i \in s^*} P_i x_i^*, \quad s^* = \{s_1, \ldots, s_n\} \tag{11.4}$$

and

$$\sum_{i \in s^{**}} P_i x_i^{**}, \quad s^{**} = \{s_1, \ldots, s_{n+1}\} \tag{11.5}$$

The maximum value of education is given by Equation 11.6, which is the integral over all future savings for as long as the education lasts, T; minus the costs, $\sum_{i \in e} P_i^o x_i$, where e is the set of resources used in education.

$$\int_0^T \left\{ \sum_{i \in s^*} P_i^t x_i^* - \sum_{i \in s^{**}} P_i^t x_i^{**} \right\} dt - \sum_{i \in e} P_i^o x_i \tag{11.6}$$

For example, suppose that an individual receives status drive fulfillment by the purchase of a Cadillac at a cost of $10,000. If the individual could be convinced that the same amount of status could be achieved by a button, the savings to society (that is, the value of the education) would be the difference between each $10,000 that this individual would have spent over his lifetime and the cost of the buttons plus the cost of the education.

Since in general the benefits of the information would be unknown to the individual, there is no particular reason for him to be on his most efficient path. In the United States today, society judges which relations are the best and then encourages a more rapid attainment of this information by a subsidy to education so that an individual's best path a priori conforms to social judgment. If in fact, after some time and a series of more or less random approaches to discovering the most believable aspects of the real world, the individual would arrive at the same conclusions as he would by following a subsidized route, there is a saving of resources. Of course, the validity of such a statement is moot. In the final analysis, it remains the judgment of those with the power to decide whether it saves resources or not, when in fact the information of each member of society is less than perfect.

MODEL 11.2—Public Education

Since the expenditure of resources on educational activities often can influence more than a single person, the value of education would be slightly different than as presented in Equation 11.6 in Model 11.1. Let G be a group of individuals that can learn from an educational activity. Let e_g be the index of resources necessary to alter the knowledge set of individual g. If the fast learners require less resource expenditure than the slow learners but can be educated simultaneously, the costs to educate the entire group G would be

$$\max_g \left\{ \sum_{i \in e_g} P_i^o x_i \right\}$$

and the value of education analogous to Equation 11.6 for a group would be

$$\int_G \int_0^T \left\{ \sum_{i \in s^*} P_i^t x_i^* - \sum_{i \in s^{**}} P_i^t x_i^{**} \right\} dt\, dg - \max_g \left\{ \sum_{i \in e_g} P_i^o x_i \right\}$$

(11.7)

Equation 11.7 is simply an aggregation over the entire group, minus the cost of educating the slowest. Thus for an efficient use of resources, the size of the group G should be expanded until the marginal cost of educating the last individual is equal to the resources saved due to the changed knowledge set for that last individual. Or, if k is the marginal individual, where

$$\left\{ \sum_{i \in e_1} P_i^o x_i \right\} \leqslant \left\{ \sum_{i \in e_2} P_i^o x_i \right\} \leqslant \ldots \leqslant \left\{ \sum_{i \in e_k} P_i^o x_i \right\}$$

then Equation 11.8 is the criterion for efficiency:

$$\int_0^T \left\{ \sum_{i \in s^*} P_i^t x_i^* - \sum_{i \in s^{**}} P_i^t x_i^{**} \right\}_g dt = \left\{ \sum_{i \in e_k} P_i^o x_i \right\} - \left\{ \sum_{i \in e_{k-1}} P_i^o x_i \right\}$$

(11.8)

or the marginal saving is equal to the marginal cost. The above holds in either the static sense or the dynamic sense. In the static sense, current drive reduction from a given knowledge set is compared to the savings in resources with an expanded knowledge set to attain the former level of drive reduction. In the dynamic sense, the above argues that the maximum drive reduction attainable by using increased available resources for education should be evaluated for each individual. These resources can be compared with the resources necessary to achieve the same higher level of drive reduction without changing the individual's knowledge set, but by increasing his wage rate or by other subsidies. (Both the drive reduction attainable from the initial knowledge set and that attainable from the altered knowledge set are the individual's own choice.) Expenditures on education should be increased as long as the marginal costs are less than the savings to the marginal individual.

This efficiency criterion does not answer the ethical or social welfare problem which is likely to arise. For example, suppose the marginal saving in resources (the savings for the last individual educated) is equal for each member of the group; but the marginal cost of educating individuals is increasing as shown in Figure 11.5.

Which members of the total group should be included in those educated $0g*$ (Fig. 11.5) and those not educated $g*g^+$? Clearly, anyone could just as well be in the benefited group $0g*$ as not. In addition, the above is a partial equilibrium analysis.

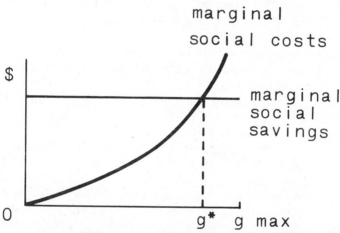

Fig. 11.5. Marginal social costs and marginal social savings of education.

Although the activities are sufficiently general to include the drive reduction derived from associating with informed people, this is not considered in a general equilibrium framework. If drive reduction were increased for other individuals as those to be educated were informed, more resources should be applied to education than Equation (11.8) implies and less if drive reduction were reduced by educating one's associates. Since implementation of the static criterion results in a savings in resources which can further be utilized by society, the argument in the general sense is one of the use to which additional resources should be put, not a reallocation of current resource use. That is, it is an argument of the direction of change for a progressing economy, not an efficiency criterion for a static economy. How to best utilize the fruits of increased productivity—through wage increases or changes in the knowledge set—is the point of Model 11.2.

An interesting application of Models 11.1 and 11.2 is "painless" taxation. Suppose one group decides to impose a tax upon another. This might be accomplished without harming those taxed by coupling the tax program with an educational program such that the value of the education (the difference between resources used in the educational process and the tax) is reaped by those imposing the tax, while those taxed are as well off as they were before, due to increased knowledge. For example, in the case where a social institution provides status through the purchase of commodities as illustrated in Model 11.1 (purchase of a Cadillac), the governing group could issue the buttons mentioned in the example and use the saved resources for other purposes.

Another possibility would be a demonstration that taxes would generate sufficient increased productivity so that the long-run effect on those taxed would be an increase in their drive reduction. For example, in the United States there are individuals who have failed to adopt the culture of the majority. They do not value the institution of working and economic betterment but live mostly from day to day just getting by. One current ethic in the United States says that individuals should be kept from starving and should be kept alive regardless of their cultural and personal values. This has led to a series of welfare programs which not only provide a bare minimum of existence but also keep these individuals in such a state of poverty that they continue to reject the majority's value system. The consequence is a self-perpetuating system of misery for the adults and the offspring as well. One proposal is to give these individuals a relatively high income which would decline over time. By having experienced the drive reduction attainable with this additional income they would learn and adopt the majority's value system. For example, the first year a family of four would receive $10,000; this would decline at the end of, say, ten years to zero. The cost of such a program might be $50,000, which would be less than $60,000, the cost of $3,000 per year at 5% for perpetuity. This ignores the additional benefits from the productivity of the family and other positive aspects of personal interaction.

An analysis similar to that of education can be given for advertising and other forms of persuasion. In this case, if the group is a firm, the goals can be more clearly defined, namely, greater profits. Obviously, advertising represents a capital expenditure, and the rate of depreciation depends upon the extent that an altered preference for its product or products is affected by other forms of advertising as well as other information.

In Models 8.2, 8.3, and 8.4 in Chapter 8 the waste of resources from the point of view of a consumer group was mentioned only as a qualification to the conclusions. In Model 11.3 this is given further consideration. The simplified assumptions of Model 11.3 lead to the conclusion that a single firm is better than two. While such a model is not difficult to generate (for example, if the equilibrium quantities of goods sold by two firms after advertising is the same as those before and if advertising adds nothing to the satisfaction of consumers, advertising is a waste of resources from the point of view of the consuming group), Model 11.3 is somewhat more general in that information is a function of advertising.

MODEL 11.3

Assume:

1. Two firms producing output q_1 and q_2 respectively.
2. Four groups of consumers $C = \{C_1, C_2, C_3, C_4\}$.
3. a. w_1^i is advertising activity undertaken by firm i.
   b. w_1^i equal one unit per period of time is the only feasible way to advertise.
4. w_2 is consumptive activity on the part of consumers, if $w_2 = \gamma_{21}(q_1)$, the individual will use firm 1's output; if $w_2 = \gamma_{22}(q_2)$, the individual will use firm 2's output.
5. The decision criterion P_o is the same for each consumer.
6. For consumer group C_1, initially, $P[\gamma_{21}(q_1)] \geqslant P_o$.
7. For group C_2, initially, $P[\gamma_{22}(q_2)] \geqslant P_o$.
8. For group C_3, initially,
   a. $P[\gamma_{21}(q_1)] < P_o$ and $P[\gamma_{22}(q_2)] < P_o$, that is, those in C_3 will not buy either q_1 or q_2 without more information.
   b. If w_1^1 is one, the experience probability with respect to $\gamma_{21}(q_1), P[E/\gamma_{21}(q_1)]$, for group C_3 is equal to μ_1.
   c. If w_1^2 is one, $P(E)$ with respect to $\gamma_{22}(q_2)$ is equal to μ_2.
   d. $P[\gamma_{21}(q_1)]$ is greater than or equal to P_o if a_1 units of x_1 are used for a_1 periods of time by firm 1.
   e. $P[\gamma_{22}(q_2)]$ is greater than or equal to P_o if $a_2 + b_2$ units

of x_1 are used for $a_2 + b_2$ units of time by firm 2 in the absence of advertising by firm 1.

9. For group C_4, initially,

   a. $P[\gamma_{21}(q_1)] < P_o$ and $P[\gamma_{22}(q_2)] < P_o$, that is, those in C_4 will not buy either q_1 or q_2 without more information.

   b. If w_1^2 is one, $P(E)$ is equivalent to μ_3 with respect to $\gamma_{22}(q_2)$.

   c. If w_1^1 is one, $P(E)$ is equivalent to μ_4 with respect to $\gamma_{21}(q_2)$.

   d. $P[\gamma_{22}(q_2)]$ is greater than or equal to P_o if a_2 units of x_1 are used by firm 2 for a_2 units of time.

   e. $P[\gamma_{21}(q_1)]$ is greater than or equal to P_o if $a_1 + b_1$ units of x_1 are used by firm 1 for $a_1 + b_1$ units of time in the absence of advertising by firm 2.

10. If $P[\gamma_{2i}(q_i)] > P[\gamma_{2j}(q_j)] \geqslant P_o$, each consumer will purchase one unit of commodity q_i. That is, for each individual if either $\gamma_{2i}(q_i)$ is sufficiently believed, the one with the greatest belief will be included in the calculus process and the result will be a point demand for one unit of q per unit of time at a price p_q. If the price rises, demand will fall to zero; if the price falls, only one unit per unit of time per person will be demanded. This is illustrated in Figure 11.6.

11. The form of advertising has no direct effect on drive reduction for any member of any group. That is, advertising per se is neither enjoyable nor irritating.

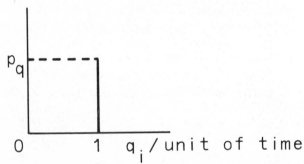

Fig. 11.6. Demand by a single consumer for commodity g_i if $P[\gamma_{2i}(q_i)] \geqslant P_0$.

Case 1—Two firms in the market

Initially, firm 1 sells C_1 units of q_1, that is, one unit to each member of C_1, while firm 2 sells C_2 units of q_2.

Assume that if both firms advertise, firm 1 will be able to sell additional quantities of C_3 to group C_3 while firm 2 will be able to sway group C_4 to his product and as long as both continue to advertise, each will maintain this share: firm 1's share = $C_1 + C_3$; firm 2's share = $C_2 + C_4$. Assume that the marginal production cost for both firms is equal and constant. Further assume it is profitable to convince groups C_3 and C_4 by firms 1 and 2 respectively, or that

$$\sum_{t=1}^{\infty} (q_1 p_{qt} - \Delta_t q_1) > \sum_{t=0}^{\infty} x_1 p_{1t}$$

and

$$\sum_{t=1}^{\infty} (q_2 p_{qt} - \Delta_t q_2) > \sum_{t=0}^{\infty} x_1 p_{1t}$$

where

$$q_1 = C_1, \quad \text{if} \quad 0 \leqslant t < a_1$$
$$q_1 = C_1 + C_3, \quad \text{if} \quad a_1 \leqslant t$$
$$q_2 = C_2, \quad \text{if} \quad 0 \leqslant t < a_2$$

and

$$q_2 = C_2 + C_4, \quad \text{if} \quad a_2 \leqslant t$$

where Δ_t is the marginal production cost at time $t \geqslant 0$ discounted to $t = 0$, and other prices are also discounted to $t = 0$. Thus, the use of resources to supply $C_1 + C_2 + C_3 + C_4$ units of q for all time is equal to

$$\sum_{t=0}^{\infty} 2(\Delta_t q_2 + p_{1t} x_1), \quad \text{if} \quad a_1 = a_2$$

Case 2—One firm in the market

Assume firm 1 can win over all four consumer groups if sufficient advertising is carried out. Further, assume that it is profitable to do so, that is,

$$\sum_{t=0}^{\infty} (q_1 p_{qt} - \Delta_t q_1) > \sum_{t=0}^{N} x_1 p_{1t}$$

where

$$q_1 = C_1, \quad \text{if} \quad 0 \leqslant t < a_1$$
$$q_1 = C_1 + C_3, \quad \text{if} \quad a_1 \leqslant t < a_1 + b_1$$
$$q_1 = C_1 + C_3 + C_4, \quad \text{if} \quad a_1 + b_1 \leqslant t < a_1 + b_1 + c_1$$
$$q_1 = C_1 + C_2 + C_3 + C_4, \quad \text{if} \quad a_1 + b_1 + c_1 \leqslant t$$

and

$$N = a_1 + b_1 + c_1$$

Use of resources here is

$$\sum_{t=0}^{\infty} \Delta_t q_2 + \sum_{t=0}^{N} p_{1t} x_1$$

Thus a monopoly will be more efficient than a two-firm oligopoly with constant marginal costs (and ignoring the fact that the monopoly takes a longer time to convince all consumers, $C_1 + C_2 + C_3 + C_4$ in this model) if

$$\int_0^{\infty} (\Delta_t \bar{q}_t + 2p_{1t} x_1)\, dt > \int_0^{\infty} \Delta_t \bar{\bar{q}}_t\, dt + \int_0^{N} p_{1t} x_1\, dt$$

where again the prices are discounted to $t = 0$ and $\bar{q}_t$ refers to the output of two firms at time t and $\bar{\bar{q}}_t$ refers to the output of the single monopolist at time t.

Since

$$\int_0^{\infty} (\Delta_t \bar{q}_t + 2p_{1t} x_1)\, dt = \int_0^{N} \Delta_t q_t\, dt + 2\int_0^{N} p_{1t} x_1\, dt$$

$$+ \int_N^{\infty} \Delta_t \bar{q}_t\, dt + 2\int_N^{\infty} p_{1t} x_1\, dt$$

and

$$\int_0^{\infty} \Delta_t \bar{\bar{q}}_t\, dt + \int_0^{N} p_{1t} x_1\, dt = \int_0^{N} \Delta_t \bar{\bar{q}}_t\, dt$$

$$+ \int_N^{\infty} \Delta_t \bar{\bar{q}}_t\, dt + \int_0^{N} p_{1t} x_1\, dt$$

and $t > N$ implies that $\bar{q}_t = \bar{\bar{q}}_t$, monopoly will be more efficient if

$$\int_0^{N} \Delta_t \bar{q}_t\, dt + \int_0^{N} p_{1t} x_1\, dt + 2\int_N^{\infty} p_{1t} x_1\, dt > \int_0^{N} \Delta_t \bar{\bar{q}}_t\, dt$$

Since we have assumed away the effects of not fulfilling total consumer demand as quickly by monopoly as by two-firm oligopoly, it can also be assumed that $\int_0^{N} \Delta_t \bar{q}_t\, dt = \int_0^{N} \Delta_t \bar{\bar{q}}_t\, dt$ so that the lost resources are essentially the duplication in advertising:

$$\int_0^N p_{1t}\, x_1\, dt + 2 \int_N^\infty p_{1t}\, x_1\, dt$$

Although this is subject to empirical investigation, it seems possible there is a great deal of waste due to competitive advertising. Advertising is perfectly rational for individual firms and is better for them than combining into a single firm, yet it exists solely due to the marketing institution. Therefore, consumers functioning as a group could eliminate this waste by changing the marketing institution. Advertising agencies, of course, would not be much in favor of such a proposal without compensation to aid transition.

In addition, if consumers decide markets should not remain underexpanded (which requires some value judgments about the distribution of income among consumers), elimination of excess profits by competitive advertising is as bad as underexpansion and not a solution for greater real income.

Another aspect affecting the welfare of consumers is the product range. Other things being equal, the wider the product range the more divisible commodities will be. However, other things are not equal in the most general case. If a firm limits the variety, it is due to the greater profitability of limited production. These economies of scale were given consideration from the firm's point of view in Chapter 8. In Model 11.4 the effect of the change in the product range with associated economies of scale is considered from the point of view of a single consumer.

MODEL 11.4—Effect of change in the product range

Assume there are 3 commodities and 3 activities x_1, x_2, x_3 and w_1, w_2, w_3, where w_2, x_2 are laboring and labor. From the feasible set for each individual, $0abc$, assume a maximizing solution along ca in Figure 11.7 or $c'a'$ in Figure 11.8, such that the quantity sold is x_1^{*i} and x_3^{*i} for individual i.

Assume one firm supplying both x_1 and x_3 and the quantity sold of each is $\Sigma_{i=1}^{G}\, x_1^{*i}$ and $\Sigma_{i=1}^{G}\, x_3^{*i}$. If $C(\Sigma x_1^i)$ is the cost of producing Σx_1^i, the initial profit is

$$\pi^* = P_3^* \, \Sigma x_3^{*i} - C(\Sigma x_3^{*i}) + P_1^* \, \Sigma x_1^{*i} - C(\Sigma x_1^{*i})$$

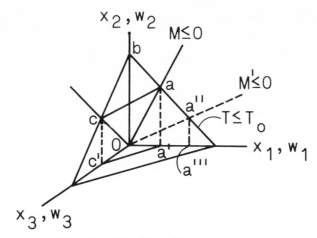

Fig. 11.7. Feasible set for a consumer.

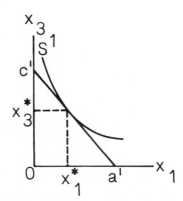

Fig. 11.8. Maximizing solution for a consumer when three commodities are available.

Suppose the firm is able to lower the price of x_1 to $\tilde{P}_1$ and concomitantly eliminate x_3 from the market so that the profit level is higher, that is, $\tilde{\pi} > \pi^*$, where

$$\tilde{\pi} = \tilde{P}_1 \sum_{i=1}^{G} \tilde{x}_1^i - C\left(\sum \tilde{x}_1^i\right)$$

The feasible set for each consumer shifts from $0abc$ (Fig. 11.7) to $0a''b$, and the change in price of x_1 is represented by a shift in the budget restriction from $M \leqslant 0$ to $M' \leqslant 0$.

The quantity sold for each individual is shown in Figure 11.9 as $0a'''$ or $\tilde{x}_1$, and it is assumed to be at a lower level of drive reduction $S^o < S^1$ is equal to the initial solution.

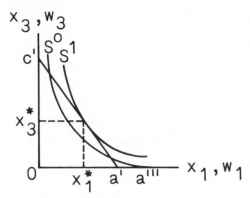

Fig. 11.9. Change in consumer demand for x_1 when x_3 is removed from the market.

Suppose that the total revenue of selling x_1^* and $\tilde{x}_1$ is the same, and letting π_3^* be equal to the profit from selling x_3^*, then $\tilde{\pi} > \pi^*$ if

$$C(\Sigma \tilde{x}_1^i) < C(\Sigma x_1^{*i}) - \pi_3^*$$

Thus given sufficient economies of scale, the firm would reduce the choice of products, thus increasing its profits and lowering the drive reduction of each consumer.

Model 11.4 is the essence of the argument by Scitovsky (1962) and others as to the absence of consumer sovereignty and the lowering of satisfaction to consumers with the advent of mass production techniques. Model 11.4 is indeed extreme, but even so the gain to the stockholders and/or managers of the firm cannot be judged against the loss to consumers. Relaxing the assumptions of Model 11.4 to allow a more competitive market structure, clearly a sufficient number of consumers must prefer the reduction in choice with the lowered price level of the mass-produced item to completely eliminate the additional product (the relative number benefited versus those made worse off depends upon the economies of scale associated with the two goods). Disregarding the effects on firms, the consumers can be classified into two groups: (1) those worse off after a change in the product set (Figure 11.9) and (2) those better off (Figure 11.10).

Whether those adversely affected by a change in the product set will be able to evoke institutional sanction against such practices will depend upon their number, threat sets, and the costs of collective action vis-à-vis those benefited.

As noted in Chapter 8, a capitalistic market structure is biased

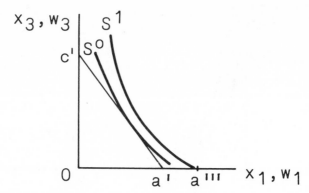

Fig. 11.10. Consumer who is benefited by a reduced product set.

toward the development of complex versus simple technologies. This is but another area where collective action may be beneficial to all concerned. By adopting an institution which would force all those benefited to contribute toward the development of the best technologies, such market failings could be corrected. For example, more funds could be collected for public research through institutions where the motivational structure is geared to the benefits of the consuming group rather than to profits alone. Although profits can represent consumer benefit, they can also represent the creation of a barrier to the benefit of a few rather than the many.

SUMMARY

The topics covered in this chapter only begin to scratch the surface of potential application of expanded models of individual behavior and social interaction. It is hoped that these examples have raised many more questions than they have answered, for the analysis is far from reaching any sort of ultimate stage. This approach is best viewed as a first step toward appropriate theory for relevant social questions. Further development awaits necessary time, interest, and empirical application.

Appendix to Chapter 2

THE SUBSTANTIAL LITERATURE on choice under uncertainty is primarily a consequence of the work of John von Neumann and Oskar Morgenstern (1947), the origins of which begin with Bernoulli (1954) in the eighteenth century and Ramsey (1931). This literature, dealing with choice when outcomes are subject to random events, has been omitted from the main body of the book since it represents a further complication to any decision process. In Chapter 4 the individual is assumed to be searching for the correct relations between products and activities and between activities and drives. Such relations are assumed to exist but are not known with certainty. The inclusion of activities whose outcome is variable when the actual relations are known would represent a further extension of the models developed. For example, in tossing a fair coin, establishing the correct relation would entail learning that the probability was equal to one-half, whereas in Chapter 4 it is assumed that the correct relations yield deterministic results.

In algebraic choice systems under uncertainty, the criterion of Bernoulli (and also that adopted by von Neumann and Morgenstern) is that the individual acts as if he maximizes expected utility. For any option open to the individual there are a series of possible outcomes. The expectation of option A is greater than option B, assuming a finite number of outcomes, if $\Sigma p_i U_{A_i} > \Sigma p_i U_{B_i}$, where p_i is either the subjective probability or the objective probability or relative frequency and where U_{A_i} and U_{B_i} are the utilities associated with outcome i under options A and B respectively.

The von Neumann-Morgenstern approach assumes numerical probability is equivalent to subjective probability and the probability of an event and its utility are independent. The axioms necessary for a slightly more general model are due to Herstein and Milnor (1953) and are as follows.

229

Assume:

A is a set of possible outcomes and there exists a binary relation on the set A.

$\gtrsim$ = preferred or indifferent to
$>$ = preferred to and implies $\gtrsim$ and not $\lesssim$
$\sim$ = indifferent to and implies $\gtrsim$ and $\lesssim$

If the following axioms of choice are satisfied for any $x, y, z \in A$ and $p, q \in [0, 1]$,

1. $\gtrsim$ is a weak ordering of A
2. $xpy \in A$
3. $xpy = y(1-p)x$
4. $(xpy)qy = xpgy$
5. $x1y = x$
6. $x \sim y$ implies $[x(1/2)z] \sim [y(1/2)z]$
7. $\{p|xpy \gtrsim z\}, \{p|z \gtrsim xpy\}$ are closed

Under these axioms of choice there exists a linear, order-preserving function $U: (A, \gtrsim) \longrightarrow R$, where U is unique up to a positive linear transformation.[1]

This result allows utility to be measured by a difference scale which is unique. By arbitrarily setting $U(x) = 1$, $U(z) = 0$, and $U(y) = p$, where $x \gtrsim y \gtrsim z$ and $y \sim xpz$, a scale of utility can be determined.

It is worth noting that serious questions can be raised with respect to the various assumptions employed. The independence of probability and outcome imply, for instance, that an individual would be indifferent between winning equal pots in a poker game with four aces and winning with a pair of deuces. The equating of numerical probability or relative frequency of an infinite number of repetitions with the subjective probability has been much criticized. This disallows such things as hunches and intuitive feels for particular outcomes. Perhaps this assumption is a normative one for "better" choice, but it does not necessarily explain and predict human behavior. In addition, the criterion of expected utility has no a priori validity. It seems reasonable that situations would arise where the various other moments of the probable utility distribution (variance, skewness, and the like) would be relevant to the final decision.[2]

Clearly axiom 6 as well as the statement of the following theorem

1. For detailed proof see Herstein and Milnor (1953) or Luce and Suppes in Luce, Bush, and Galanter (1965), pp. 284-91.
2. For extensive reviews of similar ideas see especially Luce and Raiffa (1957) and Raiffa and Schlaifer (1968).

imply that the utility function is separable and additive or that $\partial^2 U/\partial x \partial y = 0$. Axioms 1–7 place no particular restriction on the interpretation of the p's. If the p's are not interpreted as probabilities but as linear combinations of commodity bundles, even though the derived measure is unique it does not measure utility but merely commodities. Thus if the approach is going to measure utility, the p's need to be interpreted as creating gambling choices.

This von Neumann-Morgenstern (N-M) approach is a subtle but significant departure from the utility analysis under the traditional ordinal preference-ordering axioms. The analysis restricts choice to comparison of uncertain events and as such is a theory of choice among probability distributions and associated random variables; the choice set is different. The N-M axioms assert that if $z \lesssim y \lesssim x$, y is indifferent to some probabilistic combination of x and z. However, the probable combination of x and z necessary to be equal to y would depend upon the number of times the choice was going to be made. The choice between a one-time lottery ticket and a situation where the lottery ticket can be purchased an infinite number of times would in general make some difference to the individual. To this aspect the N-M axioms make no reference. In essence, the N-M approach purports to measure utility of preferences over commodities when it is actually measuring preferences of gambling events. Graphically, this means that Figures A.2 and A.3 could both be compatible with Figure A.1, yet the numerical value assigned to the U's in Figure A.2 are not equivalent to those assigned in Figure A.3.

Other unsuccessful attempts to measure utility have also been tried from a somewhat different approach.[3] The argument follows.

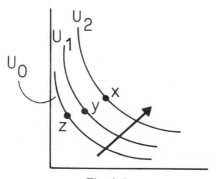

Fig. A.1

3. See Fellner (1967).

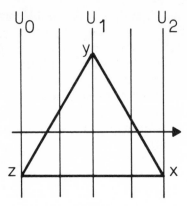

Fig. A.2

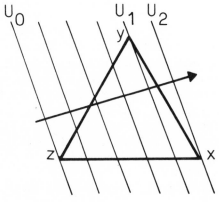

Fig. A.3

Since max U subject to $\Sigma P_i x_i = M$ results in $\partial U/\partial x_i = \lambda P_i$ as a first-order condition, if the U function is separable, that is,

$$\partial^2 U/\partial x \partial y = 0$$

under a system of changed prices and changed income levels such that the quantity of x purchased is the same in both, one should be able to measure the marginal utility of income up to a linear transformation. That is, let $\bar{x}$ be the quantity purchased under $\bar{P}$, $\bar{M}$ and $\bar{\bar{P}}$, $\bar{\bar{M}}$; let $\bar{\lambda}$ be the marginal utility of $\bar{M}$; and let $\bar{\bar{\lambda}}$ be the marginal utility of $\bar{\bar{M}}$, then

$$\partial U/\partial \bar{x} = \bar{\lambda}\bar{P}, \qquad \partial U/\partial \bar{\bar{x}} = \bar{\bar{\lambda}}\bar{\bar{P}}$$

then

$$\bar{\bar{P}}/\bar{P} = \bar{\lambda}/\bar{\bar{\lambda}}$$

This implies λ is the marginal utility of money. However, this is true only if the act of obtaining money creates neither utility nor disutility. As demonstrated in Chapter 3 and Appendix B, λ more precisely represents the marginal value of real balances. Thus if one were analyzing aristocrats who regularly clipped bond coupons with no effort, the analysis would be accurate. However, for the majority of society, the Lagrangian multiplier represents the marginal value of altering a constraint impinging upon their activities, such as market credit conditions as developed in Chapter 3.

The immediate alternative approach to choice under uncertainty is to measure subjective probability first. Ramsey (1931) suggested that finding a chance event with a subjective probability of one-half could be used to construct the utility function. Finally, the utility function is used to measure subjective probability. Extensive work with this particular approach has been done by Davidson, Suppes, and Siegel (1957), Davidson and Suppes (1956), and Suppes and Winet (1955), among others.

A theoretical approach to probability without consideration of utility originated with DeFinetti (1937)[4] and has been expanded by Savage (1954). Scott (1964) presents a more up-to-date and generalized analysis.

The application of utility under uncertain outcomes to theories of choice in games is an immediate step from the von Neumann-Morgenstern treatise and is included in their *Theory of Games and Economic Behavior*. The objection to this is that again there is no particular reason why expected utility should be maximized as opposed to the various other proposed criteria, for example, "regret" by Savage (1951), "satisficing" by Simon (1955, 1956), or "potential surprise" by Shackle (1955).[5] The problem which arises in a constant-sum game and which is intensified in a nonzero-sum game (exemplified by the "prisoner's dilemma") is twofold: (1) the relevancy of the various moments of the distributed utility outcome and (2) the assumed strategy employed by the opponent. Indeed, these aspects plus the virtual infinity of strategies available in a real-world situation and the associated lack of knowledge have dealt a severe blow to the promising applicability and usefulness that game theory held at one time.

An entirely different approach which has resulted in a great deal of theoretical verbiage and experimental application is that of the

---

4. Reprinted in Kyburg and Smokler (1964) with other similar articles.
5. For a detailed review see Luce and Raiffa (1957) or Thrall, Coombs, and Davis (1954). Also see Fellner (1965) for a survey and unique approach to choice under uncertainty.

general probabilistic choice theories. These can be summarized by the following general model.

Given that a person is in state A at time t_o, probabilities p and $1 - p$ exist such that at time $t_o + 1$ he will be in state B with a probability of p, or he will be in state C with a probability of $1 - p$. This principle assumes the response of an individual is governed by a probability. (This is quite useful for psychological experimentation, but this assumption essentially rejects a personal calculus by the decision maker.) Thus, only slight mention of the various sources will be given here.

Probabilistic choice theories can be separated into constant utility models, random utility models, probabilistic ranking theory, and probabilistic choice under uncertainty. For a review see Luce and Suppes in Luce, Bush, and Galanter, (1965) and Luce (1959).

Appendix to Chapter 3

MODEL 3.2

I.

Maximize

$$S = \phi(w_1, \ldots, w_n, \omega_1, \ldots, \omega_m) \tag{B.1}$$
$$w_i = \gamma_i(x_1, \ldots, x_k) \quad i = 1, \ldots, n \tag{B.2}$$

subject to

$$\sum_{i=1}^{k} P_i x_i \leqslant M_o \tag{B.3}$$

$$\psi(w_1, \ldots, w_n, \omega_1, \ldots, \omega_m) \leqslant T_o \tag{B.4}$$

$$x_i, w_j, \omega_l \geqslant 0, i = 1, \ldots, k; j = 1, \ldots, n; l = 1, \ldots, m \tag{B.5}$$

I is equivalent to II.

II.

Maximize

$$S = \phi^*(x_1, \ldots, x_k, \omega_1, \ldots, \omega_m) \tag{B.6}$$

subject to

$$\Sigma P_i x_i \leqslant M_o \tag{B.7}$$

$$\psi^*(x_1, \ldots, x_k, \omega_1, \ldots, \omega_m) \leqslant T_o \tag{B.8}$$

Assuming that a regular constrained maximum exists, the solution occurs on the boundary of the constraints and the inequalities in Equation B.7 and B.8 become equalities. The first-

235

order conditions are

III.

$$(\partial\phi*/\partial x_1) - \lambda_1 P_1 - \lambda_2 (\partial\psi*/\partial x_1) = 0$$

$$\vdots \qquad\qquad \vdots$$

$$(\partial\phi*/\partial x_k) - \lambda_1 P_k - \lambda_2 (\partial\psi*/\partial x_k) = 0$$

(B.9)

$$(\partial\phi*/\partial\omega_1) - \lambda_2 (\partial\psi*/\partial\omega_1) = 0$$

$$\vdots \qquad\qquad \vdots$$

$$(\partial\phi*/\partial\omega_m) - \lambda_2 (\partial\psi*/\partial\omega_m) = 0$$

$$\sum_{i=1}^{k} P_i x_i = M_o \qquad\qquad (B.10)$$

$$\psi*(x_1, \ldots, x_k) = T_o \qquad\qquad (B.11)$$

Suppose there is a parametric change in the budget or credit constraint condition M_o, dM_o. Differentiating Equation B.9 with respect to M_o and dropping the superscripts, one obtains

IV.

$$\frac{\partial^2\phi}{\partial x_i\partial x_1}\frac{\partial x_1}{\partial M_o} + \cdots + \frac{\partial^2\phi}{\partial x_i\partial x_k}\frac{\partial x_k}{\partial M_o} + \frac{\partial^2\phi}{\partial x_i\partial\omega_1}\frac{\partial\omega_1}{\partial M_o} \cdots$$

$$+ \frac{\partial^2\phi}{\partial x_i\partial\omega_m}\frac{\partial\omega_m}{\partial M_o}$$

$$- P_i\frac{\partial\lambda_1}{\partial M_o} - \frac{\partial\psi}{\partial x_i}\frac{\partial\lambda_2}{\partial M_o} - \lambda_2\frac{\partial^2\psi}{\partial x_i\partial x_1} - \cdots$$

$$- \lambda_2\frac{\partial^2\psi}{\partial x_i\partial x_k}\frac{\partial x_k}{\partial M_o} - \lambda_2\frac{\partial^2\psi}{\partial x_i\partial\omega_1}\frac{\partial\omega_1}{\partial M_o} - \cdots$$

$$- \frac{\partial^2\psi}{\partial x_i\partial\omega_m}\frac{\partial\omega_m}{\partial M_o} = 0 \text{ for all } i \qquad (B.12)$$

Letting $\partial^2\phi/\partial x_i\partial x_j = \phi_{ij}$ and $\partial^2\psi/\partial x_i\partial x_j = T_{ij}$ and differentiating all equations in III with respect to M_o and writing the resulting system of $k + m + 2$ in matrix form, system V results.

V.

$$
\begin{bmatrix}
\phi_{11} - \lambda_2 T_{11} & \cdots & \phi_{1k+1} - \lambda_2 T_{1k+1} & \cdots & \phi_{1k+m} - \lambda_2 T_{1k+m} \\
\vdots & & \vdots & & \vdots \\
\phi_{k1} - \lambda_2 T_{k1} & \cdots & \phi_{kk+1} - \lambda_2 T_{kk+1} & \cdots & \phi_{kk+m} - \lambda_2 T_{kk+m} \\
\phi_{k+11} - \lambda_2 T_{k+11} & \cdots & \phi_{k+1k+1} - \lambda_2 T_{k+1k+1} & \cdots & \phi_{k+1k+m} - \lambda_2 T_{k+1k+m} \\
\vdots & & \vdots & & \vdots \\
\phi_{k+m1} - \lambda_2 T_{k+m1} & \cdots & \phi_{k+mk+1} - \lambda_2 T_{k+mk+1} & \cdots & \phi_{k+nk+m} - \lambda_2 T_{k+nk+m} \\
-P_1 & \cdots & 0 & & 0 \\
-\dfrac{\partial \psi}{\partial x_1} & \cdots & -\dfrac{\partial \psi}{\partial \omega_1} & & -\dfrac{\partial \psi}{\partial \omega_m}
\end{bmatrix}
$$

$$
\times
\begin{bmatrix}
\dfrac{\partial x_1}{\partial M_o} \\
\vdots \\
\dfrac{\partial x_k}{\partial M_o} \\
\dfrac{\partial \omega_1}{\partial M_o} \\
\vdots \\
\dfrac{\partial \omega_m}{\partial M_o}
\end{bmatrix}
+
\begin{bmatrix}
-P_1 & -\dfrac{\partial \psi}{\partial x_1} \\
\vdots & \vdots \\
-P_k & -\dfrac{\partial \psi}{\partial x_k} \\
0 & -\dfrac{\partial \psi}{\partial \omega_1} \\
\vdots & \vdots \\
0 & -\dfrac{\partial \psi}{\partial \omega_m} \\
0 & 0 \\
0 & 0
\end{bmatrix}
\begin{bmatrix}
\dfrac{\partial \lambda_1}{\partial M_o} \\
\dfrac{\partial \lambda_2}{\partial M_o}
\end{bmatrix}
=
\begin{bmatrix}
0 \\
\vdots \\
0 \\
0 \\
\vdots \\
0 \\
-1 \\
0
\end{bmatrix}
\tag{B.13}
$$

or notationally, $[\phi] \, [\partial x/\partial M_o] = [\partial v/\partial M_o]$.

Solving by Cramer's rule,

$$
\partial x_i/\partial M_o = (-1)^{i+k+m+2} \, (|\phi_{k+m+1,i}|/|\phi|)
\tag{B.14}
$$

$$
\partial \omega_j/\partial M_o = (-1)^{j+2k+m+2} \, (|\phi_{k+m+2,j+k}|/|\phi|)
\tag{B.15}
$$

where $|\phi|$ is the determinant of $[\phi]$ and $|\phi_{ij}|$ is the determinant of the cofactor matrix of $[\phi]$.

To simplify the notation, let $\theta_{ij} = \phi_{ij} - \lambda_2 T_{ij}$ and $r = k + m$. Solving for a change in the time constraint T_o, dT_o, system VI is obtained similar to system V.

VI.

$$
\begin{bmatrix}
\theta_{11} & \cdots & \theta_{1r} & -P_1 & -\dfrac{\partial \psi}{\partial x_1} \\
\vdots & & \vdots & \vdots & \\
\theta_{k1} & \cdots & \theta_{kr} & -P_k & -\dfrac{\partial \psi}{\partial x_k} \\
\theta_{k+11} & \cdots & \theta_{k+1} & 0 & -\dfrac{\partial \psi}{\partial \omega_1} \\
\vdots & & \vdots & \vdots & \\
\theta_{r1} & \cdots & \theta_{rr} & 0 & -\dfrac{\partial \psi}{\partial \omega_m} \\
-P_1 & \cdots & 0 & 0 & 0 \\
-\dfrac{\partial \psi}{\partial x_1} & \cdots & -\dfrac{\partial \psi}{\partial \omega_m} & 0 & 0
\end{bmatrix}
\begin{bmatrix}
\dfrac{\partial x_1}{\partial T_o} \\
\vdots \\
\dfrac{\partial x_k}{\partial T_o} \\
\dfrac{\partial \omega_1}{\partial T_o} \\
\vdots \\
\dfrac{\partial \omega_m}{\partial T_o} \\
\dfrac{\partial x_1}{\partial T_o} \\
\dfrac{\partial \lambda_2}{\partial T_o}
\end{bmatrix}
=
\begin{bmatrix}
0 \\
\vdots \\
\vdots \\
\vdots \\
0 \\
0 \\
-1
\end{bmatrix}
\quad (B.16)
$$

or $[\theta] [\partial x/\partial T_o] = [\partial v/\partial T_o]$, where $[\theta] = [\phi]$ in V.
Solving Equation B.16,

$$\partial x_i/\partial T_o = (-1)^{i+r+3} \, (|\theta_{r+2,i}|/|\theta|) \tag{B.17}$$

$$\partial \omega_j/\partial T_o = (-1)^{j+k+r+3} \, (|\theta_{r+2,j+k}|/|\theta|) \tag{B.18}$$

Then by adding Equations B.13 and B.16,

VII.

$$[\theta] [\partial x/\partial M_o] + [\theta] [\partial x/\partial T_o] = [\partial v/\partial M_o + \partial v/\partial T_o] \tag{B.19}$$

or

$$[\theta] [\partial x/\partial M_o + \partial x/\partial T_o] = [\partial v/\partial M_o + \partial v/\partial T_o] \tag{B.20}$$

Let

$$[\partial x/\partial R_o] = [\partial x/\partial M_o + \partial x/\partial T_o]$$

$$[\partial v/\partial R_o] = [\partial v/\partial M_o + \partial v/\partial T_o] =
\begin{bmatrix}
0 \\
\vdots \\
0 \\
-1 \\
-1
\end{bmatrix}$$

then

$$[\theta] [\partial x/\partial R_o] = [\partial v/\partial R_o] \tag{B.21}$$

Solving Equation B.21,

$$\partial x_i / \partial R_o = \frac{(-1)^{i+r} |\theta_{r+1,i}| + (-1)^{i+r+1} |\theta_{r+2,i}|}{|\theta|} \tag{B.22}$$

The result of a price change can be similarly derived, that is, $dP_i > 0$ results in $r + 2$ equations as shown in Equation B.23.

VIII.

$$
\begin{bmatrix}
\theta_{11} \cdots & \theta_{1r} - P_1 & - \dfrac{\partial \psi}{\partial x_1} \\
\vdots & \vdots & \vdots & \vdots \\
\theta_{r1} & \theta_{rr} & 0 & -\dfrac{\partial \psi}{\partial \omega_m} \\
-P_1 & 0 & 0 & 0 \\
-\dfrac{\partial \psi}{\partial x_1} \cdots & -\dfrac{\partial \psi}{\partial \omega_m} & 0 & 0
\end{bmatrix}
\begin{bmatrix}
\dfrac{\partial x_1}{\partial P_i} \\
\vdots \\
\dfrac{\partial \omega_m}{\partial P_i} \\
\dfrac{\partial \lambda_1}{\partial P_i} \\
\dfrac{\partial \lambda_2}{\partial P_i}
\end{bmatrix}
=
\begin{bmatrix}
0 \\
\vdots \\
\lambda_1 \\
\vdots \\
0 \\
x_i \\
0
\end{bmatrix}
\tag{B.23}
$$

or

$$[\theta] [\partial x / \partial P_i] = [\partial v / \partial P_i] \tag{B.24}$$

Solving Equation B.23,

$$\frac{\partial x_j}{\partial P_i} = (-1)^{i+j} \lambda_1 \frac{|\theta_{i,j}|}{|\theta|}$$

$$+ x_1(-1)^{j+r+1} \frac{|\theta_{r+1,j}|}{|\theta|}, \quad j = 1, \ldots, k \tag{B.25}$$

$$\frac{\partial \omega_j}{\partial P_i} = (-1)^{i+k+j} \lambda_1 \frac{|\theta_{i,k+j}|}{|\theta|}$$

$$+ x_i(-1)^{j+r+1} \frac{|\theta_{1+k,r+j}|}{|\theta|}, \quad j = 1, \ldots, m \tag{B.26}$$

The foregoing analysis can be alternatively viewed in the following manner. Define Pw_i to be the price of an activity which is a function, in general, of the levels of activities undertaken.

IX.

$$Pw_i = Pw_i(w_i, \ldots, w_n) \tag{B.27}$$

Then maximize

$$S = \phi(w_1, \ldots, w_n, \omega_1, \ldots, \omega_m) \qquad (B.28)$$

subject to

$$\sum_{i=1}^{n} Pw_i w_i \leqslant 0$$

$$\psi(w_1, \ldots, w_n, \omega_1, \ldots, \omega_m) \leqslant T_0$$

gives the Lagrangian equation

$$\begin{aligned}
\lambda = \phi(w_1, \ldots, \omega_m) &- \lambda_1(\Sigma Pw_i w_i) \\
&+ \lambda_2 [T_0 - \psi(w_1, \ldots, \omega_m)] \qquad (B.29)
\end{aligned}$$

The first-order conditions are:

$$\frac{\partial \lambda}{\partial w_i} = \frac{\partial \phi}{\partial w_i} - \lambda_1 \left\{ \sum_{j=1}^{n} \frac{\partial Pw_j}{\partial w_i} w_j + Pw_i \right\}$$

$$- \lambda_2 \frac{\partial \psi}{\partial w_i} \leqslant 0, \qquad i = 1, \ldots, n \qquad (B.30)$$

$$\frac{\partial \lambda}{\partial \omega_i} = \frac{\partial \phi}{\partial \omega_i} - \lambda_2 \frac{\partial \psi}{\partial \omega_i} \leqslant 0, \qquad i = 1, \ldots, m \qquad (B.31)$$

Assuming the equality holds, dPw_i results in

$$
\begin{bmatrix}
\theta_{11} & \ldots \theta_{1r} & -\pi_1 & -\dfrac{\partial \psi}{\partial w_1} \\
\vdots & \vdots & \vdots & \vdots \\
\theta_{n1} & \ldots \theta_{nr} & -\pi_n & \dfrac{\partial \psi}{\partial w_n} \\
\theta_{n+11} & \ldots \theta_{n+1r} & 0 & -\dfrac{\partial \psi}{\partial \omega_1} \\
\vdots & \vdots & \vdots & \vdots \\
\theta_{r1} & \ldots \theta_{rr} & 0 & -\dfrac{\partial \psi}{\partial \omega_m} \\
-\pi_1 & \ldots 0 & 0 & 0 \\
-\dfrac{\partial \psi}{\partial w_1} & \ldots -\dfrac{\partial \psi}{\partial \omega_m} & 0 & 0
\end{bmatrix}
\begin{bmatrix}
\dfrac{\partial w_1}{\partial Pw_i} \\
\vdots \\
\dfrac{\partial w_n}{\partial Pw_i} \\
\dfrac{\partial \omega_1}{\partial Pw_i} \\
\vdots \\
\dfrac{\partial \omega_m}{\partial Pw_i} \\
\dfrac{\partial \lambda_1}{\partial Pw_i} \\
\dfrac{\partial \lambda_2}{\partial Pw_i}
\end{bmatrix}
=
\begin{bmatrix}
0 \\
\vdots \\
0 \\
0 \\
\vdots \\
0 \\
w_i \\
0
\end{bmatrix}
\qquad (B.32)
$$

where

$$\theta_{ij} = \frac{\partial^2 \phi}{\partial w_i \partial w_j} - \lambda_2 \frac{\partial^2 \psi}{\partial w_i \partial w_j} - \lambda_1 \frac{\partial P w_j}{\partial w_i}$$

$$- \lambda_1 \sum_{k=1}^{r} w_k \frac{\partial^2 P w_k}{\partial w_i \partial w_j} \tag{B.33}$$

$$\pi_i = \sum_{j=1}^{n} \frac{\partial P w_j}{\partial w_i} w_j + P w_i \tag{B.34}$$

$$\frac{\partial w_j}{\partial P w_i} = (-1)^{j+r+1} w_i \frac{|\theta_{r+1,j}|}{|\theta|} \tag{B.35}$$

Similarly, a parametric change in the budget and time constraints yields Equations B.36 and B.37 respectively.

$$\frac{\partial w_j}{\partial M_0} = (-1)^{r+j+2} \frac{|\theta_{r+1,j}|}{|\theta|} \tag{B.36}$$

$$\frac{\partial w_j}{\partial T_0} = (-1)^{r+j+3} \frac{|\theta_{r+2,j}|}{|\theta|} \tag{B.37}$$

As discussed in the text, a change in the knowledge set can manifest itself as equivalent to a change in the parameters of the model. This can be as any three of those discussed above or as a change in the functional form of $\psi(w_1, \ldots, \omega_m)$. If the functional change can be approximated by a small change in the first partials of ψ evaluated at max S, then $d(\partial \psi / \partial w_i) > 0$ results in the following effects.

Let $d(\partial \psi / \partial w_i) = d\psi_i$, then the analogous system of Equations B.32 is given by Equation B.38.

X.

$$
\begin{bmatrix}
\theta_{11} & \cdots & \theta_{1r} & -\pi_1 & -\dfrac{\partial \psi}{\partial w_i} \\
\vdots & & \vdots & \vdots & \vdots \\
\theta_{n+11} & \cdots & \theta_{n+1r} & 0 & -\dfrac{\partial \psi}{\partial w_1} \\
\vdots & & \vdots & \vdots & \vdots \\
\theta_{r1} & \cdots & \theta_{rr} & 0 & \dfrac{\partial \psi}{\partial w_m} \\
-\pi_1 & \cdots & 0 & 0 & 0 \\
-\dfrac{\partial \psi}{\partial w_1} & \cdots & -\dfrac{\partial \psi}{\partial w_m} & 0 & 0
\end{bmatrix}
\begin{bmatrix}
\dfrac{\partial w_i}{\partial \psi_i} \\
\vdots \\
\cdot \\
\vdots \\
\dfrac{\partial w_m}{\partial \psi_i} \\
\dfrac{\partial \lambda_1}{\partial \psi_i} \\
\dfrac{\partial \lambda_2}{\partial \psi_i}
\end{bmatrix}
=
\begin{bmatrix}
0 \\
\vdots \\
\cdot \\
\vdots \\
\cdot \\
0 \\
w_i
\end{bmatrix}
$$

(B.38)

where

$$
\theta_{ij} = \frac{\partial^2 \theta}{\partial w_i \partial w_j} - \lambda_1 \frac{\partial Pw_i}{\partial w_i} - \lambda_1 \sum_{k=1}^{r} \frac{\partial^2 Pw_i}{\partial w_i \partial w_j} w_k - \lambda_1 \frac{\partial Pw_i}{\partial w_j}
$$

$$
- \lambda_2 \frac{\partial^2 \psi}{\partial w_i \partial w_j}
$$

(B.39)

$$
\pi_i = \sum_{j=1}^{n} (\partial Pw_j / \partial w_i) w_j + Pw_i
$$

(B.40)

Solving Equation B.38, Equation B.41 is the substitution effect on activity j due to a change in the marginal time use of activity i.

$$
\partial w_j / \partial \psi_i = (-1)^{j+r+2} \frac{|\theta_{r+2,j}|}{|\theta|}
$$

(B.41)

Appendix to Chapter 4

IN THIS APPENDIX a more detailed analysis of the statistical properties of Bayesian probability theory and estimation techniques is presented. This synopsis of the relevant statistical literature can be found in further detail elsewhere.[1]

If one defines a simple sample as one generated from a binomial distribution, the probability of any sequence of r successes and s failures out of N trials, $r + s = N$, is

$$p^r(1-p)^s \qquad (C.1)$$

If p is unknown, it can be considered as a sample from a super-population with its own density function $f(x)$ and cumulative density function $F(x)$, that is, $P(p \leqslant x) = F(x)$. Then for each sequence of sample size N with r successes and s failures, the probability of each sequence is

$$\int_0^1 x^r(1-x)^s dF(x) \qquad (C.2)$$

(If the binary process is permutable—the probabilities are indepen-dent of the sequence—then any outcome of (r, s) can be expressed in this form and, furthermore, $F(p)$ is unique.)[2] Thus the probability of r successes and s failures, $P(r, s)$, would be

$$P(r, s) = \binom{N}{r} \int_0^1 x^r(1-x)^s dF(x) \qquad (C.3)$$

1. See especially Good (1965) and the references cited therein and Raiffa and Schlaifer (1968).
2. For a detailed proof of this see DeFinetti (1937) or Good (1965).

where

$$\binom{N}{r} = \frac{N!}{r!(N-r)!} = \frac{N!}{r!s!}$$

The question is, What is the nature of the superpopulation density function $f(p)$? Bayes's postulate was that $f(p) = 1$ and $F(p) = p$, which was used in Chapter 4 as a condition of ignorance.

If $F(x) = x$, then $dF(x) = f(x)dx = dx$; and the probability of r successes and s failures becomes

$$P(r, s) = \binom{N}{r} \int_0^1 x^r(1-x)^s dx \qquad (C.4)$$

and therefore the expected value of p under the Bayes postulate is $(r+1)/(N+1)$ by Laplace's rule of succession or as shown in Chapter 4.

Since Bayes's postulate is quite restrictive, it does not allow the use of prior information other than that implied by our interpretation of perfect ignorance; other forms for $f(p)$ have been promulgated. Specifically, Hardy and Lidstone (HL)[3] postulated that $f(p)$ is a beta function with parameters α, β, that is,

$$f(p) = p^\alpha(1-p)^\beta, \alpha > -1, \beta > -1$$

Since $dF(p) = f(p)dp$, the expected value of p after r successes and s failures under the HL postulate is:

$$\int_0^1 p^{r+1}(1-p)^s \, dF(p) = \int_0^1 p^{r+1}(1-p)^s f(p)dp$$

$$\int_0^1 p^{r+\alpha+1}(1-p)^{\beta+s}dp = (r+\alpha+1)/(\alpha+\beta+N+2) \qquad (C.5)$$

Clearly this amounts to adding α successes and β failures to the observed successes and failures (r,s). For example, α and β could be generated by an "imaginary" experiment. This amounts to a subjective alteration of the probability estimation processes.

Suppose that one wants to estimate the value of p. Then by familiar maximum likelihood techniques (ML) the estimate would be r/N. However, for an analysis of individual behavior, and especially when the sample size N is small, this estimator is clearly unsatisfactory. Suppose that $r = N$, then the ML estimate of p would be 1. Yet one can easily give examples where individuals would not act in this

3. See Hardy (1949) and Lidstone (1920).

manner, that is, assign complete certainty of success to future samples.

While adding parameters such as α and β is somewhat arbitrary, it is no more so than the ML estimator which implicitly uses a superpopulation density function of $p^{-1}(1-p)^{-1}$, that is, $\alpha = -1$, $\beta = -1$.

However, distinction between the degree of subjectivity in altering estimation techniques is really not relevant to Chapter 4 in general, since even the assigning of observed successes and failures was analyzed as being a subjective process on the part of the individual.

The entire approach with a binomial distribution can be generalized to a multinomial distribution as demonstrated in Good (1965). In a multinomial sample there are t categories (or characteristics or classifications) with probabilities p_i such that $\Sigma_{i=1}^{t} p_i = 1$. If n_i is the frequency of category i in the sample N (that is, $\Sigma_{i=1}^{t} n_i = N =$ sample size), the probability of such a sequence is

$$p_1^{n_1} p_2^{n_2} \cdots p_{t-1}^{n_{t-1}} \left(1 - \sum_{i=1}^{t-1} p_i\right)^{n_t} \tag{C.6}$$

which is the generalization of Equation C.1. Again, if the p_i's are unknown, the probability of such a sequence is

$$\int_0^1 \int_0^1 \cdots \int_0^1 p_1^{n_1} \cdots p_{t-1} \left(1 - \sum_{i=1}^{t-1} p_i\right)^{n_t} d_1 d_2$$

$$\cdots d_{t-1} F(p_1, \ldots, p_{t-1}) \tag{C.7}$$

The natural generalization of Bayes's postulate is to assume $F(p_1, \ldots, p_{t-1})$ is uniform in the simplex $\Sigma_{i=1}^{t} p_i = 1$. The analogous expected value of p_i is

$$\bar{p}_i = (n_i + 1)/(N + t) \tag{C.8}$$

compared to the ML estimate of p,

$$\bar{p}_i = n_i/N \tag{C.9}$$

Similarly, the implementation of a more general superpopulation density function for the p_i's is the Dirichlet distribution with parameters k_i, $i = 1, \ldots, t$:

$$\Gamma(\Sigma k_i) \prod_i \left\{\frac{p_i^{k_i-1}}{(k_i)}\right\} = \text{Dirichlet distribution} \tag{C.10}$$

This can easily be shown to be equivalent to a Beta distribution if $t = 2$, that is,

$$\Gamma(\Sigma k_i) \prod_i \left\{ \frac{p_i^{k_i-1}}{(k_i)} \right\} = \frac{\Gamma(k_1 + k_2)}{\Gamma(k_1)\Gamma(k_2)} p^{k_1-1} (1-p)^{k_2-1} \qquad (C.11)$$

Since

$$\frac{\Gamma(k_1)\Gamma(k_2)}{\Gamma(k_1 + k_2)} = B(k_1, k_2) = \text{Beta distribution}$$

Equation C.11 becomes

$$\frac{p^{k_1-1}(1-p)^{k_2-1}}{B(k_1, k_2)} = \frac{p^{k_1-1}(1-p)^{k_2-1}}{p^{-k_1}(1-p)^{-k_2}} = p^{2k_1-1}(1-p)^{2k_2-1} \qquad (C.12)$$

Equation C.12 is equal to $p^{\alpha}(1-p)^{\beta}$, where $\alpha = 2k_1 - 1$, $\beta = 2k_2 - 1$. Therefore the estimate for p_i becomes

$$\overline{p}_i = (n_i + k_i)/(N + k_i t) \qquad (C.13)$$

Clearly, the generalization of the Bayes's postulate implies that $k_i = 1$, while the ML estimation implies that $k_i = 0$. In any case the value of each k_i is a subjective value depending upon the individual, the essence of others' information, and the specific problem.[4]

The implications of the above generalization of the binomial probability distribution relieve many of the "interpretative" aspects of the special analysis of Chapter 4 but do not change the essence of the simplified argument.

With the multinomial approach one can view the individual as partitioning an activity into several characteristics or categories and from past experience, assigning a number of successes to each category. Again the only important aspect of the assigning of successes n_i to each category is their relativity. $N = \Sigma n_i$ is the intensity of the actual, observed experience and the k_i's result from imagined experiences such as those from advertising and the like.

The estimation procedure and the changing of the knowledge set as developed in Chapter 4 would be essentially unchanged. The difference, of course, would be the jointness of the multinomial distribution to estimating arbitrary categories of the activities carried out and/or imagined. Note, however, that the modification to the estimation procedure as shown in Equation C.13 is slight, but depen-

---

4. Jeffreys (1961) suggested $k = 1/2$, while Perks (1947) advocated $k = 1/t$. While each have some merits, neither is sufficiently general for all situations.

dent upon the number of categories. This in turn would alter the specific analysis of special cases such as the quantity of advertising necessary to "alter" preferences, for example. However, the more general analysis of cases I.1 and I.2 in Chapter 4, where μ_i^j's, $P[E_j/(x_s)] = \mu_i^j$, are assigned by any method remains unchanged.

Bibliography

Ackoff, R. L. 1962. Scientific Methods. New York, Wiley.

Anspach, Ralph. 1966. The general incompatibility of the traditional consumer equilibrium with economic rationality—an exploratory analysis. *Oxford Econ. Papers* 18: 71-82.

Arrow, K. J. 1962. The economic implications of learning by doing. *Rev. Econ. Stud.* 29: 152-73.

_____. 1963. Social Choice and Individual Values, 2nd ed. New York, Wiley.

_____. 1969. Classificatory notes on the production and transmission of technological knowledge. *Am. Econ. Assoc. Papers and Proc.*, pp. 29-35.

Arrow, K. J., and Enthoven, A. C. 1961. Quasi-concave programming. *Econometrica* 29: 779-800.

Ayres, C. E. 1962. The Theory of Economic Progress, 2nd ed. New York, Schocken.

Bailey, M. 1959. Formal criteria for investment decisions. *J. Polit. Econ.* 67: 476-88.

Baldwin, W. L., and Childs, G. L. 1969. The fast second and rivalry in research and development. *Southern Econ. J.* 35: 18-24.

Bain, Joe S. 1956. Barriers to New Competition. Cambridge, Harvard Univ. Press.

_____. 1959. Industrial Organization. New York, Wiley.

Baumol, W. J., and Goldfeld, S. M. 1968. Precursors in Mathematical Economics. London, London School of Econ.

Baumol, W. J., and Quandt, R. E. 1964. Rules of thumb and optimally imperfect decisions. *Am. Econ. Rev.* 54: 23-41.

Becker, Gary S. 1964. Human Capital. New York, Columbia Univ. Press.

_____. 1965. A theory of the allocation of time. *Econ. J.* 75: 493-517.

Bernoulli, Daniel. 1954. Exposition of a new theory on measurement of risk. *Econometrica* 22: 23-36.

Blaug, Mark. 1968. The private and social returns on investment in education: Some results from Great Britain. *J. Hum. Resources* 2: 330-46.

_____. 1969. Economic Theory in Retrospect. Homewood, Ill., Irwin.

Breton, A., and Breton, R. 1969. An economic theory of social movements. *Am. Econ. Rev.* 59: 198-205.

Buchanan, J. M., and Tullock, G. 1962. Calculus of Consent. Ann Arbor, Univ. of Mich. Press.

Chamberlin, Edward. 1948. The Theory of Monopolistic Competition, 6th ed. Cambridge, Harvard Univ. Press.

Chipman, John S. 1960. The foundations of utility. Econometrica 28: 193-224.

Chipman, John, Hurwicz, Leonid, Richter, Marcel, and Sonnenschein, Hugo. 1971. Preferences, Utility, and Demand. New York, Harcourt Brace Jovanovich.

Coase, Ronald. 1937. The nature of the firm. Econometrica 4: 386-405.

Coats, A. W. 1969. Is there a structure of scientific revolutions in economics? Kyklos 22: 250-65.

Collins, B., and Guetzkow, H. 1964. A Social Psychology of Group Processes for Decision Making. New York, Wiley.

Commons, J. R. 1934. Institutional Economics. Vols. 1 and 2. New York, Macmillan.

Davidson, Donald, and Suppes, Patrick. 1956. A finitistic axiomatization of subjective probability and utility. Econometrica 24: 264-75.

———, Suppes, Patrick, and Siegel, Sidney. 1957. Decision Making: An Experimental Approach. Stanford, Stanford Univ. Press.

DeFinetti, Bruno. 1937. La prevision, ses lois logiques, ses sources subjectives. Ann. Inst. Poincari 7: 1-68. Translated in H. E. Kyburg and H. E. Smokler, eds., Studies in Subjective Probability, pp. 93-158. New York, Wiley, 1964.

Dember, William N. 1961. The Psychology of Perception. New York, Holt, Rinehart, and Winston.

Demsetz, Harold. 1970. The private production of public goods. J. Law Econ. 13: 293-306.

Dewey, Donald. 1965. Modern Capital Theory. New York, Columbia Univ. Press.

Dollard, John, and Miller, N. E. 1950. Personality and Psychotherapy. New York, McGraw-Hill.

Doyle, Peter. 1968a. Advertising expenditure and consumer demand. Oxford Econ. Papers 20: 394-416.

———. 1968b. Economic aspects of advertising: A survey. Econ. J. 78: 570-602.

Durkheim, Emile. 1947. Division of Labor in Society. Reprint. New York, Free Press.

Etzioni, A. 1968. The Active Society. New York, Free Press.

Etzioni, A., and Etzioni, E. 1964. Social Change. New York, Basic Books.

Fellner, William. 1962. Rate and Direction of Inventive Activity. Princeton, Princeton Univ. Press.

———. 1965. Probability and Profit. Homewood, Ill., Irwin.

———. 1967. Operational utility: The theoretical background and a measurement. In W. Fellner et al., Ten Economic Studies in the Tradition of Irving Fisher, pp. 39-74. New York, Wiley.

Fisher, Irving. 1930. The Theory of Interest. New York, Macmillan.

Fortes, M., ed. 1965. African Systems of Thought. London, Oxford Univ. Press.

Friedman, M. 1953. Essays in Positive Economics. Chicago, Univ. of Chicago Press.

Galbraith, J. K. 1956. American Capitalism. Boston, Houghton Mifflin.

———. 1967. The New Industrial State. New York, Houghton Mifflin.

General Electric Corporation. Annual report. 1968.

Gherity, J. A., ed. 1965. Economic Thought: An Historical Anthology. New York, Random House.

Good, I. J. 1965. The Estimation of Probabilities: An Essay on Modern Bayesian Methods. Cambridge, MIT Press.

Griliches, Zvi. 1957. Hybrid corn: An exploration in the economics of technical change. Econometrica 25: 501–22.

Haavelmo, T. 1960. Study in the Pure Theory of Investment. Chicago, Univ. of Chicago Press.

Hadley, G. 1964. Nonlinear and Dynamic Programming. Reading, Addison-Wesley.

Hardy, G. H. 1949. Divergent Series. London, Oxford Univ. Press.

Helson, Harry. 1964. Adaptation-Level Theory. New York, Harper and Row.

Hirshleifer, J. 1958. On the theory of optimal investment decisions. J. Polit. Econ. 66: 329–52.

Herstein, I. N., and Milnor, J. 1953. An axiomatic approach to measurable utility. Econometrica 21: 291–97.

Holdren, Bob R. 1968. The Structure of a Retail Market and the Market Behavior of Retail Firms. Ames, Iowa State Univ. Press.

Houthakker, H. S. 1961. The present state of consumption theory: A survey article. Econometrica 29: 704–40.

Hull, C. L. 1943. Principles of Behavior. New York, Appleton-Century-Crofts.

Hurwicz, Leonid. 1969. On the concept and possibility of informational decentralization. Am. Econ. Assoc. Papers and Proc., pp. 513–24.

Isaacs, Rufus. 1965. Differential Games. New York, Wiley.

Jeffreys, Harold. 1961. Theory of Probability, 3rd ed. London, Clarendon Press.

Jen, F. C., and Southwick, L. 1969. Implications of dynamic monopoly behavior. Am. Econ. Rev. 59: 149–58.

Johnson, Harry G. 1958. Demand theory further revised, or goods are goods. Econometrica 25: 149.

Jorgenson, D. W., and Stephenson, J. A. 1967a. The time structure of investment in U.S. manufacturing. Rev. Econ. Studies 34: 16–27.

———, 1967b. Investment behavior in U.S. manufacturing. Econometrica 35: 169–220.

Kalman, Peter J. 1968. Theory of consumer behavior when prices enter the utility function. Econometrica 36: 497–510.

Katz, D., and Kahn, R. L. 1966. Social Psychology of Organizations. New York, Wiley.

Kennedy, C. 1964. Induced bias in innovation and the theory of distribution. Econ. J. 74: 541–47.

Koopman, Bernard O. 1940. The bases of probability. Am. Math. Soc. Bull. 46: 763–74.

Koopmans, T. C. 1957. Three Essays on the State of Economic Science. New York, McGraw-Hill.

_____. 1960. Stationary ordinal utility and impatience. *Econometrica* 28: 287-309.

Koopmans, T., Diamond, Peter, and Williamson, R. E. 1964. Stationary utility and time perspective. *Econometrica* 32:82-100.

Kornhauser, W. 1959. The Politics of Mass Society. New York, Free Press.

Kraemer, H. C. 1964. Point estimation in learning models. *J. Math. Psychol.* 1: 28-53.

Kuhn, T. S. 1962. The Structure of Scientific Revolutions. Chicago, Univ. of Chicago Press.

Kyburg, H. E., and Smokler, H. E. 1964. Studies in Subjective Probability. New York, Wiley.

Lancaster, Kelvin J. 1965. Change and innovation in the technology of consumption. *Am. Econ. Assoc., Papers and Proc.*, pp. 14-23.

_____. 1966. A new approach to consumer theory. *J. Polit. Econ.* 74: 132-57.

Levhari, D., and Srinivasan, T. N. 1969. Durability of consumption goods: Competition versus monopoly. *Am. Econ. Rev.* 59: 102-9.

Lewin, K. 1942. The psychology of learning. *Natl. Soc. Studies Educ. Year-book* 41, 2: 215-42.

Lidstone, G. J. 1920. Note on the general case of Bayes-Laplace formula for inductive or a posteriori probabilities. *Fac. Actuar. Trans.* 8: 182-92.

Luce, R. Duncan. 1959. Individual Choice Behavior. New York, Wiley.

Luce, R. Duncan, and Raiffa, Howard. 1957. Games and Decisions. New York, Wiley.

Luce, R. Duncan, Bush, R. R., and Galanter, Eugene, eds. 1963, 1964, and 1965. Handbook of Mathematical Psychology, vols. 1, 2, and 3. New York, Wiley.

Machlup, F. 1962. The Supply of Inventors and Inventions, in the Rate and Direction of Inventive Activity, R. Nelson, ed. Princeton, Princeton Univ. Press.

McKeachie, Wilbert J., and Doyle Charlotte L. 1966. Psychology. Reading, Addison-Wesley.

Mansfield, Edwin. 1968a. Industrial Research and Technological Innovation New York, Norton.

_____. 1968b. The Economics of Technological Change. New York, Norton.

_____. 1969. Industrial research and development. *Am. Econ. Rev.* 59: 65-71.

March, J. G., and Simon, H. 1958. Organizations. New York, Wiley.

Marx, Karl. 1865. Capital, trans. by Frederick Engles, 1886. Modern Library ed., 1906. New York, Random House.

Maslow, A. H., and Mintz, N. L. 1956. Effects of aesthetic surroundings. *J. Psychol.* 41: 247-54.

Melitz, J. 1965. Freedman and Machlup on the significance of testing economic assumptions. *J. Polit. Econ.* 71: 394-416.

Menger, Carl. 1881. The Collected Works of Carl Menger. London, London School of Econ.

Modigliani, F. 1958. New developments on the oligopoly front. *J. Polit. Econ.* 66: 215-32.

Murdock, G. P. 1959. Africa: Its Peoples and Their Culture. New York, McGraw-Hill.

Myers, J. L., and Atkinson, R. C. 1964. Choice behavior and reward structure. *J. Math. Psychol.* 1: 170–203.

Neyman, J., ed. 1951. Proceedings of the Second Berkeley Symposium on Mathematical Statistics and Probability. Berkeley, Univ. of Calif. Press.

Page, Alfred N., ed. 1968. Utility Theory: A Book of Readings. New York, Wiley.

Perks, Wilfred. 1947. Some observations on inverse probability including a new indifference rule. *J. Inst. Actuar.* 73: 385–312.

Pfanzagl, J. 1968. Theory of Measurement. New York, Wiley.

Pontryagin, L. S., et al. 1962. Mathematical Theory of Optimal Processes. New York, Wiley.

Raiffa, Howard, and Schlaifer, Robert. 1968. Applied Statistical Decision Theory. Cambridge, MIT Press.

Ramsey, F. P. 1931. The Foundations of Mathematics and Other Logical Essays. New York, Harcourt, Brace, and World.

Roberts, Blaine. 1971. Individual influence over group decisions. *South. Econ. J.* 37: 434–44.

Roberts, Blaine, and Schulze, David. 1972. Modern Mathematics and Economic Analysis. New York, Norton.

Samuelson, P. A. 1947. The Foundations of Economic Analysis. Cambridge, Harvard Univ. Press.

——. 1954a. The pure theory of public expenditure. *Rev. Econ. Stat.* 36: 387–89.

——. 1954b. Diagrammatic exposition of a theory of public expenditure. *Rev. Econ. Stat.* 37: 350–56.

Savage, L. J. 1951. The theory of statistical decision. *J. Am. Stat. Assoc.* 46: 55–67.

——. 1954. The Foundations of Statistics. New York, Wiley.

Scherer, F. M. 1967. Research and development resource allocation under rivalry. *Q. J. Econ.* 81: 359–94.

Schlaifer, Robert. 1959. Probability and Statistics for Business Decisions. New York, McGraw-Hill.

Schultz, T. W. 1960. The formation of human capital by education. *J. Polit. Econ.* 68: 571–83.

Schumpeter, J. A. 1950. Capitalism, Socialism, and Democracy, 3rd ed. New York, Harper.

Scitovsky, Tibor. 1962. On the principle of consumers' sovereignty. *Am. Econ. Rev.* 52: 262–66.

Scott, D. 1964. Measurement structures and linear inequalities. *J. Math. Psychol.* 1: 233–47.

Shackle, G. L. S. 1955. Uncertainty in Economics. Cambridge, Cambridge Univ. Press.

Simon, H. A. 1955. A behavioral model of rational choice. *Q. J. Econ.* 69: 99–118.

——. 1956. Rational choice and the structure of the environment. *Psychol. Rev.* 63: 129–38.

Smelser, N. J. 1963. Theory of Collective Behavior. New York, Free Press.

Southall, A. 1961. Social Change in Modern Africa. London, Oxford Univ. Press.

Stigler, George. 1950. The development of utility theory. *J. Polit. Econ.* 58: 307-27, 373-96.

Suppes, Patrick. 1961. Behavioristic foundations of utility. *Econometrica* 29: 186-202.

Suppes, P., and Ginsberg, R. 1963. A fundamental property of all-or-none models, binomial distribution of responses prior to conditioning with applications to concept formation in children. *Psychol. Rev.* 70: 139-61.

Suppes, P., and Winet, M. 1955. An axiomatization of utility based on the notion of utility differences. *Manage. Sci.* 1: 259-70.

Swan, Peter L. 1970. Durability of consumption goods. *Am. Econ. Rev.* 60: 884-94.

Thompson, Earl. 1968. The perfectly competitive production of collective goods. *Rev. Econ. Stat.* 50: 1-12.

Thrall, R. M., Coombs, C. H., and Davis, R. L., eds. 1954. Decision Processes. New York, Wiley.

Tolman, E. C. 1955. Principles of performance. *Psychol. Rev.* 62: 315-26.

Uzawa, H. 1960. Preference and choice in the theory of consumption. In K. J. Arrow, Samuel Karlin, and Patrick Suppes, eds, Mathematical Methods in the Social Sciences, pp. 129-50. Stanford, Stanford Univ. Press.

Veblen, Thorstein. 1899. The Theory of the Leisure Class. New York, Macmillan.

———. 1904. The Theory of the Business Enterprise. New York, Scribner's Sons.

Viner, Jacob. 1925. The utility concept in value theory and its critics. *J. Polit. Econ.* 33: 369-87.

von Neumann, John, and Morgenstern, Oskar. 1947. Theory of Games and Economic Behavior, 2nd ed. Princeton, Princeton Univ. Press.

Watts, H. 1969. Graduated work incentives: An experiment in negative taxation. *Am. Econ. Assoc. Papers and Proc.*, pp. 463-72.

Weber, Max. 1904. The protestant ethic and the spirit of capitalism. *Arch. Sozialwiss. Sozialpol.*, vols. 20-21, 1904-1905. Trans. Talcott Parsons, New York, Scribner's Sons, 1930.

Weisbrod, B. A. 1966. Investing in human capital. *J. Human Resources* 1: 1-21.

Wilson, R. B. 1969. An axiomatic model of logrolling. *Am. Econ. Rev.* 59: 331-41.

Index